RECRUITING, INTERVIEWING, SELECTING & ORIENTING NEW EMPLOYEES

Third Edition

Other Books by Diane Arthur

Success Through Assertiveness (1980)

Recruiting, Interviewing, Selecting & Orienting New Employees (1986)

Managing Human Resources in Small and Mid-Sized Companies (1987)

Recruiting, Interviewing, Selecting & Orienting New Employees, Second Edition (1991)

Workplace Testing: An Employer's Guide to Policies and Practices (1994)

Managing Human Resources in Small and Mid-Sized Companies, Second Edition (1995)

The Complete Human Resources Writing Guide (1997)

RECRUITING, INTERVIEWING, SELECTING & ORIENTING NEW EMPLOYEES

Third Edition

Diane Arthur

AMACOM
American Management Association

New York • Atlanta • Boston • Chicago • Kansas City • San Francisco • Washington, D.C.
Brussels • Mexico City • Tokyo • Toronto

This publication is designed to provide accurate and authoritative information in regard to the subject matter covered. It is sold with the
understanding that the publisher is not engaged in rendering legal,
accounting, or other professional service. If legal advice or other expert
assistance is required, the services of a competent professional person
should be sought.

Library of Congress Cataloging-in-Publication Data

Arthur, Diane.
    Recruiting, interviewing, selecting & orienting new employees /
Diane Arthur. — 3rd ed.
      p. cm.
   Includes index.
   ISBN 0-8144-0401-4
   1. Employees — Recruiting. 2. Employment interviewing.
3. Employee selection. 4. Employee orientation. I. Title.
HF5549.5.R44A75 1998
658.3'11 — dc21   98-16733
                                          CIP

Printing number

10 9 8 7 6 5 4 3 2 1

To Warren, Valerie, and Victoria
wisdom, humor, and joy

Contents

Preface

This third edition of *Recruiting, Interviewing, Selecting & Orienting New Employees,* like its predecessors, is designed as a comprehensive guide through the four stages of the employment process. For those who are not human resources (HR) professionals but whose jobs encompass HR responsibilities, it provides the skills, tools, and techniques needed to operate effectively in this field. For those recently hired as HR specialists or who lack formal training in this area, this book provides step-by-step guidance, beginning with recruitment challenges through an employee's first weeks at work. It is also a useful refresher for those who have worked in the field for some time and wish to update or upgrade their skills.

The methods and techniques described in this book are applicable to all work environments: corporate and nonprofit, union and nonunion, technical and nontechnical, large and small. They may also be applied to professional and nonprofessional positions. Consider the particulars of your own environment and tailor the concepts accordingly.

The book may also be used as a reference for training workshops in various aspects of the employment process, and as a textbook for college, university, and other courses dealing with employment issues.

Although the basics of hiring new employees have not changed since the first two editions of this book were published (1986, 1991), other factors affecting our work culture have, warranting the revisions contained in this edition. These begin with Chapter 1, which explores emerging recruitment challenges, such as integrating a contingent workforce, tapping a growing low-wage workforce, and dealing with workplace violence. Employers must also identify the implications of workplace diversity and achieve a diversity "comfort level" if they hope to attract and retain qualified employees. Hence, a new chapter, on workplace diversity, has been added to this edition. Recruitment has changed considerably since the second edition in terms of proactively finding candidates, with an emphasis on electronic recruitment. Accordingly, Chapter 3, on recruitment sources, has been revamped, and a new Chapter 4, concerning online recruiting, has been added. Chapter 6, on employment law, has also been updated and expanded.

Different approaches to interviewing are explored in the third edition. Chapter 7 focuses on a competency-based technique that links past and future behaviors, and Chapter 8 probes additional employment interview questioning techniques that are more likely to result in prudent hiring decisions. Various aspects of the actual face-to-face interview have also been expanded in Chapter 9.

A unique feature of this book, as with the first and second editions, is the recognition that selection is not the end of the employment process. With all the time, energy, and resources expended toward hiring the best candidate, to begin over again for the same position soon after hire, is counterproductive. Yet this can, and frequently does, happen when a new employee quickly grows disenchanted with the new job and surroundings. One way to avoid this is to make certain that all employees are indoctrinated into their new work culture using a comprehensive orientation process. This book addresses the role that orientation plays in the employee's introduction to a new job by discussing the all-important first day of work, companywide orientation, and the less formal, but no less important, departmental orientation. The third edition goes on to advise employers how to customize and evaluate the success of an orientation program as well as providing sample organizational programs (Chapters 13 and 14).

Many of these revisions have also affected the appendixes appearing in the first two editions.

Readers are cautioned on two points: first, any reference made to specific publications, services, or institutions is for informational purposes only and is not to be considered an endorsement; second, this book is not intended to provide legal advice.

Recruiting, interviewing, selecting, and orienting new employees are specific skills. How well you practice these skills can directly affect many common organizational problems, such as turnover, employee morale, and absenteeism. By carefully implementing the methods described in this book, your organization can greatly improve its employer-employee relations and its level of productivity.

D.A.

Chapter 1
Recruitment Challenges and Opportunities

Increasingly, human resources (HR) specialists and managers involved in the hiring process view future job openings with a combination of excitement and apprehension. It is becoming apparent that the labor pool from which employers select new employees is changing at every level, from minimum wage and hourly paid workers right up the ranks to professionals and executives. Unless companies understand, and ultimately embrace, the expectations of tomorrow's workforce, they may find unnerving the inevitable transition from traditional work schedules performed by current employee populations, to more innovative work arrangements required to draw on the talents of diverse human resources groups.

Identifying the Changing Workforce

Tomorrow's workforce will reflect some of the economic changes that have occurred over the past two decades. The labor shortage that arose during the 1980s, due primarily to the low retraining potential of millions of displaced workers affected by closings, mergers, and takeovers, continued into the 1990s. The problem was compounded by lower birthrates as compared with the flood of baby boomers' entering the labor market in the mid-1960s. The demographic picture has started to change, however. In 1996, the U.S. population was around 263 million. By 2020, that number is expected to increase by 63 million in the following increments: in 2005, 288 million; in 2010, 300 million; in 2015, 313 million; and by 2020, about 326 million. It is anticipated that 65 percent of this increase will be the result of more births than deaths, with the remainder due to increased immigration.

We expect, then, to have a greater number of people in the workforce. Who will these workers be?

The age mix is expected to change significantly, with workers aged forty-five to sixty-four consistently outnumbering those under twenty-five and over sixty-five (population figures are noted in millions):

	18–24	25–34	35–44	45–54	55–64	65–74	75+
1996	25.5	41.7	42.2	30.2	21.2	19.0	14.7
2005	28.2	36.8	43.1	41.2	28.9	18.6	18.3
2010	30.2	38.2	39.7	44.1	34.6	21.0	19.1
2015	31.3	41.1	38.2	42.1	39.4	25.7	20.1
2020	30.5	43.6	39.7	38.9	42.3	30.9	22.4

The ethnic composition will become more diverse, as more African-Americans, Hispanics, and Asian-Americans enter the labor market. Between 1996 and 2015, the African-American population is projected to go from 12 percent to 13 percent, Hispanics from 10 percent to 15 percent, and Asian-Americans from 3.5 percent to 6 percent. Overall, the so-called minority population will rise from 25 percent in 1996, to 37 percent in 2020, to over 50 percent in 2060. Conversely, fewer whites will comprise the workforce, down from 74 percent in 1996 to 66 percent in 2015. This shift will be due, in part, to whites' constituting more than 80 percent of the retirees in the early twenty-first century. However, there will be fewer early retirements. By 2020, 89 percent of the men aged fifty-five to sixty-four will still be working, as opposed to 67 percent in 1996; for women, the number will increase from 50 percent to 77 percent. Most employees will retire between ages sixty-five and seventy, although many will combine retirement and work by accepting part-time jobs.

The educational picture is changing as well. As of 1996 (the last year for which figures are available), Asian-Americans lead, with 40 percent of those twenty-five years and older having earned a college degree, as compared with 24 percent for whites, 13 percent for African-Americans, and 9 percent for Hispanics. Overall, high school and college enrollment will grow, especially in the western states.

Regarding gender, employers can expect more women and fewer men in the job market. (*A Special Kiplinger Report: The Next 20 Years;* The Kiplinger Washington Editors, Inc.; Washington, D.C.; January, 1996.)

All of this means that companies must become more innovative in their recruitment efforts. The greatest demand will be for workers in the areas of:

Foreign trade	Entertainment
Biotechnology	Computer maintenance
Drugs and medical devices	Telecommunications
Home health care	Paralegal
Health care billing and management	Security
	Internet services
Physical and occupational therapy	Finance
Engineering	Sales and marketing

Although high school and college enrollment is expected to grow, many graduates will not have learned or developed the skills needed to perform many of the jobs in these and other fields, even at an entry level. Hence, companies are advised to offer on- and off-site training. It is also a good idea to work in partnership with schools to prepare students better for the work environment.

Preparing now for the anticipated employment changes will enable employers to confront recruitment challenges and opportunities instead of problems.

Integrating a Contingent Workforce

A significant challenge confronting employers has to do with an increase in the number and job categories of contingent workers—those who work less than a full forty-hour week without comprehensive benefits, carrying portable skills from job to job. Part-timers, temps, freelancers, contract employees, and consultants all fall under the "contingent" umbrella. Their work is literally contingent on an employer's need for them. Most hold from one to two assignments within a six-month period. Experts project that up to a third of all individuals will be employed on a contingent basis by the year 2005. Many of these workers will be in their twenties and early thirties.

People take contingent jobs for a variety of reasons. Many teachers seek additional income during summer and other school vacations. Retirees who no longer want to work full time, women with child or elder care responsibilities, and college students too seek out contingent assignments for additional income. Others look to contingent work as a path to full-time employment. Some take temporary assignments to improve skills or gain exposure to a particular work environment. Many enjoy the flexible work schedules that can accompany contingent assignments. Still others accept contingent work as a stop-gap between full-time jobs.

There was a time when contingent work was considered strictly clerical. Now contingent assignments are available in virtually every field and profession. Attorneys, business executives, clerical and hotel workers, industrial laborers, nurses and other medical personnel, restaurant workers, and technical support staff can all work on a contingent basis.

Companies generally hire contingent workers to provide flexibility in the number of workers hired and how much this labor costs. Unfortunately, many employers fail to calculate in advance the cost-effectiveness of hiring contingents. To figure out the true productivity of contingent workers, determine the output of goods and services produced per hour by contingents, divided by the input, which is the cost of employment per hours worked. High-wage labor might be cost-effective if it is also high output; low-wage labor may not be cost-effective if the output is low also. Another factor to be calculated is training costs. After training, the output that workers produce for the company should exceed the cost of their wages and benefits. One of the challenges is finding enough qualified contingent workers to fill all the available positions and then retaining them long enough to maximize the benefits they can provide.

Many businesses now operate with a core group of regular employees whose skills are critical to the business and then contract for contingent workers as needed. To do this, evaluate your company's staffing needs and determine which employees should form the core workforce and what positions can be more flexible. Look at the nature of the work that needs to be done, the volume of the workload, the timing required to complete a project, and the cyclical nature of the business to determine whether to hire core employees or contingent workers. Examine your company's business plan over the short term and the long term. Is the goal to save money? Increase profitability? Expand operations? The kinds of workers you hire—core or contingent—will depend on your industry and the answers to these questions.

Regardless of how skilled your core employees and contingent workers may be, productivity is likely to suffer if the two groups do not work harmoniously. Avoid a two-tier labor force, in which regular staff receive all the best assignments and contingent workers are left to perform the undesirable tasks or higher-risk work.

Contingent workers emphasize eight key concerns in their relationships with employers:

1. They are treated impersonally.
2. They receive inaccurate or incomplete information about job assignments.

3. They are given little information about the nature of the company's product or services.
4. Their performance is evaluated according to different standards than those of regular employees.
5. They are overlooked when there are job openings.
6. They are excluded from company social events.
7. They lack a sense of job security.
8. They do not receive benefits.

In addition, contingent workers reportedly feel underemployed, bored, and unchallenged.

Employers can improve relations between themselves and contingent workers by being forthright about the nature and length of an assignment, encourage regular employees to treat contingent workers with respect, avoid dumping undesirable or menial tasks on them, and provide better training and orientation for these short-term workers.

Employers should also be selective in choosing contingent help agencies. This can be accomplished through a series of questions:

1. How do you recruit your contingent workers?
2. How much training do your workers receive?
3. Do you check on the progress of your contingent workers?
4. What benefits do you offer your contingency workers?
5. What guarantees do you offer in case one of your workers does not measure up?

Many businesses using contingent labor work jointly with contingent help agencies, permitting workers recourse against both the agency and the employer. This means that each employer bears the burden of whatever liability arises as a result of its own relationship with the contingent workers. However, the liability resulting from a co-employment relationship is not such that one employer can be held liable for the wrongful acts of the others. The courts are increasingly examining the relationship between companies and their contingent workers, often siding with the employees in areas of benefits and workers' compensation. Currently, U.S. and state labor laws, including civil rights laws, the Occupational Safety and Health Act (OSHA), the National Labor Relations Act, and minimum wage and overtime laws apply to contingent workers. New legislation is expected to be introduced regulating the hiring of contingent workers.

Tapping a Low-Wage Workforce

Society's move from an industrial-based economy to a service economy is changing the fundamental nature of work. In many cases, service jobs pay less than comparable unskilled jobs in the manufacturing sector. As better-paying manufacturing jobs vanish with each round of layoffs and corporate downsizings, lower-wage jobs flourish. Many leading industries are populated by low-wage and minimum-wage employees, with a heavy concentration in food service, health care, agricultural, hotel, and retailing.

Finding dependable entry-level workers willing to accept minimum or low wages is becoming a challenge. Employers must find qualified prospective workers, sell them on the company, and entice them. Here are some ways employers can attract low-wage workers:

- General equivalency diploma programs
- College tuition reimbursement programs
- Training for employees and family members
- Stock purchase plans
- Membership on strategic group planning teams
- Promotional opportunities
- Increased responsibilities
- Career counseling
- Retention bonuses
- Bonus points redeemable for gifts
- Flexible schedules
- Incentive rewards

Targeting Special Interest Groups

As the composition of the workforce changes, employers must reconsider who will make the best workers. Traditional views that certain jobs are appropriate for men or women only, unsuitable for older people, or undesirable for minorities may be discriminatory and in violation of certain equal employment opportunity laws. As well, they may be impractical and self-defeating from the standpoint of productivity and profitability.

Older Workers

The employee age mix is shifting. By the year 2020, approximately a third of all workers will be between ages forty-five and sixty-four; more than one-fifth will be age sixty-five and older—nearly double the number of workers ages eighteen to twenty-four. Baby boomers will continue productive working lives much longer than their parents and grandparents did.

A number of factors will greatly affect this aging workforce, compelling them to work into their seventies and maybe even their eighties. Many women are delaying the start of families until in their late thirties and forties, thus assuming the burden of their childrens' rising college costs later in life. Additionally, many older workers are financially responsible for the care of elderly parents, either at home, where support nursing or aide care is required, or in outside care facilities. The social security system is also changing. The protection it provided past workers in their retirement years may not be available to the current workforce. Major changes to Medicare are projected, and many employers will no longer take responsibility for the health care needs of their retiring employees.

In spite of the growing number of older workers, many employers resist hiring this increasingly visible group. The list of reasons is topped by the belief that older people have more accidents on the job, poorer attendance, and lower productivity. In addition, many managers assume that older workers are less able or willing to learn new ideas or skills. Each of these statements is easily refuted by Ken Dychtwald, the "guru of aging," and founder/chairman of Age Wave Inc., an organization that promotes the value of older workers. He tells us that older workers are responsible for far fewer on-the-job accidents than twenty to twenty-four-year-old workers; they have fewer avoidable absences than do younger workers and good attendance records overall.

Additionally, there are no data available to indicate that one age group is superior to another when it comes to productivity. In fact, with the exception of a slight decline in productivity in jobs requiring a great deal of physical exertion, many studies indicate that older workers perform at least as well as, and in many instances better than, younger workers do. As for an unwillingness or inability to change, historically older workers have experienced a great deal of social and technological change and are familiar with the necessity for change. Older workers also exhibit less stress on the job, have a lower rate of illegal drug use, and have a lower rate of admission to psychiatric facilities.

As Dychtwald says, people do not grow old at sixty-five anymore. In addition, not all older people want or need the same benefits or rewards from employment. Many "younger" workers, between the ages of fifty and sixty-two, are looking for advancement opportunities and more money. Translated, that means full-time employment and full benefits. Retirees over the age of sixty-two are often on social security; therefore, they may be seeking part-time work for a supplemental income. But this is not always the case. Other reasons older people give for returning to work include the desire to feel useful and needed, an interest in staying in touch with current developments, a need to provide structure to their days, and a need to retain a sense of productivity and worth. It would appear to be in the best interests of American businesses to sweep aside traditional generalizations about an entire population of people who may prove to be among our most valuable assets.

The process of recruiting older workers may require some deviation from customary hiring practices. It is a good idea to seek out older candidates actively, as opposed to expecting them to come to you through traditional recruitment avenues, such as job ads or employment agencies. Many retirement-age job hunters have been rejected a number of times, and some may have been victims of age-related jokes and age discrimination. Consequently, they may feel written off by potential employers.

One way of recruiting older workers is to contact the Senior Employment Service, which maintains a job clearinghouse and can put you in touch with qualified older candidates. Visiting senior citizen community centers with information about available job openings is another recruitment technique that has proved to be successful. Approaching social service agencies and organizations with large senior memberships is another avenue. Contacting Forty Plus, a national organization that helps those over age forty to find employment, is yet another way of recruiting older workers. The American Association of Retired Persons offers a free booklet, *How to Recruit Older Workers,* which can help employers with their recruitment efforts. Also, do not overlook the obvious resource of your company's own retirees. In addition, if you run advertisements, use language that encourages older workers to apply—for example, "This job is suitable for retired persons." Also, describe the kind of employees your company wants to hire in terms of qualities and not just qualifications. Since many older adults are not actively seeking employment, advertise in sections other than the classified ads, say, the television or sports sections. You might also want to have pictures of older workers in your ads. Consider, too, sponsoring open houses and second-career fairs specifically for older adults.

When hiring older workers, recruiters should be prepared to answer questions as to how the return to work will affect a retiree's income. Limitations on the amount that social security recipients can earn without penalty have been reduced in recent years, but regular employment could still produce too high a level of income for some. Also, be familiar with the benefits that full- and part-time workers may be entitled to, including medical and life insurance, sick leave, paid vacations, and holidays.

Once hired, ensure older employees that their work is valued by offering the same opportunities for advancement and challenging work available to their younger colleagues. Develop training programs to help older workers redirect their skills and knowledge and provide counseling to aid in the transition to their new status.

Youth

A shortage of younger workers is imminent. In 1996, workers aged eighteen to thirty-four represented approximately 35 percent of the labor force. In 2005, that percentage drops to 30 percent; ten years later, it drops again, significantly, to a mere 20 percent.

This group, referred to as generation X, with those born between 1985 and 1993 known as generation Y, presents unique recruitment challenges, especially because of job expectations that envision a balance between fulfilling careers and familial responsibilities, including child care and elder care, as well as the pursuit of personal interests. Work must be interesting and reflect leading-edge technology. Not wedded to one job or even one field, younger workers are open to alternatives and look for exciting and entertaining opportunities that will expand their skills, knowledge, and interests.

Methods for recruiting younger workers include using interactive techniques, such as CD-ROMs, and revising company brochures to focus on new technology, promotional opportunities, geographic alternatives, and family leave policies.

One technique for attracting a segment of youthful workers is to provide funding for scholarships. Increasingly, businesses are offering scholarships to employees attending college or technical school. Others provide scholarship funding to local schools in the hope that graduates will seek employment with them. Some businesses go a step further, enticing top students from select colleges to commit to employment by granting 100 percent tuition aid from the second or third year of school through graduation. In turn, students must commit to work for that organization for a minimum period of time, ranging from one summer to one year after graduation. Information regarding the management of scholarship programs is available to employers from the Council for Aid to Education (212/689-2400).

Businesses are starting to use innovative techniques to attract the dwindling number of young workers. For example, one fast food company experimented with uniforms until it found one that particularly appealed to teenage applicants. Moreover, to retain younger workers, employers are offering alternative work arrangements, such as job sharing, flextime, and telecommuting (discussed later in this chapter). Businesses are also providing financial incentives, career opportunities, and comprehensive benefits.

Women

According to the employment statistics for the year 2000, as prepared by the U.S. Department of Labor in *Facts on Working Women* and *Working Women: A Chartbook*, women will represent approximately 50 percent of the workforce. Currently, however, only 3 percent are corporate executives; of the four thousand highest-paid executives in the country, a mere 0.5 percent are women. Relatively few women are found at the upper levels of management, on corporate boards, and in chief executive officer positions. Also, within every work, educational, and age category, men continue to earn more than women. These statistics should send a clear advisory to every company in the United States to examine its structure and environment for compatibility when it comes to hiring women at all levels.

Many of the women in the workforce are mothers who look for alternative work arrangements—for example, flexible work schedules, job sharing, at-home work arrangements, and on-site child care facilities or support.

Although gains have been made toward eliminating discrimination against women in nontraditional female jobs, bias still prevails. Equal employment opportunities are still not available for qualified women at all types and levels of work. This is something that needs to change if employers are to avail themselves fully of this valuable pool of human resources.

Minorities

It is projected that the term *minority*, here intended to encompass a broad spectrum of ethnic groups including, but not limited to, African-Americans, Hispanics (e.g., Puerto Ricans, Cuban- and Mexican-Americans, as well as people originally from more than twenty additional Central and South American nations, and Spain), Asian-Americans (e.g., Korean-, Japanese-, Chinese-, and Filipino-Americans), and Native American, will soon disappear from our employment vocabulary. How can we call "minority" a collective group of people representing 37 percent of the labor market in 2020 and over 50 percent in 2060?

Although these groups may represent a large percentage of tomorrow's workforce, few will be targeted for professional positions. Those qualified will be drawn to employers offering not only the usual growth opportunities and benefits, but also a multicultural or diverse environment, a concept that is still difficult for some employers to grasp. Traditionally, employers have tended to hire candidates most resembling themselves in terms of skills, interests, background, and even appearance. That simply will not work anymore. Chapter 2 addresses the issue of workplace diversity in depth. For now, suffice it to say that recruiters are advised to concentrate on ability, not ethnicity.

Businesses are encouraged to develop and maintain an ongoing relationship with various minority professional associations to aid in recruitment efforts. There are numerous national associations with local chapters that can be sources of job candidates—for example, the National Black MBA Association, the American Association of Hispanic CPAs, Latin Business Association, National Association of Asian-American Professionals, and the American Indian Science and Engineering Society.

One minority recruitment source that is often overlooked is a company's own employees. Training existing staff for higher-level jobs can both resolve recruitment woes and help to establish management as committed to minority development and placement.

Applicants With Disabilities

In 1997 there were reportedly about 50 million people in the United States with disabilities—roughly 26 percent of the workforce, according to *Mosaics SHRM Focuses on Workplace Diversity*, July–August 1997. Legislation, such as the Americans with Disabilities Act of 1990, has drawn greater attention to workers with disabilities and the contributions they can make. Still, people with disabilities have the highest unemployment rate of any other group. Why is there such resistance in hiring them?

One of the primary reasons has to do with how we perceive people with disabilities. In reality, the term *disabled* encompasses a broad spectrum of impairments. More than half of those with disabilities have hearing impairments, and only a small percentage of these are totally deaf, according to Arlene Vernon-Oehmke (*Effective Hiring and ADA Compliance*, AMACOM, 1994). Other categories include visual impairments, speech impairments, heart disease, developmental disabilities such as cerebral palsy, mental illness, acquired immune deficiency syndrome (AIDS) or human immunodeficiency virus (HIV)-positive status, and limitations resulting from accidents. We also have a tendency to feel uncomfortable around people with disabilities.

Another reason commonly cited for rejecting applicants with disabilities is the cost, since laws require that employers make reasonable accommodations, which do not create undue hardship, for applicants with disabilities (Chapter 6). In determining whether a particular accommodation would result in an undue hardship, the law assesses employers on the basis of the overall size of the business, the nature of their business, and the nature and cost of the required accommodation. If a job should require the modification of certain equipment or procedures to accommodate a worker, employers are advised to contact organizations such as the Job Accommodations Network, established by the President's Committee on Employment of People with Disabilities, at 800/JAN-PCEH, or the National Support Center for Persons with Disabilities, established by IBM, at 800/IBM-2133, for advice and assistance.

As with older workers, traditional recruitment methods are not usually successful when applied to people with disabilities. In this regard, many employers find networking with civic centers and associations such as the National Association of Rehabilitation Facilities (703/648-9300) to be helpful. The workplace should be made accessible to applicants, including going beyond any legal requirements (e.g., ramps for people with physical disabilities). For example, consider installing a telephone device for the deaf (TDD) so applicants with hearing impairments can call to discuss job openings. Also, do not overlook internal candidates: Are job postings accessible to all employees? Put bulletin board postings at lower levels for access to people with physical disabilities and add a mechanism to computers so visually impaired employees can retrieve e-mail postings.

Interviewing applicants with disabilities can initially be an unsettling experience if bias and stereotypical thinking get in the way. Many companies run training programs to help interviewers and other employees develop a keener sense of understanding toward, and a greater tolerance for, people with disabilities. These workshops may recommend changing certain standard application and interview procedures, such as permitting blind applicants to submit employment applications through the mail or having someone help with the completion process, and writing out interview questions and showing them to hearing-impaired applicants.

Beyond such preparatory steps, the format of the actual employment interview should be essentially the same as with any other candidate. All questions should be job related and tied in to the skills, education, and experience required to perform the job.

Be careful about making assumptions—for example, that a person cannot perform a task because of an apparent disability or that a person with one disability has others. If you have legitimate concerns that a person's impairment might interfere with performance of the essential job functions, then ask the candidate a series of pertinent questions—for example, "Approximately 50 percent of this job requires keyboarding. Can you perform this task, with or without accommodation?"

Carefully evaluate the responses to questions such as these to determine whether a reasonable accommodation may be made without creating an undue hardship for the company. If a person cannot perform the essential functions of a job without creating an undue hardship for the company, then he or she does not qualify for the position.

Immigrants

The U.S. Census Bureau reports that 9.3 percent of the population living in the United States is foreign born. That number is steadily climbing toward the peak percentage reached in 1920, when the foreign-born composed 13 percent of the population. After 1920, the numbers dropped steadily until the 1970s, when they began their climb back to their current high of 24.5 million.

The influx of immigrants into the United States is expected to continue, although the racial and ethnic makeup will differ from past years. For example, in 1970, most immigrants were from Mexico, Germany, Italy, Canada, and Great Britain. High numbers of immigrants from Mexico are expected to continue, but the other countries will be replaced by the Philippines, China, Cuba, India, and Vietnam, according to *Workplace Visions* (September–October 1997).

The growing number of immigrants is slated to have two key effects on U.S. employers. First, employers must be certain to hire only those who have the legal right to work in this country. That means carefully checking documents and dealing with periodic government intervention. Second, with more immigrants arriving in the United States, the issue of speaking only English at work will continue to be an important human resources issue.

Combating Workplace Illiteracy

Department of Labor statistics reveal that 2.5 million illiterate Americans enter the workforce each year. In the immediate future, 80 percent of all available jobs will require at least a high school education, but only 74 percent of Americans finish high school. In addition, only approximately 66 percent graduate with adequate skills.

The U.S. Department of Education offers additional disturbing statistics:

- One in every seven American adults is a functional illiterate, unable to read, write, calculate, or solve even simple problems.
- Functionally illiterate people comprise 30 percent of unskilled workers, 29 percent of semiskilled workers, and 11 percent of all managers, professionals, and technicians.
- Forty-seven million adults are borderline illiterates.
- Half of our nation's industrial workers read at or below the eighth-grade level.

The impact of illiteracy on business is far-reaching. In addition to accounting for a loss of billions of dollars in profits each year, there are problems of lowered productivity, declining international competitiveness, and reduced promotability. The pool of available workers that industries can hire from is affected; workers who cannot read instructions may endanger the lives of coworkers, illiterate customers cannot read advertisements, and illiterate consumers cannot read instructions. The problem has become so severe that a toll-free hot line (800/228-8813) has been set up enabling companies to find groups within their community that can help fight illiteracy.

As part of the effort to reduce the growing gap between the reading, writing, and math skills of the workforce and the current and future needs of industry, many businesses offer in-house programs and encourage outside education and training. Among those companies providing basic skills training are the following:

- American Telephone & Telegraph has offered remedial courses to its employees.
- General Motors and International Business Machines have financed adult education for many of their employees.
- Ford Motor Co. offered basic reading courses at many of its plants.
- Texas Instruments reimbursed the tuition of thousands of employees each semester.
- New York Telephone provided a program designed to elevate the educational level of barely literate employees to ninth- and tenth-grade levels.
- Aetna Life and Casualty and United Technologies imple-

mented a tutorial program whereby employees tutored co-workers one on one.

- B. Dalton Bookseller launched a national literacy campaign.
- Standard Oil Co. employed former teachers to conduct classes in grammar and spelling for newly hired secretaries.
- Nabisco Brands offered several hours of elementary school courses weekly.
- Polaroid identified hundreds of employees each year for remedial programs.
- Liberty Mutual Insurance Group offered remedial and advanced literacy training.
- Olsten Corp. sponsored spelling bees and provided how-to guides for its employees in grammar, spelling, and punctuation.
- Spring Industries provided on-site facilities for classes in basic literacy and basic technical skills.
- Travelers Insurance Co. established MOST (Modern Office Skills Training) and BEST (Business English for Spanish-speaking Trainees).
- The UAW-Ford Eastern Michigan University Academy offered classes in reading, writing, speaking, and listening.
- Rocco, Inc. launched a companywide campaign against illiteracy through its Career Enhancement Program.

Preemployment screening offers an opportunity for employers to identify job applicants with skill deficiencies that require remedial training. Unfortunately, recruiters and interviewers often assume that a business school or college graduate has mastered basic reading, writing, and match skills. This, sadly, is not so. It has been found that many college graduates cannot write a coherent business letter, and many are deficient in critical reasoning skills.

Some HR departments unintentionally help illiterate applicants conceal deficiencies by allowing them to take employment applications home to complete. Such illiteracy may be concealed further when employers shy away from preemployment tests out of fear of discrimination charges. In addition, employment and educational reference checks are increasingly difficult to conduct, and many employers do not even attempt them. Consequently, employees are placed on the payroll even though their literacy levels are unknown.

Many employers, concerned with screening potential employees for basic literacy, have found the following techniques helpful:

1. Require applicants to complete the employment application form by themselves, at the time of the interview.

2. Show applicants job descriptions, defining both the requirements for the job and primary duties and responsibilities, during the course of the interview. Allow sufficient time for the applicant to read the contents and ask questions.

3. Use job-related, validated tests as one of the selection criteria. Chapter 11 addresses this area in detail.

4. Conduct thorough employment and educational references, whenever possible. See Chapter 12 for additional information on references.

5. Conduct in-depth face-to-face interviews. Emphasize open-ended and behavioral, competency-related questions, so you can evaluate such factors as word use, clarity of thought, organization of information, and analytical ability relevant to a given job opening. Details regarding employment interviews appear in Chapters 7 and 8.

Providing Alternative Work Arrangements

As American businesses strive both to recruit qualified workers and accommodate changing work ethics, it is becoming increasingly evident that alternatives to the traditional workweek and work schedule must be considered if effective levels of productivity are to be maintained. Many of these alternative work arrangements, such as part-time employment, telecommuting, and contingent work (discussed earlier in this chapter), have found limited use in the past. But now these options are being considered for many different levels of employees, and with some creative twists. Of course, not all arrangements work equally well in every environment. It is significant, however, that more organizations are willing to test diverse work options and are reporting positive results.

As this trend toward varying work schedules continues, it is projected that the typical American company will soon consist of workers from the lowest-paid entry level up to the highest levels of management in several different work arrangements. In fact, it may very well be that at some point in the near future, regular, full-time employment will be the exception.

Regular Part Time

Traditionally, candidates completing job applications have been asked to check off one of two boxes for their desired work schedule:

full time or part time. The latter usually referred to schedules of up to twenty hours per week and ineligibility for benefits. It also generally applied to nonexempt-level employees, usually women with child care responsibilities, and students.

As employment concepts continue to change, the term *regular part time* has expanded in meaning and scope. The traditional part-timer still exists in many industries, but increasingly the term refers to varying levels of employees, male and female, on a reduced work-time schedule, who are entitled to many of the privileges and benefits available to full-time workers. The trend is also spreading up through the ranks, as many more professionals (e.g., attorneys) are being granted part-time work arrangements.

The change in definition clearly indicates a redirection in thinking. Employers are coming to realize that there is a great deal of competition for qualified candidates who are striving to balance family, job responsibilities, and outside interests.

Job Sharing

Job sharing may be defined as an arrangement in which two employees divide the responsibilities of one full-time job. It is distinguishable from regular part-time employment in that it applies to positions that cannot be separated into two definitive part-time jobs. Although the concept of job sharing has been around for about thirty years, only since the mid-1980s have organizations such as Quaker Oats Co. and Levi Strauss & Co. started viewing it as a viable work arrangement. Initially it was viewed as a female-related issue; now it is seen as a solution to the needs of many employees, including parents, older workers, and students.

Numerous employer benefits are reportedly derived from job sharing, including the broader range of skills brought to the position, the retention of valuable workers who might otherwise leave, a higher level of energy, and reduced absenteeism. In addition, job sharing virtually eliminates the need for employees to take care of personal business while on the job. Also, if one partner terminates, the job is still half filled.

There are some drawbacks to job sharing: Twice as much payroll and personnel record keeping is required, an overlap in scheduling can create a logistics problem, and clients or customers may complain about not being able to deal with the same person consistently. The issue of benefits can also create problems. Some employers offer full benefits to both partners, and others elect to divide a single package.

Organizations considering job sharing should conduct a full

analysis, including consideration of the job's requirements and responsibilities; an assessment of each partner's skills, abilities, shortcomings, and interests; a clear definition of how matters of salary and benefits are to be handled; and a schedule that is acceptable and workable for all concerned.

Flextime

The classic definition of flextime requires each worker to put in the same number of hours each day, with identical core hours, but varying starting and quitting times. Employers may vary the amount of flexibility granted workers in establishing their schedules according to the specific needs of the organization and the employees concerned.

Flextime, the first alternative work arrangement to gain acceptance, was implemented at a Hewlett-Packard company plant beginning in 1972. Indications are that it is gaining in popularity; more private and public sector organizations now offer flextime.

Flextime allows employees to balance work demands with those of home, school, and outside activities. It also helps relieve transit and commuting problems. In addition, given a voice in the scheduling of their workday, employees tend to feel involved in the company's decision-making process. This, in turn, may strengthen employer-employee relations. Employees are also able to schedule work more in tune with their own "biological clocks"; that is, they can choose to work during those hours when their skill and response levels are most keen.

Benefits to the employer include extended hours of coverage or service, which reduces or eliminates the need for overtime; reduced tardiness, absenteeism, and turnover; an expanded and improved recruitment pool; and improved work performance attributable to higher employee morale. As a system, it is also adaptable to many situations and can easily be implemented in most environments. It tends to function best in work environments that promote independence and self-motivation and is least effective in assembly-line work or situations in which the work must be accomplished in a short time span.

As with any other system, flextime has some drawbacks. The number one problem appears to have less to do with the employees than with supervisors, who are uncomfortable with having workers unsupervised on the job, during noncore hours. A sufficient level of discomfort may compel some supervisors to put in longer hours in order to make certain work is being accomplished during noncore hours. Other concerns include difficulty in scheduling meetings, not having key employees available when needed, and employee abuse of flextime. In addition, overhead costs are increased by keeping facilities open for longer periods of time.

Compressed Workweek

Following close on the heels of flextime in the early 1970s was the idea of the compressed workweek. This alternative arrangement allows employees to work the required forty hours in fewer than five days. The most popular schedule remains four ten-hour days.

The compressed workweek has received mixed reviews from both employees and management. Positive votes come from employees, who react favorably to the longer periods of personal time the compressed workweek allows. They also prefer commuting during nonrush hours and saving money by not working a fifth day. In addition, many workers reportedly accomplish more in a day during hours when telephone calls from customers or clients are less likely to interrupt them. Employers have reported that the compressed workweek works well as a recruitment tool. Some improvement in rates of absenteeism, tardiness, and turnover has also been reported.

On the other hand, workers and managers alike have complained about excessive fatigue brought by the length of the workday. This is troublesome to older employees, young singles with active social lives, and employees with families. Long-term effects on health are also of concern. Both factors can adversely affect productivity.

Many long-term users of the compressed workweek have nothing but praise for the system; others who have tried it have abandoned it.

Companies that are considering this alternative work arrangement should make certain that state laws do not prohibit a compressed workweek. Some states require the payment of overtime compensation for hours worked in excess of eight hours on any given day.

Telecommuting

Also known as remote access work, flexplace, at-home work, telework, or satellite office work, the concept of telecommuting has been around since the 1970s. It did not gain popularity until some ten years later, with the explosion of personal computers and facsimile machines. Today, telecommuting is one of the fastest-growing components of the labor market. In 1985, the U.S. Department of Labor reported approximately 5 million full- and part-time at-home workers; ten years later, that number tripled to 15 million.

Many companies maintain that there are advantages to having some employees work at home, at least part of the time. Reduced utility and office space leasing costs, as well as increased productivity, are two of the most common reasons for hiring telecommuters. Several employers have also reported that this work option has proved to be an effective recruitment tool. It both attracts employees and allows the employer to expand its recruiting base beyond the normal commutation area. In addition, organizations have been able to hire people who might not be able to travel to an office to work, such as those who are elderly and or have certain disabilities. Employers with telecomuting workers also report less absenteeism, since these employees often work at home even if they are not feeling well.

Many employees also appreciate the arrangement. For example, parents who want to work and care for their children can more readily manage both. In addition, at-home workers report being able to perform their duties without the typical office interruptions and enjoy the freedom of working during "off hours." Other benefits cited include not having to commute and being able to wear whatever they want while working.

But there are drawbacks as well. For employers, there is the lack of direct control over an employee's work. In addition, when computers are involved, there is concern over unsupervised access to data and theft of equipment. And some employees complain of a sense of isolation and worry whether they have the self-discipline required to meet deadlines.

Companies considering telecommuting work arrangements for some employees should consult with legal and tax experts regarding employee classifications, local zoning regulations, and insurance requirements.

Additional Alternative Work Arrangements

Contingent work, part-time employment, job sharing, flextime, compressed workweeks, and telecommuting are the six primary alternative work arrangements available today. There are additional arrangements that employers may find suitable, too.

Sabbaticals represent a lesser known but increasingly popular work arrangement, in recognition of our long-lived workforce. Formal sabbatical programs offer employees periods of time to pursue other interests or tend to familial obligations with a job guarantee upon return. Actually, this is not a new idea; academic sabbaticals are common at colleges and universities. Although seldom used in business in the past, sabbaticals are now starting to catch on. Most arrangements are for unpaid leaves of from three to six months.

The *supplemental workforce* is a variation on an old theme. These are employees who are recruited and hired through conventional means and then trained in job- and industry-specific matters. Here is the twist: They are then placed in a standby pool for work as needed, with the company committing to weekly or longer work assignments. This program provides a consistency and level of skill not usually available in temporary employees.

Voluntary reduced work-time programs (v-time) allow full-time employees to become part time for a certain period, usually six to twelve months. During their tenure as part-timers, their salaries and benefits are adjusted accordingly. After the agreed-upon period of reduced work time is completed, the employees are able to return to their original full-time status. Full pay and benefits are also restored.

Employees benefit from v-time by having maximum flexibility in scheduling, on an as-needed basis. Employers find the arrangement cost-effective. V-time can be disruptive, however, and make the scheduling of work difficult. Other employees may also resent the latitude v-time employees enjoy.

Work sharing is an alternative work arrangement generally used by companies as a cost-reduction strategy and an attempt to avoid layoffs. The hours and salary of some or all of a company's employees are reduced until such time as regular pay and status can be restored. In some states, work sharing is combined with short-term compensation, whereby employees receive partial unemployment insurance payments to compensate for part of the reduced salary.

Independent contractors are self-employed workers in a variety of fields in exempt and nonexempt capacities. Companies may employ independent contractors for short- or long-term assignments without any of the commitments or obligations that accompany an employer-employee relationship. Generally there is a written contract outlining the services to be provided, the approximate or specific period of time for the services, and the amount and schedule of payment. Conditions governing severance of the agreement may be outlined in the contract as well.

Employee leasing is a unique work arrangement, used primarily by small companies with fewer than 300 employees, in an effort to avoid some of the headaches of administration. The system allows for an entire group of employees to be fired from a company, hired by a professional employer organization (PEO), and then contracted back to the original employer. The PEO handles all the administrative paperwork, provides fringe benefits to the employees, and charges the employer approximately 20 to 35 percent above gross payroll. Currently, there are more than 2,500 PEOs managing in excess of 2 million workers. The industry as a whole is growing at a rate of 30 percent a year, according to *HR Magazine* (September 1997).

Phased or *partial retirement* enables employees to retire voluntarily over a period of years by gradually reducing their full-time work schedule. This process results in improved employment and advancement possibilities for younger workers. In many instances, the retiring employees are able to mentor the incoming workers.

Phased or partial retirement originated in Europe during the early 1970s, but did not gain a foothold in the United States until 1987, when mandatory retirement was banned. It gained momentum in 1988 with requirements that employers continue pension plan contributions for workers aged sixty-five and over.

In most instances, phased retirement programs allow participants to retain their rate of pay, prorated to reflect a reduced work schedule. Benefits, too, may be adjusted to reflect a part-time schedule.

Although implementation of phased retirement is limited, more companies are beginning to turn to it. Organizations that have implemented phased retirement programs in recent years include Aetna, Levi Straus, and Polaroid.

Other Responses to Employee Needs

Besides innovative programs and techniques, what else can companies do to attract and motivate the workers of tomorrow? They can start by recognizing that, unlike generations before, this new workforce is more interested in opportunity than job security; they are more willing to take risks and less concerned with financial stability. Hence, employers need to provide challenging and varying work assignments. In addition, participative management, in which all employee levels are involved in at least some aspect of the decision-making process, is becoming of greater importance to workers. Workers have also expressed the need to be recognized and rewarded for their specific contributions. Furthermore, they are seeking greater autonomy with fewer levels of management.

Flexibility with regard to work schedules and work arrangements will be a key element in the near future. Flexible benefits plans are increasingly being sought. Also growing in significance is an interest in encouraging social relationships among coworkers off the job. Managers will therefore need to plan more social activities and sponsor company outings. The continuing interest in physical fitness will also affect employment, as more workers favor employers' providing workout rooms or health club memberships.

Preventing Workplace Violence

We have all heard about disgruntled former employees' returning to the workplace, seeking revenge for termination or lack of promotion. In most instances, employers are stunned by the events, maintaining that there were no warning signs or any way the violence could have been prevented. We read about these events, shaking our heads over the tragedy, and certain it could never occur where we work. Don't be so sure.

We tend to think of workplace violence as physical harm, but it also includes threats of injury, harassment, and damage to company property. In addition to former workers, violence may involve co-workers, bosses, customers and clients, employee family members, and total strangers. According to the Society for Human Resource Management, most acts of workplace violence are prompted by personality conflicts, followed by family and marital problems. Other factors are drug or alcohol abuse, stress, and firings or layoffs. The Northwestern National Life Insurance Institute for Occupational Safety and Health adds additional motives for acts of violence, including dissatisfaction with service, anger with disciplinary proceedings, and prejudice.

Statistics on workplace violence are alarming. The U.S. Department of Justice reports that one out of every six crimes committed in the United States occurs at work, affecting over 1 million victims annually. According to the National Institute for Occupational Safety and Health (NIOSH), homicide and other acts of workplace violence have become the second leading cause of death in the workplace overall and the number one cause of on-the-job death for women. Guns are reportedly used in 75 percent of these cases. For every murder that takes place in the workplace, there are numerous violent assaults or threats and destruction of company property, all of which can result in physical injury, trauma, and decreased productivity—suffering and damage that cannot be measured by statistics.

In addition, many injured workers, or families of murdered workers, sue employers for not having protected the employees. Employers can be held liable for prior indications of potential violence and failure to warn the ultimate victim. Also, if an employer knows, or should have known, of certain characteristics of an individual that indicate a propensity for violent behavior and hires or retains the person anyway, the employer may be responsible for any resulting harm.

Violence in the workplace cannot be stopped entirely, but employers can take certain preventive and protective measures. Begin by carefully prescreening potential employees. In addition to exploring competency-based areas of skills and knowledge, explore job-related intangibles that will reveal information about the person's temperament and character. Ask questions that reflect specific experiences, since the best indicator of future behavior is past behavior. Possible indications of future violence include a history that reflects a low tolerance for frustration, frequent outbursts of anger, blaming others for mistakes, suspicion of others' motives, lack of empathy for others, negative interpersonal relationships, and the inability to adapt to new work situations.

You might also want to implement job-related psychological testing designed to assess a propensity for workplace violence. London House/Science Research Associates (9701 West Higgins Road, Rosemont, IL 60018, (800/221-8378), for example, offers the Personnel Selection Inventory, which is designed to evaluate violent or nonviolent tendencies. Test results alone, however, are insufficient to establish that someone poses a direct threat.

Reference checks on applicants under consideration for hire may prove helpful, assuming you ask the right questions and the former employer is forthcoming with information. As you will learn in Chapter 12, however, ascertaining substantive background information is not always feasible.

Since prescreening applicants cannot, with absolute certainty, ferret out potentially violent workers, employers must also be alert to warning signs exhibited by employees; frequent angry outbursts, intimidation of others, veiled threats, obsessions, sullen withdrawal, and persistent discussion of weapons. Note that these characteristics may be exhibited by employees who performed well in the past and never before gave any indication of violent behavior. These behaviors may be triggered by any number of aggravating factors, such as a bad performance review, being bypassed for a promotion, a conflict with a coworker or boss, drug or alcohol use, financial or family problems, and involuntary termination. Employers are urged to investigate thoroughly and immediately and document all allegations or actual acts of violence. Also, provide avenues for disgruntled or otherwise troubled employees to receive relief, such as employee assistance programs and formal grievance proceedings.

Many resources are available to assist employers in dealing with potential workplace violence, including:

Institute for Human Resources
P.O. Box 1373, Mail Route 6320
Minneapolis, MN 55440
612/945-6620

CONCERN Employee Assistance Program
2635 North First Street, Suite 23
San Jose, CA 95134
408/432-0616

Work Trauma Services
110 Sutter Street, Suite 710
San Francisco, CA 94104
415/398-3966

National Crisis Prevention Institute
3315 K, North 124th Street
Brookfield, WI 53005
800/558-8976

Institute for Crisis Management
710 West Main Street, Suite 200
Louisville, KY 40202
502/584-0402

Crisis Management International
8 Piedmont Center, Suite 420
Atlanta, GA 30305
404/841-3400

Summary

Tomorrow's workforce offers employers many challenges. We are seeing increasing numbers of older workers, women, minorities, and applicants with disabilities enter the job market to compete for available work. But not all workers are necessarily prepared. One in every seven American adults is a functional illiterate. Since the fastest-growing industries require higher levels of skills and knowledge than ever before, businesses must pay greater attention to education and training.

We are also witnessing an influx of contingent workers—people carrying portable skills from job to job, their work literally contingent on an employer's timely need. Additionally, employers are finding it increasingly difficult to attract and maintain low- and minimum-wage workers.

The traditional five-day workweek and nine-to-five work schedule must allow room for alternative arrangements. Employees at all levels will require flexible scheduling to fit in with the other aspects of their lives. Hence, arrangements such as regular part time, job sharing, flextime, compressed workweeks, and telecommuting will become increasingly more commonplace.

Finally, businesses must take preventive and protective measures to protect employees against workplace violence.

For employers accepting these changes and preparing for them accordingly, the next few decades will be filled with many productive recruitment opportunities.

Chapter 2
Workplace Diversity

Workplace diversity first received serious attention in the 1960s, with the onset of major equal employment opportunity and affirmative action legislation. It was not until the early 1990s, however, that diversity was viewed as a separate HR matter. Now it is one of the most significant issues affecting the workplace. More companies understand the need for a diverse workplace, as they see that the global market is growing increasingly competitive, the pool of human resources continues to change, and an increasing number of workers are demanding a multicultural work environment. The result has been a gradual shift from merely accepting diversity to valuing it.

Understanding Diversity

Diversity reflects all the factors that identify us. The term goes far beyond our ethnicity or sex, and includes the multitude of ways in which we are unique and, at the same time, similar:

age	marital status
behavioral style	mental abilities
communication style	national origin
customs	personality
education	physical abilities
ethnicity	physical characteristics
family status	religious beliefs
gender	sexual orientation
goals and aspirations	skills
health	socioeconomic status
interests	talents
language	values
lifestyle	work styles

This broad definition sends a significant message to those resisting diversity: that we are all unique; hence, a diverse workplace benefits everyone.

The ultimate goal of a diverse workplace is for all involved to work together toward achieving common organizational objectives, while prospering individually. To achieve organizational goals, employees need to be flexible and cooperative; however, the onus for adaptation cannot be placed solely on employees outside the dominant culture, i.e., the one to which the people in power belong. In order for a business to grow and profit, commitment and adaptation to diversity must be made by everyone, beginning with senior management. Indeed, without top-level support, diversity efforts are certain to fail. Senior executives must emphasize that diversity is a business issue, and not some altruistic cause to be given lip-service. If senior management is the only group committed, however, diversity will remain a goodwill gesture and never achieve bottom-line focus. Accordingly, a growing number of organizations, understanding the connection between diversity and business, are linking a manager's evaluation with progress in the area of diversity. They are requiring accountability for results that reflect a maximum utilization of the skills, abilities, and interests of all staff members. This communicates to managers and supervisors that commitment to diversity is part of their job.

There are many advantages to seeking a diverse workforce. Employers are able to select from a larger labor pool, improving their chances of finding outstanding candidates. Candidates reflect a variety of backgrounds and experience, increasing the talents and contributions they bring to the organization. Employees will appreciate the multicultural environment provided; consequently, they are likely to be more motivated and have a better attitude, resulting in higher productivity. A diversity-driven work environment can also result in fewer discrimination charges and lawsuits.

Having a diverse workforce is especially critical in companies that reach out to a diverse customer or consumer base. With changing demographics in the United States and many businesses operating internationally, it makes good business sense to have a workforce that reflects the needs of the organization's diverse customers.

Companies that invest in diversity as a long-term commitment may enjoy significantly better financial results than those that do not. But committing to diversity appears to be easier for large companies than for smaller ones. According to a recent survey conducted by the Work Force Programs Department of the American Association of Retired Persons (AARP), the larger the organization, the more likely it is to have a diversity program. The discrepancy ranged from 71 percent for companies with 10,000 or more employees to 18 percent for companies with fewer than 500 workers (*MOSAICS: SHRM Focuses on Workplace Diversity*, September 1996).

Affirmative Action Versus Diversity-Driven Work Environments

Affirmative action and diversity are often, but incorrectly, considered synonymous; sometimes, too, diversity is thought to be the politically correct version of affirmative action.

Although both affirmative action and diversity are intended to bring into an organization people from various backgrounds with different characteristics, the similarity stops there. Affirmative action is a legally driven tool that came about in the 1960s as an attempt to rectify past discriminatory practices in business (see Chapter 6). Organizations were required to set goals and hire, train, and promote a certain percentage of qualified representatives of underutilized groups. The emphasis was on increasing the numbers of employees from these groups. While hired to be part of the organization, employees brought in as part of affirmative action were often excluded within the organization in various ways, from decision making to company-sponsored social events. A hierarchy prevailed, with control in the hands of the dominant culture, almost exclusively white males.

Diversity-driven work environments go beyond affirmative action by nurturing individuality and making changes to suit the needs of its employees, customers, and the organization. Differences in opinion and experience are viewed as leading to a more creative approach to problem solving and decision making. A sense of inclusion leads to shared power, collaboration, and consensus. The work environment is healthier, and everyone feels more nearly equal.

This description of a diverse workforce is achievable if businesses are willing to examine and initiate changes in organizational structure. Senior management is responsible for beginning the process by supporting and committing to the concept of a diversity-driven workforce, overseeing a program that includes an assessment of existing policies and practices. With organizational goals in mind, systems currently in place that do not promote inclusion should be revamped or replaced. This process includes a look at the distribution of work assignments, how employees are evaluated, the basis for promotions, the composition of work teams, and behaviors warranting special recognition, such as suggestions leading to increased productivity or profits. The prevailing objective should be to create a model of inclusion that enables the workforce to become more productive and the organization more efficient and competitive.

To accomplish this end, an increasing number of organizations are establishing cultural diversity assessment committees, with representatives from all employee levels and backgrounds. Their analysis of existing policies and practices begins with an evaluation of the company's affirmative action program. Here are some of the questions they are asking themselves:

- Do we have a history of exclusion based on ethnic or gender bias?
- What are the historical and current goals of our affirmative action program?
- Are we motivated solely by meeting legal requirements, or do we have a sense of social and moral responsibility?
- How do we go about recruiting applicants and training and promoting our employees in relation to these goals?
- Do we ever hire or promote women and minorities who are not qualified, merely to meet legal requirements?
- Once our goals are met, do we continue to recruit, train, and promote women and minorities?
- Do women and minorities work in all or most of our departments at varying levels of responsibility and authority?
- Have we successfully mainstreamed affirmative action new employees into the corporate culture?
- Once we have succeeded in attracting qualified women and minorities, do we respect their abilities and contributions and feel comfortable working with them?
- Have we made certain that our affirmative action efforts have not backfired, that is, resulted in discrimination against white males?
- How would we rate our affirmative action accomplishments?
- How do employees perceive our affirmative action program, and what could we do to strengthen our image?

The conclusions businesses often draw from these probing questions is that affirmative action, although good in many respects, is limited in terms of the results produced. True, the programs usually result in hiring large numbers of women and minorities, but then what? Too often, these new employees start out at the bottom of the corporate ladder and remain there. Few are treated as part of the governing inner circle. This situation triggers a collective sense of job dissatisfaction and disproportionately low morale, which impairs productivity and results in excessively high turnover. Then the cycle begins again, with the company searching for more women and minorities to fill the vacancies created by their disgruntled predecessors. While this cycle of recruitment reoccurs, white males grumble about reverse discrimination and preferential treatment. The result is that everyone is unhappy and no one wins.

Diversity and Recruiting

After an assessment of their affirmative action programs, most companies agree that affirmative action alone cannot help achieve organizational objectives. They need to move to a diversity-driven work environment. Since the composition of a diverse workforce is not unlike that of an affirmative action workforce, employers may initially think that their recruiting efforts need not be reexamined. That is not a wise assumption. Recruiting for a diversity-driven work environment requires tailoring recruitment sources to target representatives of diverse groups. The specific recruitment sources used are not as relevant as how they are applied. The next step for a cultural diversity assessment committee, then, is to review the company's current recruiting practices and resources. Here are some ways to improve diversity recruiting efforts:

• Look for applicants in-house by posting job openings for interested staff. Encourage training for employees who may fall short of possessing concrete requirements but show potential and interest.

• Encourage representatives from diverse groups within the organization, such as older employees, minorities, women, and people with disabilities, to assist in referring applicants. This word-of-mouth method of recruitment has been around for years and has always worked as a reliable, cost-effective, quick recruitment source. Traditionally, however, the word has generally spread from one white male to other white males. The twist here is that you are turning for assistance to employees who are more likely to refer applicants with diverse backgrounds.

• Actively seek out applicants with diverse qualities by advertising in publications that target women, minorities, and other diverse groups. Be sure to promote your company as a supporter of diversity.

• Visit colleges that have ethnically diverse populations. Meet first with administrators and professors, describing your corporate culture and the type of jobs you need to fill. Distribute literature that boasts of your diversity-driven work environment.

• Meet with local professional organizations that represent diverse groups. They can provide tips on how to attract more people from diverse groups, as well as serve as a recruitment resource.

• Send company representatives to speak at professional organizations that represent diverse groups. Talk about the work you have done to date in the area of diversity and describe available job openings. Representatives should include women, minorities, people with disabilities, and older people, in addition to white males.

• Include photographs of employees representing different ethnic backgrounds, as well as women, people with disabilities, and older employees, all performing work at varying levels in organizational publications, such as annual reports, recruiting brochures, and advertisements.

Diversity Education and Training

Assuming you are sold on the benefits of a diversity-driven workforce and have successfully recruited employees with diverse traits, you probably think your job is now done. After all, you have proved your commitment to diversity and should be able to sit back and watch your newly shaped workforce produce.

True, you have made a good start, but the job is far from complete. Confronting you now is the issue of acceptance by your existing workforce, so that increased productivity can be realized. Acceptance will come about through diversity education and training: education for how employees think about others and related issues and training to develop new skills that will affect productivity.

Although a discussion of education and training falls beyond the scope of this book, employers will find that a basic awareness of the issues and practices will improve their ability to attract and retain a diverse workforce. The following brief discussion should be helpful. For further information, readers might wish to consult *Redefining Diversity* (AMACOM, 1996) and *Beyond Race and Gender* (AMACOM, 1991) by R. Roosevelt Thomas, Jr. and *A Practical Guide to Working With Diversity* by Joy Leach et al. (AMACOM, 1995).

In her classic book on workplace equality, *A Tale of "O" On Being Different in an Organization* (Harper & Row, 1980), Rosabeth Moss

Kanter talks about the two groups of people who exist in every organization: the X's, who are found in large numbers, and the O's, scarce and "different." After a handful of O's are hired, they often continue to feel different. X's view them as outsiders, and O's feel like observers. Sadly, Kanter's observations from almost twenty years ago continue to ring true in many work environments. This is certainly the case with companies that are stuck at the affirmative action level of mainstreaming, uncertain of how to progress to the diversity level of inclusion.

Successful diversity education and training begins with putting this two-tiered, complementary process in the right context. The objective of any educational program is to raise awareness and increase knowledge; training builds specific skills. But neither alone can solve problems or change the way a system functions. In fact, education or training in a vacuum can actually be harmful. Employees are given the impression that they are what is wrong with the company and a new mind-set or set of skills will "fix" them. Employees are also likely to leave a training session with a set of expectations that the organization is often not prepared to meet. Education and training need to be part of an ongoing, multifaceted process in which the organization assumes responsibility for a targeted direction and desired goals.

Diversity education and training are no different. Employers who pluck workers from their jobs for several hours or days to show a film, distribute some handouts, and lecture on the merits of diversity are setting themselves up for failure. They need instead a plan that begins with executive commitment—not merely on-paper commitment, but a continuous, visible demonstration to all employees that senior management believes diversity is a vital business issue, necessary for the company's continued growth and success. This is part of the educational process. Then the cultural diversity assessment committee can continue its work by assessing specific in-house issues. After identifying a "benchmark" of the company's current diversity culture, the committee can conduct individual interviews, hold focus groups, or distribute surveys to identify the kinds of problems employees perceive in relation to a diverse workforce. Specific objections, attitudes, and assumptions can also be isolated.

Once the results have been analyzed, the committee can identify the issues to be addressed through employee diversity education and training. (Note that not everything wrong with an organization can be fixed by training.) The committee can then proceed to set clear goals that meet both employee needs and organizational objectives. These goals need to be realistic in terms of a time frame and expected results. Start with educating employees about global objectives, such as improving understanding and acceptance of diversity efforts and reducing existing barriers to diversity. Then focus on the specific issues identified in the assessment stage. The most successful diversity training takes place over an extended period of time, with modest expectations at each level. A permanent change in how your employees work together and perceive one another will take time.

Everyone in the organization, from senior management to entry-level workers, should be part of diversity education and training workshops. However, mandating attendance could create a backlash before the process even begins. Connect the program to an overall organizational objective and present it as one in which everyone benefits. Time it so that the sessions do not interfere with other organizational priorities. And make certain that literature describing the workshops does not divide the workforce into perpetrators and victims, with the former depicted as exclusively white males.

Your company probably has a general training format it follows with regard to group composition, class sizes, training materials, and duration. Diversity training may not fit the standard model, however. Every training activity and method selected should stress diversity as it relates to the success of the company and the growth of all employees. Employees need to be reminded frequently that what they are learning applies to each of them.

Sessions consisting of mixed levels, departments, or functions may prove more effective than isolating employees who perform the same work at the same level. This employee mixing facilitates an exploration of a variety of diversity issues like job function, gender, and personality. Small groups of six to eight employees may be more efficient than standard classes of fifteen or more. Pairing up for case studies could yield better results than group activities. And video-taped role playing could produce eye-opening results—or greater resistance if it is introduced too early or with the wrong mix of employees. Consider, too, the merits of self-assessments, the results of which may be shared with others.

Session leaders should be experienced facilitators knowledgeable in the subject matter, sensitive to the concerns of all attendees, effective with group dynamics, able to field questions, and able to defuse potentially volatile issues. Leaders must establish credibility at the outset, to gain and maintain the attention of the attendees. The team can consist entirely of in-house HR staff, all outside "neutral" educators and trainers, or a combination of both. Consider, too, the merits of sending employees off-site, where there are no distractions or the temptation to return to work during breaks. Off-site training also sends the message that this topic is of primary importance to the organization.

The topics addressed in education and training workshops are varied. Although each organization should be guided by the results of the surveys conducted by its cultural diversity assessment committee, here are some general categories:

- Defining diversity
- Valuing diversity
- Facilitating organizational change
- Building a diverse workforce
- The benefits of working with diversity
- Promoting diversity
- Understanding inclusion
- Identifying personal prejudices
- Cross-cultural communication
- The problems with stereotyping
- Removing obstacles to diversity
- Multicultural management

Other topics may be more suitable for a specific group of employees. For example, HR staff may benefit from diversity-driven sessions on developing nonbiased job descriptions, increased sensitivity to people of diverse groups during job interviews, and career planning in a diverse workplace. Managers and supervisors will benefit from programs that address supervising in a diverse workplace, diverse staff development, and coaching and counseling members of a diverse workforce. Also, HR staff and managers and supervisors together may find helpful workshops focusing on hiring people with disabilities, maintaining a harassment-free work environment, and cross-gender teamwork.

In order to ensure education and training effectiveness, feedback is critical—not just a course evaluation, but feedback over time that is tied directly to specific goals. Periodically hold focus groups or conduct surveys to assess the usefulness of the diversity sessions. Since diversity education and training is an ongoing, often repetitive process, feedback needs to be ongoing as well. Formal training may need to be supplemented by coaching—informal, one-on-one discussions—to help certain employees cope with specific diversity issues, or perhaps segments of the workshops need to be isolated and reexamined. Focused and customized diversity education and training is likely to prove the most effective.

Compliance Issues

Diversity makes good business sense. Furthermore, a diverse work-force may preclude legal complications resulting from job discrimination charges. Specific equal employment opportunity laws and related issues will be discussed in Chapter 6. Here we consider several diversity groups and key questions to ask concerning them. Implementing changes based on the answers can make the workplace more diversity friendly and, hence, in compliance with the law.

Women

Legislation prohibiting discrimination against women includes Title VII of the federal Civil Rights Act of 1964, the Equal Employment Opportunity Commission's 1980 guidelines on sexual harassment, Executive Order 11246, the federal Equal Pay Act of 1963, the federal Pregnancy Discrimination Act of 1978, and the Civil Rights Act of 1991. Yet women still find it difficult to achieve an equal footing with men in business: they earn less, have less prestigious jobs, and are promoted less often. In addition, many must wrestle with the issue of child care and the balancing of work, as well as family issues.

To evaluate your organization with regard to its employment of women, conduct a thorough internal audit of current female employees:

- Do women plateau at a certain level?
- Are women overrepresented in some areas and underrepresented in others?
- Do women have levels of responsibility comparable to men?
- Are women considered equally for those jobs requiring travel?
- Are women offered international assignments?
- Does the organization make certain assumptions about women with children? Are women with children treated differently from child-free women, in terms of being offered less meaty assignments or work that requires less of an overtime commitment?

Also, meet with the women in your organization, and ask how they are being treated and perceived by colleagues, management, and customers:

- When members of a team, are they ever leaders?
- If they have supervisory responsibilities, how are they viewed by their employees?

- Are their proposals or solutions to problems taken seriously?
- What do women in your organization want to achieve in terms of growth and responsibility?
- Is there an invisible or "glass" ceiling preventing women from rising to senior positions?
- How do women want to be viewed?
- What are some of the work-related issues that women feel are important?
- How do women rate your company's child care arrangements?
- Do your work schedule alternatives allow women to balance work-family issues?

Examine career development opportunities for women:

- Are the women in your company asked about their aspirations and interests?
- Are women given an equal shot at education and training to acquire the knowledge and skills currently lacking?
- Are career paths charted for women who are interested?
- Are women excluded from informal networking and social affairs?

Posing and addressing these and other questions will help you to establish goals of inclusion and development for current, as well as incoming, women workers.

Older Workers

Assessing how well your organization is serving the needs of older workers begins with defining the term *old*. Ask someone aged twenty-something what "old" means, and you are likely to get a response that is substantially different from someone in her fifties. Although technically the federal Age Discrimination in Employment Act of 1967 (amended in 1978 and again in 1986) offers some guidelines by protecting workers aged forty and over, it is generally accepted that forty is far from old. We could turn to traditional views on retirement for guidance: early retirement at fifty-five (not too old), likely retirement by age sixty-five (pretty old), and almost sure to retire by age seventy (old). Of course, these views are countered by numerous articles describing the continuously improving health and physical condition of older Americans. More significant, companies are recognizing the business benefits to hiring older workers. Companies such as Kentucky Fried Chicken, the Home Shopping Network, and McDonald's have made a commitment to hiring older adults, and with good results.

Hiring older workers is also no more costly than hiring younger ones. A study conducted by Yankelovich, Skelly and White Inc. revealed that health care costs between thirty-year-old and sixty-five-year-old retirees are comparable. And the American Association of Retired Persons (AARP) reports that workers between the ages of fifty and sixty stay on the job an average of fifteen years and that their attendance and safety records are as good as or better than other age groups. In fact, mature workers have a lower accident rate in most occupations, *Personnel Journal* reported in October 1995.

Determining where your organization stands with regard to older workers begins with an examination of your current workforce:

- Do you discourage early retirement?
- What percentage of your staff consists of workers aged fifty-five and over?
- Sixty-five and over?
- Seventy and over?
- If older workers cannot continue to perform every aspect of their jobs successfully, do you modify the assignments or offer retraining?
- Since one of the most common midcareer problems is career burnout, do you offer job redesign or job rotation?
- Another common midcareer problem is career plateauing; one viable solution is assigning employees to special projects and assigning them as mentors for new employees.
- Is there a health and fitness program available (this benefits workers or all ages)?
- Does senior management stress compliance with the Age Discrimination in Employment Act, in both policy and practice?
- Is there an overall atmosphere of acceptance and encouragement for older workers?
- When hiring, do recruiters reach out to older adults in places they may frequent, such as senior centers and mall-walker groups?
- Are younger recruiters and managers coached in how to interview applicants old enough to be their grandparents? For example, rather than asking someone returning to work after retiring about career goals, focus on how the company can benefit from their skills and knowledge.

• Do older applicants receive the same alternative work schedule options as other candidates?

• Are managers educated in how to acclimate older workers into their departments?

Viewing older workers as assets will not only help you comply with legal requirements, but improve your pool of human resources.

Younger Workers

It may seem that younger workers could not possibly have any workplace bias issues. In their twenties and early thirties, there is a seemingly abundant supply of opportunities and options from which they can choose, something that many baby boomers and older workers envy. Nevertheless, there are certain perceptions and mind-sets that can adversely affect their chances for employment.

The work ethics of today and tomorrow's youth differ from those of previous generations. With a greater interest in balancing a fulfilling career with familial responsibilities and outside interests, young employees focus on salary, benefits, and flexible scheduling. Baby boomers and older workers may view this as self-serving and indicating a lack of initiative and dedication. Younger workers also seek out jobs that are fulfilling, meaningful, or interesting. They are more likely to change jobs when the level of satisfaction drops below a certain point. Employers who believe that work for work's sake is important and value the idea of developing a career with one company over a long period of time may perceive these workers as less dedicated and perhaps even "spoiled." Of course, younger workers are quick to point out that loyalty is difficult to sustain with all the mergers, acquisitions, and cutbacks in today's economy.

Boundaries established by hierarchy, position, and authority are viewed as lacking merit by many younger workers, creating a conflict with employers valuing such concepts. Problems with promotions can arise as well; younger workers expect to move up faster than older managers are prepared to implement.

Credibility is another area of concern. Despite younger workers' knowledge and expertise, the work of young executives may not be taken seriously. Jokes and demeaning remarks may be made, especially about those achieving high levels of success at a young age.

Since employers will be competing to attract the limited number of youthful workers projected for the near future, it makes good business sense to tune in to the concerns of this important group.

People With Disabilities

The Americans with Disabilities Act of 1990 prohibits employers from discriminating against employees or job applicants with disabilities. It affects millions of people with physical, mental, or emotional impairments. Most employers have no problem complying with the requirement of reasonable accommodation: 31 percent of the accommodations cost nothing, and 50 percent cost less than $50 per person; only 11 percent cost in excess of $1,000, according to the President's Committee on Employment of People with Disabilities (*Employer Incentives When Hiring People with Disabilities*, September 1992). These same employers, however, experience varying levels of discomfort, embarrassment, and even resentment when talking to or working with someone with a disability.

Many workers complain of being defined by their disability, frequently patronized, and excluded from social activities. They are made to feel they should be grateful for any job, and their advancement opportunities may be limited. People with "invisible" disabilities, such as AIDS, cancer, or emotional illness, hesitate to make their disabilities known because of anticipated negative reactions.

Where does your organization stand when it comes to hiring, training, and promoting workers with disabilities? The President's Committee on Employment of People with Disabilities has published an educational kit, "Ability for Hire," that offers practical do's and don'ts for hiring people with disabilities. Here are some of the questions to ask yourself based on the kit's guidelines:

• Is our workplace accessible to people with physical disabilities?

• Does my organization have written job descriptions that define the essential functions of the job and the approximate percentage of time each task requires?

• Does our HR department go out of its way to recruit people with disabilities, for example, by attending specialized job fairs?

• Do managers understand and comply with the concept of "reasonable accommodation"?

• Do interviewers know not to ask applicants if they have a disability?

• Is our staff sensitive to basic issues of disability etiquette? For example, do they know not to shout or speak very slowly when conversing with someone who is blind?

• Do we have procedures for maintaining and protecting confidential medical records?

• Do we treat people with disabilities the same as any other applicant or employee?

• Perhaps most important, do we treat people with disabilities the way *we* expect to be treated?

Minorities

This collective group, rapidly outgrowing the term *minority*, will represent a large percentage of tomorrow's workforce, but few will be targeted for professional positions. In far too many environments, race and ethnicity continue to identify nonwhite workers, regardless of levels of achievement. They may be referred to as the company's African-American attorney, Chinese financial officer, or Hispanic vice president. For those reaching high levels within an organization, the assumption often is that they rode on the coattails of affirmative action or are the exception.

Legislation protecting people from race or ethnic discrimination abounds: the federal Civil Rights Acts of 1866, 1964, and 1990; Executive Order 11246; and the Equal Employment Opportunity Commission's Guidelines on Discrimination Because of National Origin are examples. Yet discrimination based on ethnicity continues. Although overt bias is less frequently demonstrated than in the past, the message in many businesses is clear: Minorities can work in certain positions, but rarely at the higher levels.

To achieve a diversity-driven work environment, employers must strive to eliminate even subtle messages of bias. You may be making a concerted effort to recruit minorities, but what happens once they are hired? Conduct an assessment of your workforce by asking yourself some tough questions:

• What percentage of professional or executive positions are filled by minorities? For those that are, does positive stereotyping prevail (e.g., steering Asian-Americans into technical jobs)?

• Are minorities in high-level positions resented by other employees?

• Do these high-level minorities receive less respect or have less credibility because of their ethnicity?

• Do whites supervised by a minority feel they have less status in the organization?

• Do whites take seriously ideas and suggestions made by minorities?

• Are minorities given equal amounts of feedback and supervision, or are managers who impart criticism as part of feedback fearful of being called "racists"?

• Do managers have lower expectations of minorities?

• Are harsher judgments made about the performance of minorities than about anyone else's?

• Does your organization ever hire or promote unqualified minorities to satisfy affirmative action goals, and then fail to provide them with sufficient education or training, effectively setting them up for failure?

• Does management see all nonwhite employees as representing their race?

• Do minorities participate in the normal socializing that goes on in your organization?

When employers stop identifying workers by their ethnicity and instead see them as productive colleagues, businesses will be that much closer to achieving true workplace diversity.

Immigrants

The United States has always been viewed as a land of opportunity. Before 1965, most immigrants came from Europe and Canada; since then, the majority have come from Asia and Latin America. In addition to immigrants, waves of refugees continue to arrive in the United States, predominantly from Southeast Asian and Central American countries. Some are highly skilled and educated; others are illiterate. Many face language problems and have difficulty adjusting to the American culture.

Many experts agree that immigrants help expand the economy by starting their own businesses. In addition, they often fill jobs rejected by American workers, since many immigrants come to the United States virtually penniless and view any work as an opportunity. It is also apparent that many highly educated and technically expert immigrants can fill scientific and engineering jobs. Nevertheless, many native-born Americans resent immigrants, believing that they are taking jobs away from those born in the United States. This attitude, along with adjusting to a different work ethic, makes assimilation difficult for immigrants intent on making the United States their home.

Certainly employers ensure compliance with the requirements of the Immigration Reform and Control Act of 1986 (IRCA) by certifying that all employees hired after November 6, 1986, are eligible to work in the United States. But it also makes good business sense to go beyond compliance and help immigrants integrate. Consider some key questions:

• Are your native-born employees impatient with immigrant workers because they speak English slowly or are unfamiliar with certain words and expressions?

• Do you have a policy requiring that only English can be spoken?

• Do your native-born employees assume that negative news concerning the national group of some immigrant workers is typical (e.g., assuming that all Colombian immigrants are drug dealers)?

• Are the technical skills and educational accomplishments of immigrants recognized and rewarded?

• Does HR assume that immigrants prefer working together, even if they are from different cultures?

• Is there tolerance shown immigrants with a different sense of time, punctuality, and deadlines?

• Are cultural mannerisms and dress ridiculed?

• Does management respect and allow time off for an immigrant's religious observances or holidays?

• Is the body language of people from other cultures misunderstood?

• Do employees make an effort to help immigrants ease the stresses of being in a new country, culture, and work environment?

• Are immigrant employees invited to social affairs?

• Perhaps most important, are you treating immigrant employees with the same patience, tolerance, and understanding that *you* would expect, having moved to a new country with an entirely new language, culture, and work ethic?

White Males

American-born white male workers, still the dominant culture, are witnessing a host of changes affecting their coveted role in the organizational hierarchy. Blue- and white-collar jobs, almost exclusively theirs in the past, are increasingly going to women and minorities: women are driving trucks, and women and minorities are moving, albeit slowly, into management positions. Work-related social events for men only have all but fallen by the wayside. Race and gender lines are blurred. The result is a sense of loss, anger, and disorientation.

Many white men feel the finger of accountability pointing at them for much of what is wrong with the culture of an organization, such as an environment that is not diverse. To them, this translates into an assumption that most white men are racists or sexists. Their sincere efforts to assist women or minorities in their work may be viewed as patronizing. Improper etiquette with a woman can lead to charges of sexual harassment. The reactions to this broad categorizing and white male bashing range from quiet resentment to rage. Many are afraid to speak out for fear of being misinterpreted. Productivity is affected, and the relationships between white males and other workers widen.

Because they must accommodate different groups in nonstereotypical roles, white males may become less productive; in turn, they may lose out on growth opportunities due to a lack of effort. The organization loses the benefits of their skill and knowledge, and other workers may lose them as mentors.

Employers need to ask themselves: Can we continue our diversity efforts without alienating white males? If you implement diversity from an approach encompassing everyone, and communicate this to your workforce through repeated action, then the answer is yes.

Resources on Diversity

Resources on diversity include:

MOSAICS: SHRM Focuses on Workplace Diversity
Society for Human Resource Management
606 North Washington Street
Alexandria, VA 22314
703/548-3440

Diversity Marketing Outlook
Gil Deane Group
13751 Lake City Way Northeast, Suite 210
Seattle, WA 98125
206/362-0336

Managing Diversity
Jamestown Area Labor Management Committee
P.O. Box 819
Jamestown, NY 14702
716/665-3654

WD—The Journal of Work Force Diversity
Equal Opportunity Publications
150 Motor Parkway, Suite 420
Hauppauge, NY 11788
516/273-0066

Workforce Diversity
350 West Hubbard Street, Suite 440
Chicago, IL 60610
312/464-0300

The Diversity Bookstore catalog, *Cultural Diversity at Work*
13751 Lake City Way Northeast, Suite 210
Seattle, WA 98125
206/362-0336

Summary

Diversity is one of the most significant HR issues affecting the workplace today. It reflects the multitude of ways in which workers are both unique and similar. The ultimate goal of a diversity-driven work environment is for everyone to work together toward achieving common organizational objectives, while prospering individually. This requires commitment and adaptation by all involved, beginning with senior management. To succeed, diversity must be viewed not only as an altruistic gesture but as an important business issue.

Diversity differs from affirmative action in its emphasis on inclusion as opposed to mainstreaming. Employers often establish cultural diversity assessment committees to evaluate their affirmative action programs. This analysis leads to a review of the company's recruitment practices and resources, to ensure the targeting of representatives from diverse groups. In addition, the committee can recommend diversity education and training to encourage the existing workforce to accept diversity.

Having a diversity-driven workforce may also preclude charges of job discrimination. By integrating into the workforce women, older and younger workers, people with disabilities, minorities, recent immigrants, and white males, organizations can ensure greater compliance with equal employment opportunity laws.

Chapter 3
Recruitment Sources

As Chapter 1 revealed, the labor pool from which employers may select new employees is changing at every level. In order to attract outstanding candidates to their organizations, employers are becoming more aggressive, approaching recruiting proactively, and carefully weighing the benefits and drawbacks of various resources before proceeding. Reliable recruitment sources may be approached differently or abandoned entirely, and more creative techniques may emerge. Online recruiting, the newest and, according to many recruiters, most effective means of attracting candidates, will be discussed at length in Chapter 4.

Prerecruitment Considerations

Deciding which recruitment source to tap each time you have an opening may prove difficult. Some organizations ignore the multitude of options and use the same sources each time, with mixed results. For example, a company that relies heavily on newspaper ads should consider the time of year (ads running just before Christmas generally do not do well) and even the day of the week (certain jobs attract more applicants in the middle of the week than on weekends).

Avoid using the same recruitment source every time an opening is available for a similar position. Aside from the possibility that market conditions and certain internal factors may have changed, there is the possibility that this practice could lead to charges of *systemic discrimination*—the denial of equal employment opportunity through an established business practice, such as recruitment. Even though the discrimination may be inadvertent, the disparate effect it produces may develop into a prime area of vulnerability for employers. Relying on the same recruitment source each time a particular position becomes available could have an adverse impact on members of certain protected groups who lack the same access as others to that source. This, in turn, could translate into the denial of equal employment opportunity.

Before embarking on a recruitment campaign, employers should consider four factors: how much money is available, how quickly the opening must be filled, whether a wide audience must be reached, and the exemption level of the position.

Recruitment Budget

The amount of money allocated for recruitment can reduce options considerably. Display ads and search firms can be extremely costly, with no guarantee of attracting a substantial number of qualified candidates. On the other hand, some of the most effective recruitment sources cost very little or nothing at all.

If money is of primary concern when it comes to recruiting, explore the possibility of using job posting, HR files, employee referrals, government agencies, direct mail, referrals from clients and customers, and school placement offices.

Quick-Results Recruitment Sources

No matter how well you anticipate staffing needs, an opening may occur suddenly and unexpectedly. When this happens, focus on recruitment sources that are most likely to yield immediate results.

Advertising in professional journals, attending job fairs, and running an open house will take too long. But going through your HR files may prove effective, since these candidates have already been interviewed and assessed. More important, they have already expressed an interest in working for your company.

Other options are employee referrals, employment agencies, search firms, newspaper ads, and inter-HR networking. If you are really pressed, you might want to hire contingent workers or, if you have one, turn to your preemployment training pool.

Broad-Based Recruiting

Some positions are highly specialized and more difficult to fill. To improve the chances of a job match, you will want to reach as many candidates as possible. Also, if you are uncertain as to the type of individual being sought, interview as many applicants as possible.

Employment agencies and search firms may be helpful in these instances, although they tend to recommend nearly everyone when the requirements are broad. Ads in newspapers and journals can be effective also. Consider advertising in out-of-town publications for hard-to-fill openings, being prepared to accommodate the travel needs of viable candidates.

Exemption Status

Exempt employees are defined by the Fair Labor Standards Act as workers legally exempt from receiving overtime compensation; that is, employers do not have to pay professionals for overtime. The term *nonexempt* literally means not exempt from overtime compensation, or, stated another way, entitled to receive overtime pay. (Exemption status is discussed at greater length in Chapter 5.)

Recruitment sources that produce qualified exempt or professional candidates may not work as well for nonexempt applicants. Effective resources for exempt-level, professional positions include direct mail recruitment, search firms, campus recruiting, job fairs, research firms, and professional associations. Nonexempt applicants are frequently found through employee referrals, high school guidance counselors, government agencies, advertising in the classified section of newspapers, and employment agencies. In addition, most walk-in candidates are looking for nonexempt-level employment.

Of the factors indicated—cost, immediacy, audience, and level—each recruitment source may meet some criteria but not others. Employers are advised to explore the ramifications of using each resource in relation to these four factors, deciding which are most important for each job opening.

Newspaper ads provide a prime example. They are expensive but more likely to yield immediate results. Assuming they appear in the most-likely-to-be-read section of an appropriate paper, on the right day of the week, at the right time of year, and contain the necessary text, newspaper ads will reach a wide audience consisting of the level you are trying to reach. A separate section in this chapter is devoted to advertising, since newspapers and magazines are widely relied upon as recruitment sources.

Proactive and Reactive Recruitment

After examining the four criteria, consider how aggressive you must be in order to fill a particular opening. If immediacy is a primary factor, search out proactive recruitment sources that will make a concerted effort to find employees. This is the reverse of reactive recruitment, where you wait for applicants to apply, hoping that the right person is among them.

Some recruitment sources are inherently reactive, by their very nature prohibiting recruiters from aggressively pursuing candidates. The responsibility for finding applicants is placed elsewhere. Consider one of the most popular recruitment sources, employee referrals (discussed in detail later in this chapter). HR provides employees with the job description and a list of requirements, then waits to see who applies. The onus for referring candidates is on the employees. This is fine (and cost-effective) if time is not a factor. Perhaps you have an employee who wants to retire but is willing to wait until a replacement is found. Or maybe one department is thinking about creating a new position but is not pressured to fill it immediately. Whatever the scenario, time is not a key issue; hence, reactive recruitment can work under the right circumstances. More often than not, however, time is crucial. When an employee resigns, giving two weeks' notice (if you are lucky), you must move fast; that means being proactive in your attempts to find a replacement.

Proactive recruiters start recruitment efforts as soon as they learn that there will be an opening. They expand their recruitment pool to encompass other than traditional recruiting sources and aggressively go after candidates, luring them with attractive employment packages. Such packages are not offered by large, money-is-no-object companies only. Any organization can put together a tempting offer reflecting such items as shared decision making, child and elder care referrals, suggestion and award programs, health club memberships, and company-sponsored social affairs. One small publishing firm provides each employee with a complete turkey dinner at Thanksgiving. An electronics company, located in snowy New Hampshire, gives each worker ten free skiing lessons. Once free of traditional thoughts when it comes to perks, there is no limit to the extras you can offer applicants, and many cost very little.

Being proactive means more than avoiding a lengthy gap between the time an incumbent vacates a position and someone new is hired. It also provides a clearer shot at attracting outstanding candidates and making a hiring decision after interviewing a number of *qualified* applicants. That is because you are in control of who are targeted as candidates. With direct mail recruiting, for example, employers contact specific candidates known to have certain skills and knowledge. Although the response rate is usually low, around 2 percent, you at least know that those responding are viable candidates.

Another example of proactive recruitment is preemployment training that provides a supplemental workforce. These are employees recruited through conventional means over time and trained in job- and industry-specific matters. They are then placed in a standby pool. When there is an opening, employers can turn to their supplemental workforce and select a suitable candidate. Of course, there is no guarantee that the right person will remain in the pool, waiting to be offered a job.

Professional associations and inter-HR networking can also provide employers with the opportunity to recruit proactively. Direct contact with potential employees or communication with others in your field can often put you in touch with qualified applicants.

Employee Referrals

One of the most expeditious recruitment sources is a company's own employee referral program, also known as word of mouth. In spite of the fact that this form of recruitment is reactive, it is frequently used because of its cost-effectiveness and positive impact on employee morale.

In basic terms, this method entails spreading the word as soon as a position becomes available. The department head in charge of the area with the opening tells other department heads; employees talk to one another; word may be carried outside the organization to family, friends, and acquaintances. Employees, especially those proved to be valuable and reliable human resources, can often lead their company to good candidates. To make this method more effective, incentives of varying worth are offered to encourage employees to refer qualified candidates.

In an employee referral program, employees are advised every time an opening becomes available. They are provided with a job description, highlighting the education and experience requirements, as well as the responsibilities of the job. Employees may then refer people meeting the requirements of the job. If the new employee is an employee referral, an award is given to the person who made the referral.

Employee referral programs work most effectively when ground rules are clearly defined. Certain restrictions may apply that preclude referrals of either current employees or relatives to work in one's own department. Also, HR employees and company officers are usually prohibited from participating. The granting of awards is customarily conditioned on the new employee's satisfactorily completing a predetermined period of employment and receiving a minimum-level evaluation during that time.

The awards or bonuses are often in the form of cash, generally ranging from twenty-five dollars for a nonexempt worker to several thousand dollars for a top-level executive. Rewards may take other forms too. Growing in popularity is the concept of a drawing. In addition to cash bonuses, employees successfully referring a new employee may enter a drawing to be held after a certain number of referral-based applicants are hired and win even bigger prizes. The greater the number of referrals, the grander the prizes, which may include trips, over and above accrued vacation time, and cars, with taxes and the first year's insurance paid. Other offerings include savings bonds, gift certificates, and merchandise.

Employee referral programs generally work well. Employees respond favorably to the incentives offered, usually costing the company considerably less than expenditures for other recruitment sources, such as advertising or search firms and employment agencies. Caution must be exercised in their use, however. Because it has been shown that "like tends to refer like" (for example, white males tend to refer other white males), women and minorities may not receive equal employment opportunities if they are not proportionately represented in your organization. Indeed, employee referral programs are one of the primary sources of systemic discrimination. Hence, they should be used only in conjunction with other recruitment sources or in a highly diversity-driven work environment.

Advertising

Advertising in both newspapers and professional publications remains a popular and often effective means for soliciting applications. Careful planning in terms of content, timing, and location is likely to generate a large response and result in a hiring.

To increase your chances of finding top-notch candidates through advertising, begin with these powerful ad placement strategies:

• Capture the job hunter's attention through the location of the ad, an appropriate job title, graphics, use of white space, and the placement of a logo.

• Hold the job hunter's attention. Provide enough information to pique readers' interest so that they establish a connection between your needs and their skills. Also, omit some information so potential candidates will want to make contact and learn more.

• Design your ad to be the last one a job hunter wants to read. Use language that creates an image of how great employment with your company would be.

When designing the contents of an ad, define those you want to reach. If you are looking for individuals with specialized skills, the ad should clearly enumerate those skills. If, on the other hand, you are scouting for talent, the wording should be less specific. The same holds true for the extent to which the job's duties and responsibilities are spelled out. Some employers want applicants to know virtually everything about a job before they apply. Others prefer to learn about the candidates and establish their interest before describing the details of the job. When advertising, make certain that enough information is provided for applicants to determine whether it is worth applying. Also be sure to include the method of contact: resumé, telephone call, fax, or walk-in.

Regardless of how explicit the ad is, it is generally best to be direct in your wording. Job hunters should not be required to wade through cute, nondescriptive, or unprofessional jargon to determine what positions are available or the qualities being sought. This kind of language may succeed in catching the reader's eye, but it is not likely to generate the desired response.

This caution does not preclude designing an ad that will stand out. Use of creative graphics, color, clever job-related language, and tasteful humor can accomplish this objective and still project an appropriate image. Keep in mind that the contents and appearance of your ad are a reflection of your organization. Consider the image you wish to project, and proceed accordingly.

If you have not developed ads before, consider enlisting the services of an agency to help write the copy, select the categories under which an ad should appear, and determine the most effective combination of spacing, boldness and size of letters, layout, and other graphic elements. Agencies may also offer advice as to the best day of the week to run an ad for a specific job category. The issue of timing can make a substantial difference in the number of responses received. Not only can specific days of the week be significant, but the time of the year can also influence responsiveness. As stated earlier, ads running just before Christmas generally do not do well, except perhaps during times of high unemployment. January, on the other hand, is traditionally the time when soon-to-be college graduates begin thinking about employment opportunities.

Where you choose to advertise will have an effect on responsiveness. Begin by scouting a variety of newspapers both in your area and outside it. Note the frequency with which ads for certain jobs appear in specific publications. Consider newspapers that have broad appeal as well, especially if you are seeking to attract candidates for a hard-to-fill position. In addition, consider publications that are read mainly by women or minorities. Ads placed in these publications can reach highly qualified applicants and, at the same time, help your company meet its affirmative action goals and diversity objectives.

If you are not in a hurry to fill a position and can wait for the issue carrying your ad to be published, you may choose to advertise in a bimonthly or monthly business magazine. Many professional journals have a classified section reaching a wide audience of specialists in their field that is generally not costly.

Researching the circulation and readership of publications that may carry your ads also makes sense. In addition to contacting the publication directly, review standard media guides, available in most public libraries. These list national and regional newspapers and various professional magazines, along with information relating to audience profile and circulation.

Advertising can be a costly means of recruitment. Generally if you are seeking candidates for a highly competitive field, you must compete visually with other ads through eye-catching displays with large type, logos, and borders. Make certain that the ad conveys your message precisely. In order to outshine competitors, brag about your company's standing in the industry, outstanding benefits package, and other perks offered. Commenting on some key attractions within striking distance of the company can also draw applicants.

Some organizations run blind ads that do not reveal the company's identity, instead giving a box number to which a resumé may be forwarded. This is usually done to avoid a flood of telephone calls. On the other hand, with hard-to-fill positions where the number of responses will be limited, interested individuals should be encouraged to get in touch with you as soon as possible. Blind ads may discourage potential applicants from applying altogether. Without knowing the source of an ad, there is always the danger of someone's applying to one's own company for a new job.

As a final comment with regard to advertising, make certain that the language used does not violate equal employment opportunity laws and regulations. This language would include an age preference using terminology such as *young man* or *mature woman*, using certain other subjective terms, such as *attractive*, or stating a preference for either gender. With regard to the last, note that masculine or feminine terms do not automatically constitute an equal employment opportunity (EEO) violation. The Equal Employment Opportunity Commission (EEOC) has issued a policy statement regarding sex-referent language in employment advertising, noting that terms such as *patrolman* or *meter maid* have become "colloquial ways of denoting particular jobs rather than the sex of the individuals who perform those jobs." The statement continues, "The use of sex-referent language in employment opportunity advertisements and other recruitment practices is suspect but is not a per se violation of Title VII." The EEOC goes on to urge employers to indicate clearly their intent to consider applicants of both genders whenever sex-referent language is used. A statement in a recruitment ad confirming nondiscriminatory intent, such as "equal employment opportunity employer, male/female," should be included.

A sampling of ads appears in Appendix A.

Additional Recruitment Sources

There are many effective ways of finding candidates in addition to employee referrals and advertising. Each of these recruitment sources should be evaluated in relation to the four factors, determining which factors are most important, and deciding if proactive or reactive recruitment is the better approach. Then assess each recruitment source in terms of its advantages and disadvantages (summarized at the end of this chapter). The following discussion includes some commonly used recruitment sources, as well as some relatively lesser-known methods for filling positions.

Job Posting

Almost without exception, the first recruitment source to be explored should be your own organization. Promoting or transferring employees from within offers several advantages:

- It usually creates an opening at a lower, easier-to-fill level.
- The company saves considerable time and money by transferring someone already familiar with the organizational structure and methodology.
- Employee morale is boosted.
- Hidden talent may be uncovered.

The process by which internal recruitment is accomplished is called *job posting*. With this proactive system, available positions are offered to employees before recruitment using outside sources. A simplified job description, citing the department, location, exemption status, salary grade and range, work schedule, requirements, primary duties and responsibilities, and working conditions, is posted in central locations, such as outside the company cafeteria or on bulletin boards outside rest rooms, or is transmitted to all employees via printed form or e-mail. Also included is a closing date by which time all applications must be submitted. The standard deadline is generally from one to two weeks.

Organizations may require that interested employees receive permission from their supervisors before applying, others require notification, and still others respect the confidentiality of the process until a decision has been reached. A sample job posting form appears in Appendix B, and a sample job posting application form is shown in Appendix C.

All applicants are considered in the same manner as any outside candidate. If a qualified applicant is found, arrangements for a starting date in the new position are made by the existing department head, HR, and the new department head. Anywhere from two to four weeks is generally allowed for finding a replacement to fill the position being vacated.

Some organizations have a policy of posting all openings; others post only nonexempt positions. Some steer clear of job posting altogether, for the following reasons:

• Supervisors and managers may want to promote someone they have groomed for a position. Therefore, they do not want to consider other candidates.

• Some managers may resent employees who apply for jobs outside their department, tending to take such a move personally.

• Losing an employee to job posting may mean waiting for a replacement who may not be as qualified.

• Some companies prefer to bring in new blood rather than recycle existing employees.

The success of a job posting system depends largely on how well it is designed and monitored. For example, an organization may stipulate that employees must be with a company for at least one year, as well as in their current position for at least six months, before using the job posting system. The number of jobs that an individual may apply for within one year may also be limited, generally to three. In addition, a rating of satisfactory or better on the most recent performance appraisal may be required in order for an employee to use the job posting system. These guidelines may mitigate the problem of the "revolving-door" employee who may opt to apply for virtually every job posted. It also treats the process in a serious manner and lends it credibility, thereby increasing its effectiveness.

Employment Agencies and Search Firms

Two popular reactive recruitment sources are employment agencies and search firms. Generally search firms handle only professional openings, while employment agencies recruit for all other types of jobs. A minimum dollar figure is generally used to determine the level of job a search firm will recruit.

There are two primary reasons that organizations turn to agencies and search firms frequently. First, they have access to a large labor pool and can readily scout the market for qualified candidates. This includes seeking out applicants seemingly content with their current jobs. Second, they can often fill a position more quickly than a company could on its own.

The most significant reason for not retaining the services of an agency or search firm is the cost. Although the fee structure of each employment service varies somewhat, most work on a contingency basis; that is, they do not collect the fee until a referred applicant is hired. The cost then ranges from 1 percent per $1,000 of salary, all the way up to a straight 25 percent of the annual salary. Executive search firms may charge more, ranging from 25 to 30 percent of the new employee's salary for the first year. For example, at 30 percent, an employee earning $75,000 would cost a company $22,500 in fees. There may be additional charges for related out-of-pocket expenses. (Fees charged for sales positions may take into account incentive or bonus compensation.)

Before agreeing to register an opening with either an employment agency or a search firm, consider these five guidelines:

1. Be certain that the agency will evaluate applicants and refer only those who meet the standards stipulated. Too often agencies merely forward resumés to a client, expecting the company's interviewer to do the screening.

2. Be firm about the job's requirements, and refuse to consider anyone who does not meet them. In this regard it is prudent to forward a copy of the job description for the available position.

3. Ask for a written agreement detailing the fee arrangement: how much, when it is to be paid, and any other stipulations. For

instance, some search firms refund a percentage of the fee paid if employees placed as a result of their efforts are terminated within the first three to six months of work.

4. Be selective in determining which agencies and search firms will receive your business. Meet with and interview representatives to make certain that they clearly understand your objectives. Establish their degree of knowledge in the specific field for which they will be recruiting, and make certain that you feel comfortable working with them. Ask for information regarding their methodology, experience, and track record. Do not hesitate to ask for references and to gauge their reputation in the field. Also be sure that the person with whom you meet is the person actually handling your company's account.

5. Formally notify all agencies and search firms with which you will be working that you are an equal opportunity employer. Also, share information regarding your organization's affirmative action plan and diverse workforce program. Make it very clear that you expect them to comply fully with all equal employment opportunity and affirmative actions laws and regulations and that you will terminate your relationship if they should violate these laws at any time.

Once you have decided to work with a particular employment agency or search firm, encourage agency representatives to learn as much as possible about both your organization and the specific job opening. The more information the agency has, the better able it will be to meet your needs effectively and expeditiously.

Employers should note that private employment services may be regulated by state and federal laws. Coverage varies among the states and may regulate such facets as annual licensing, fees, and certain practices, such as misrepresenting a job or advertising without identifying the source as an employment service.

With more than twenty thousand placement agencies in the United States, employers can afford to be selective when choosing an employment service. Recommendations from satisfied clients can assist in the process, as can publications such as *The Directory of Executive Recruiters*, published by Consultants News.

HR Files

In some instances, the expense of an agency or ad can be avoided simply by referring to the company's HR files. This is a proactive, cost-effective recruitment source. It is quite possible that someone applied for a similar position not too long ago and was a viable candidate. Perhaps there were several qualified applicants at the time, or perhaps there were no suitable openings when this individual applied. Possibly the applicant's salary requirements exceeded the amount then being offered.

When scanning HR files for existing applications, carefully compare background and skills with the requirements of the available position. Also, review the notes of the previous interviewer and try to talk to that person. The previous interviewer may recall the applicant well enough to provide you with valuable insights.

Walk-Ins, Call-Ins, and Write-Ins

Other reactive recruitment sources that do not cost anything are walk-ins, call-ins, and write-ins. Walk-ins and call-ins usually consist of nonexempt applications; write-ins are usually professionals. These unsolicited applications can often result in the hiring of outstanding employees. Too often, however, walk-ins, call-ins, and write-ins are not treated seriously. Walk-ins are automatically told by the receptionist that there are no openings at the time. If they are permitted to complete an application, these forms are quickly filed away, without an interviewer's reviewing them. Call-ins are generally told to apply in person, only to be informed that there are no openings. And unsolicited resumés are given a cursory glance, at best, before being filed. Sometimes letters of acknowledgment are sent, but more often than not, there is no communication whatsoever.

A simply monitored system for handling such applicants can yield excellent results. Make certain that the receptionist in the HR department has an up-to-date list of job openings, accompanied by a simplified job description for each. This list should be referred to every time a walk-in applies for a job. If the applicant has expressed an interest in a position that appears on that list, an interviewer should be so informed. If time is not available for an immediate conference, arrangements should be made for the candidate to return at a specified time.

Call-ins should be treated in a similar fashion. The receptionist can check the list of openings and refer callers to the interviewer in charge of a particular job. A brief telephone interview can usually be conducted on the spot to establish sufficient interest. An appointment can then be scheduled.

Unsolicited resumés can also be reviewed with the list of openings in mind. Possible job matches can then be pursued, by telephone or mail.

These three recruitment sources can be especially valuable when you must meet the requirements of certain hard-to-fill positions.

School Recruiting

School recruiting, a proactive form of finding employees, is not what it used to be. Not so long ago, representatives from companies would visit selected campuses, high schools, and trade schools, selecting the names of candidates to interview from the placement office's resumé book. If mutual interest was established, follow-up interviews at the company would be arranged. Or companies would conduct an open house on campus to promote the benefits and advantages they offered. Letters would then be sent to promising graduates, inviting job applications.

On-campus recruiting has always required careful planning and preparation, because of the high degree of competition for those graduating from the nation's top schools. But now a subtle shift has developed in bargaining position. Today's graduates, in greater demand, expect to be courted and can be very selective. In particular, graduates with information technology (IT) skills can pretty much write their own ticket. According to a survey conducted by the National Association of Colleges and Employers (NACE) and reported in May 1997 in *HR Magazine*, almost 8 percent of all job offers for college graduates in 1996 went to computer science majors. Other highly sought after graduates included those with majors in management information systems, business, math, and electrical and software engineering. The need for college graduates with computer skills is so great that in Virginia, a coalition of technology employers has asked that all incoming students at colleges and universities be required to develop computer literacy, regardless of their projected major. Going a step further, some companies are trying to beat the competition by paying college placement offices to provide resumés of students with IT skills as early as a year before graduation.

This change in attitude is attributable, for the most part, to those changes in the workforce described in Chapter 1—specifically, an increased number of positions requiring higher levels of education, a decline in the number of potential new employees from known populations, and a national shift to a service economy, prompting companies to rely more on the quality of management than on the quality of manufactured goods.

These factors have resulted in new forms of school recruitment. An increased number of organizations are now promoting educational assistance programs. By offering scholarships, low-interest loans, internships, and work-study programs, companies hope to nurture the educational and professional development of students as early as the beginning of high school.

"Professor programs" are another relatively new method of school recruitment. Professors not only identify students who are high-potential candidates, but also take information about a company back to their students after meeting with management and observing company employees at work. A variation of the professor program occurs when company executives teach courses at selected schools, giving them direct access to students with demonstrated potential. Sign-on bonuses are also increasingly offered as an effort to garner commitment from a candidate, as is selling long-term employability through formal career-growth programs.

Moreover, the traditional company recruitment brochure, describing the organization in terms of its origins, products, and objectives, is being updated. Today's students are attracted to companies that enjoy a good reputation, are successful, and are on the leading edge of technological change. And, let's face it, a company that will look good on a resumé does not hurt either. In addition, students want in-depth information about career paths, training programs, and specific benefits, and frequently they request details about the city or town that will provide their living and working environment.

Although printed brochures identifying various aspects of employment are still the norm, there are more technologically advanced means of communicating this information. To attract students, companies have developed intriguing videotapes, emphasizing the positive aspects of employment with them. Others distribute CD-ROMs that present company history, products, services, customers, work environment, and culture, including answers to anticipated questions. In many cases, these CD-ROMs are preferable to brochures, offering students a clearer sense of what working for a company would be like. Consequently, many companies now substitute the CD-ROM presentation for an on-campus information session, cutting travel costs for recruiting in half.

School recruitment can prove costly, and if the end result is the hiring of only a few students, the cost per new employee may not be economical. Although there are no standard cost-per-hire guidelines, the following rule of thumb may be helpful: If an organization is spending at least two-thirds of its recruitment budget on students who never become employees, the recruiting program should be revamped.

Many companies continue to conduct back-to-back on-campus interviews of approximately fifteen to thirty minutes in duration. Increasingly, however, employers are turning to videoconferencing job interviews. Although nearly half of the Fortune 500 companies currently use videoconferencing to deliver corporate training programs, videoconference job interviewing for campus recruiting is an innovative technique. Used by employers unable to commit to extensive on-campus recruiting, this technology allows recruiters to interview students "live" through audio and visual contact on large-screen monitors. The communication is interactive, allowing the candidate to observe the image being viewed by the recruiter via picture-in-picture technology.

Videoconferenced job interviews save employers time, speeding up the recruiting process by allowing HR representatives and department managers to conduct follow-up interviews before deciding to bring students for on-site meetings. It can also extend an employer's diversity efforts. On the other hand, the process lacks the personal face-to-face element of traditional interviews. Some students report an uneasiness with being scrutinized on camera, knowing that recruiters can pan and zoom using a control pad.

The cost of the equipment ranges from $5,000 for a basic system to $25,000 for a system that provides broad videoconferencing capabilities. Additional information regarding videoconferencing is available in the brochure, *Power User's Guide—Tips for Better Videoconferences* from Picturetel Corporation (800/716-6000).

Employers unable to compete for the top students from prestigious institutions are urged to recruit from lesser-known schools. For many jobs, even at a management level, educational credentials may take a back seat to other skills and job-related knowledge not necessarily acquired through formal education.

Aside from cost, there is a major disadvantage to school recruiting: Because most students have limited work experience, interviewers must face the difficult task of selection based almost exclusively on intangible factors. Although a student's chosen field of study is useful for determining suitability for the job, recruiters must still concentrate on evaluating potential, that is, the probability of a particular student's becoming an asset to their organization. If effective recruiting and interviewing skills are applied, however, many candidates selected through school recruiting efforts will develop a keen sense of company loyalty and go on to become valued, long-term employees.

Job Fairs

An increasingly popular and proactive recruitment technique is the job fair. Organizational representatives gather to interview sev-

eral applicants over a period of one or two days, often for a specialized field such as engineering. Job fairs may also be designed to
specialize in placing women, minorities, or people with disabilities.

Approaches may vary somewhat, but most companies essentially operate through newspaper advertisements announcing the location and date of a job fair. Other organizations are invited by the
hosting company to call for additional details. Company recruiters
doing so receive a notebook filled with resumés of prescreened, qualified candidates for specific positions. Candidates' names are omitted,
but other pertinent information, including salary history, education,
and work experience, is included. After reviewing the resumés, recruiters contact the hosting company, identify the candidates they
wish to interview by number, and set up appointments during the job
fair. The fairs are usually held over a weekend in a hotel or conference
center. For a flat fee paid to the host, recruiters can interview and hire
an unlimited number of qualified candidates.

To get the most for your money, conduct brief interviews during
the fair. Make them in-depth enough to establish further interest, but
not so detailed as to result in a hiring decision. In this way, a maximum number of candidates can be screened, but only potential employees called to company offices for a full interview at a later date.

If all goes well, you may hire several people for what it would
cost to hire one employee using a search firm. It is also possible that
no one suitable will be found. Even if this should occur, your efforts
are not wasted. Job fairs usually include social functions in the evenings, a wonderful opportunity to meet and exchange information
with recruiters from other organizations. This type of networking
among recruiters often results in a sharing of resumés and leads for
those hard-to-fill positions.

Open House

Another proactive recruitment effort occurring outside of the
company is the open house. Organizations generally place newspaper ads covering various geographic locations, announcing a recruitment drive on specific dates. Unless the company is well known, a
lengthy description of the company's product and reputation is included, along with starting salaries and benefit packages. All available jobs are listed as well.

On the advertised date of the open house, company recruiters
gather to greet and interview interested candidates. Either hiring decisions are made during the open house, or arrangements are made
for additional interviews on company premises.

An open house is usually a risky proposition in terms of cost and time. It is difficult to predict whether there will be a large turnout of qualified candidates and whether such candidates will ultimately be hired. Prescreening applicants by telephone or asking them to submit resumés in advance are two ways of safeguarding against this occurrence.

Government Agencies

Another reactive recruitment source is the state or federal employment agency. These agencies are cost free; they screen and refer many applicants, usually for entry-level or nonspecialized positions. Because they keep such detailed EEO records, government agencies can be counted on to help organizations meet their affirmative action goals.

An additional advantage is that candidates referred by government agencies are currently unemployed, so anyone selected can usually begin working immediately. If the person were working, anywhere from one to four weeks' notice to the current employer would be commonplace. When you have deadlines to meet and work to get out, those four weeks can seem like an eternity.

Although government agencies can provide assistance, they frequently refer unqualified job applicants in spite of the specified requirements. In addition, they often challenge the reasons given for rejecting a candidate. Therefore, it is important that recruiters use appropriate rejection language, a topic covered in Chapter 12.

Direct Mail Recruitment

A proactive recruitment source less frequently used but effective is the direct mail campaign, whereby specific individuals are contacted by a company with an opening, hoping for a job match.

The first step in this type of recruitment is determining the person to contact. Since the expected response rate is between 0.5 and 2 percent, you will need several different mailing lists. These lists and list information may be obtained through professional associations, business directories, trade groups, and magazine subscription lists. *Direct Mail List Rates and Data*, published by Standard Rate and Data Service, 5201 Old Orchard Road, Skokie, Illinois 60077, can offer additional assistance. You may also opt to hire the services of direct mail specialists or consultants to help plan and implement your mail campaign.

If you are embarking on an extensive mailing effort, it is advisable to have a mailing house help you fold, stuff, seal, and mail every-thing. If the mailing list is rather small, you can do everything yourself. Obtain a copy of the *Mailer's Guide* from the local post office for guidance.

Direct mail campaigns often fail because recipients do not even open the envelope. Sometimes this problem can be mitigated by put-ting an attention getter on the envelope. Teasers, such as "We want to give you $75,000!" are unprofessional and therefore not advisable. Instead, print "personal" or "confidential" on the outside. Not only is it more likely that the addressee will open the envelope, but others, such as clerks or secretaries, are less likely to do so. The letter should contain a clear, brief, easy-to-read message. The first sentence should inform the reader of your purpose and interest. Include information about the requirements of the job, its duties and responsibilities, and its benefits. Try to anticipate any relevant questions an applicant might ask and provide appropriate answers. Enclose a response card (see the section on response cards later in this chapter) or ask to be contacted by telephone. If possible, also provide a brochure or CD-ROM promoting your company.

One final suggestion: Ask for a referral. In the event that your initial prospect is not interested in the position, she may know of someone who is.

Radio and Television

There are two main advantages to using radio or television ad-vertising to fill an opening. First, you will appeal to a large audience in a short period of time. Second, you can reach and tempt prospects not actually looking for a job—a real plus when you have a hard-to-fill position.

In the past, employers have tended to shy away from radio and television advertising as a proactive source, primarily because of the cost. No doubt among the most costly recruitment sources, radio and television nevertheless have become more accessible media. Radio spots in communities outside major metropolitan areas, for example, are more affordable by comparison and still reach a good-sized audi-ence. And since advertising on television no longer necessitates deal-ing with the major networks, it too has become more affordable. The growth of independent stations and cable television has created greater opportunities for employers with limited budgets.

Proponents of radio advertising emphasize that radio often reaches people when "their guard is down," that is, when they are not necessarily thinking about job hunting. For example, they may have the radio on while getting ready for work in the morning or sitting in traffic as they commute. Television advertising receives high marks from supporters because aspects of the job can be demonstrated as well as described. Done well, this can compel job seekers to respond.

To get your money's worth, make certain that your radio or television message is believable. The speaker's voice should be sincere and pleasing to the ear. The person's appearance and attire should set an appropriate tone and reflect the image your company wants to project. No matter how short your ad may be, make it a point to repeat the name of your company and how you may be reached. If possible, your telephone number should be particularly easy to remember in the event that the viewer or listener does not have a pad and pen handy.

As with newspaper or magazine advertising, consider those you want to reach, and prepare the ad contents accordingly. Your objective is to capture their attention within the first few seconds, keep them listening or watching, and then solicit calls or written responses. Be careful not to throw so much at your audience that prospects will be unable to retain what you have said. This usually means limiting the contents of the ad to no more than three key statements or ideas.

Research Firms

Research firms may be described as abbreviated versions of fullservice executive search firms, providing essentially half the services. Their primary function is to provide organizations with information about potential high-level professional employees; the interview and evaluation are then up to the employer. Research firms generally charge by the hour, as opposed to a percentage basis, although some offer flat-rate fees.

Most research firms begin by ascertaining the specifications of available positions within the company. Then, target companies— those likely to have employees meeting the job's specifications—are identified. Following this, specific employees within the target companies are researched, with any relevant information being turned over to the client company in written form. Contacting well-established persons within a given industry to request personal recommendations of potential employees is a variation on this procedure.

At this point, most research firms terminate their services, although occasionally the client company may ask the firm to make the initial contact with the targeted candidates. This phase is intended to clarify qualifications and to determine mutual interest.

Research firms are considered reactive and are most useful when a company is looking for a cost-effective way to recruit top-level professionals or when more hands-on involvement in the interviewing process is desired.

When evaluating the services of a research firm, consider whether the company services a wide range of industries or specializes in one particular field. Also, determine its success rate and reputation. Ask for references from satisfied clients to determine the extent to which the research firm provided client companies with candidates whose qualifications reflected the job's specifications. In addition, find out how long it took for an organization to produce the candidates. Finally, ask how many job offers were extended to applicants as a result of the research firm's efforts.

Preemployment Training

Preemployment training is a proactive means for employers to ensure the hiring of those candidates "guaranteed" to possess the basic knowledge and skills needed to perform a given job. This may be accomplished through advertising a program that offers skill training free of cost to participants. Such prospects are not necessarily being trained for specific jobs, nor are they being offered employment. The emphasis is on preparation, so that when jobs do become available, the trained individuals will be considered first.

Pretraining programs usually include a companywide orientation. A tour of the premises is conducted; the history, products, and goals of the company are described; and salary and benefits information is provided. Interviews are scheduled for those who are interested.

Throughout the process, it should be stressed that the successful completion of the pretraining program does not imply or guarantee a job. Rather, it ensures eligibility if and when an appropriate opening becomes available.

Selecting employees from a pool of pretrained candidates generally works best in plant or manufacturing environments requiring the operation of equipment or machinery. Employers benefit by having an available workforce of skilled individuals from which to choose, without wasting time to screen a group of unknown applicants. In addition, once hired, program graduates need not devote the first several days, or even weeks, to learning their jobs. Program participants benefit by acquiring marketable skills and being first in line for employment opportunities. Of course, there is no guarantee the acquired skills will not ultimately benefit another company. In this regard, pretraining may not be cost-effective.

Outplacement Firms

Outplacement firms are generally retained by companies to help higher-level managers and executives find new employment after termination. Lower-level management and nonexempt workers who have lost their jobs through plant closings or other major workforce reductions may be provided with partial, or group outplacement, services.

Outplacement firms can be very effective for those seeking advice and guidance in finding new employment, and they can also be a valuable reactive recruitment source. Most of these organizations are staffed with generalists who do not specialize in placing people in particular occupations or fields. Therefore, they may know of a number of candidates meeting various job specifications. In addition, the immediate availability of candidates referred by outplacement firms is a big plus. Since most recipients of outplacement services are at a professional level, this translates into a savings of at least two to four weeks in starting time.

Another benefit in dealing with a reputable outplacement firm has to do with the degree of information that can be provided about a candidate. Part of the firm's responsibility is to become thoroughly familiar with a terminating person's skills and interests. Some may even conduct career or psychological assessment testing to confirm information acquired through multiple interviews with the individual, his or her peers, and supervisors. Having a thorough profile of the job candidate can assist an employer in deciding whether to pursue employment possibilities.

Having obtained a complete picture of a job candidate, employers may still be concerned with the accuracy of the representations. One of the most challenging areas to evaluate is why people leave a job; indeed, it is often difficult, if not impossible, to determine the true reason. Reference checks, explored in Chapter 12, cannot always be relied on to reveal the actual set of circumstances surrounding a person's termination; the candidate may also be an unreliable source. Outplacement firms, however, usually have access to this information.

One significant disadvantage of interviewing outplacement firm referrals is that these candidates may not project a clear overview of their intangible qualities. The traumatic experience of losing a job, in some cases after twenty or more years of service, and the stress of having to market oneself, added to the pressure of finding new employment, can greatly affect an applicant's self-image. This, in turn, affects how the applicant comes across and is perceived.

Full-service outplacement firms receive a fee from the candidate's former employer in the range of 10 percent to 25 percent of annual salary, with most averaging around 15 percent.

Billboard Advertising

Billboard advertising is still a relatively new and virtually unexplored proactive recruitment source. Since most people view billboards while driving, often at high speeds, they do not have much time to take in the details (unless, of course, they are stuck in traffic). Therefore, an effective billboard ad must immediately catch the eye and offer a limited amount of information that the average person can both understand and remember (it is unlikely that a pad and pen will be handy). These stipulations usually limit a company to a statement about employment advantages, available jobs, an enlarged logo, company name, and telephone number in an easy-to-read recall format. Since so many people use car phones, encouraging calls at all hours can increase the number of applicants who respond.

Billboard ads seem to work most effectively for hotel-motel chains, restaurants, and airlines and are generally targeted toward nonexempt-level workers.

Response Cards

Response cards may be viewed as a spin-off of direct mail recruitment in that cards are mailed to the homes of targeted candidates. The language on the card is designed to pique the interest of even those not interested in seeking new employment. After a brief description of the job opportunities available, potential applicants are invited to complete a brief questionnaire that can easily be detached from the informative portion of the card and mailed, postage paid.

Response cards may also be attached to ads appearing in magazines or other publications. General information about the company and available jobs is provided; those interested are invited to complete the card and mail it in.

Some companies report that they continue to receive responses to this proactive form of recruitment for as long as a year after they have run ads with detachable cards. Although the return rate is not especially high (under 5 percent), many employers report a high ratio of new employees as a result.

Employers can also add a twist to using response cards. Try sending out letters inviting people to return an accompanying coupon entitling them to receive a free poster or calendar. Ask them to provide basic information about their skills and knowledge. They get a free poster; you get names for your data bank.

Military

Mention the military and words like *self-disciplined, traditional, structured, orderly, organized, adaptable*, and *responsive* come to mind. Although these are qualities many employers seek in their workers, few have considered the military as a recruitment source. However, with the changing job market compelling employers to explore different resources, more companies are starting to turn to military recruiting firms (reactive), military career conferences (proactive), and military job fairs (proactive) for future employees.

Military personnel frequently have a great deal of hands-on experience in a variety of tasks but lack general business knowledge. For this reason, they often start in entry-level sales, technical, or staff positions, although some do go directly into management.

Newspaper Inserts

Newspaper inserts represent a relatively untapped proactive recruitment source. Arguments against their use include the possibility that they will fall out of the paper or be overlooked as job hunters head straight for the classified or special employment sections. Others feel that inserts will not be taken seriously.

Proponents, on the other hand, view newspaper inserts as a refreshing approach to advertising and consider the fact that this is an infrequently used medium a plus. In addition, unlike ads that must be cut or torn out, insert ads can easily be slipped out of the newspaper. The higher quality of the paper used for inserts, as well as the absence of newsprint on one's clothing and hands, might also appeal to job seekers. Moreover, because they are generally larger than standard newspaper ads, inserts are less likely to be misplaced. Finally, newspaper inserts may use several colors, making them visually appealing.

Professional Associations

Most employers agree that the primary benefit of joining a professional association is the opportunity to network with colleagues from other organizations.

For HR specialists, this can mean exchanging information about selected job applicants and sharing the resumés of candidates deemed unsuitable for specific openings in a particular company but perhaps well suited for positions in another organization. The process is simple: Working with two or three other HR representatives belonging to the association, agree to review, on a monthly basis, a list from within each of your companies of job openings, accompanied by abbreviated job descriptions. If the list indicates some viable candidates you have either interviewed or whose resumé or application you have reviewed, this information can be shared with your colleagues. They will do the same for you. In addition to the cost-effectiveness of these exchanges, you may also benefit from a professional impression of particular candidates.

A variation on this proactive technique is to join professional associations in fields related to your recruitment responsibilities. The associations' membership directory, mailing list, placement service, and publications can provide the names of potential employees.

On-Site Recruitment

On-site recruitment, proactive in nature, is limited to the types of businesses that attract large numbers of people to their locations each day. Still, it can be quite effective, usually for various nonexempt-level positions. For example, railroad companies may place pamphlets describing employment opportunities on car seats at various times of the day; airlines might do the same with seats on planes; department stores might attach fliers to packages at cashier stations; and fast food chains, as well as family restaurants, might describe job openings on tray liners and table tents.

The brief message, which usually describes the benefits or working for the company, is often framed by bright, eye-catching colors and graphics. Pictured, too, may be people representing diverse traits and characteristics. Interested candidates are invited to see or call the employment manager (or equivalent) to obtain an application form. In some instances, postage-paid applications are attached to the message; anyone interested can complete the form for submission.

Bumper Sticker Advertisements

Like billboard advertisements, bumper sticker ads are a relatively new and virtually unexplored proactive recruitment source. Space is limited, and there is not much one can do to make the stickers visually outstanding. Also, unless someone is stuck in traffic directly behind a car sporting a bumper sticker advertisement, there is little time to read what is written. For these reasons, companies that advertise on bumper stickers usually include merely a generic statement about employment opportunities and note, in large letters, their telephone number.

From company employees willing to place this inexpensive form of advertisement on their car bumpers, employers may get some viable nonexempt candidates. On the other hand, bumper sticker ads may not be taken seriously by job seekers.

Clients and Customers

Approaching clients and customers about possible candidates to fill openings is another proactive technique. Applicants referred this way come with personal recommendations; in addition, you will probably learn more about their work habits than in a reference check to a former employer.

Deciding against a candidate referred by a client or customer, however, can lead to strained business relations. So, too, can hiring a referral, only to end up disciplining or terminating that person.

Of course, you can also ask customers and clients to work for you. You have probably learned a great deal about their skills, abilities, and interests. Be careful, however, about how you steal someone from the competition. It could damage future business relations and your reputation.

Banners and Signs

You can use banners and signs as successful proactive recruitment tools if your business or store occupies a separate building that is located on a main street. Drape a banner across the front or post a sign, inviting customers, clients, and passers-by to stop in and inquire about employment opportunities. The banner or sign can simply state that there are jobs available, or it can list the openings (which means you must prepare a new banner or sign each time there are different jobs to fill). Companies using this technique may list their main benefits to lure potential employees. Also, unless the nature of your business is well known or understood from its name, identify your product in a few words. Be sure to specify if interested candidates should walk in and apply, or call for an appointment.

Banners and signs are a real "you never know" recruitment source. The investment is minimal, and the payoff could be big.

Voice Ads

Most employers who use proactive telephone voice ads prerecord a message on a weekly basis, listing all available openings. Interested candidates leave their names and telephone numbers, and the employer takes it from there. Some messages include a request for a resumé to be faxed or mailed by a certain date. Others ask only for a telephone number so they may call back and conduct a screening interview. Companies that have volume openings with tight production schedules may encourage callers to leave specific job-related information, such as length and type of experience, or to walk in for an interview during specified days and times.

This recruitment technique requires a minimum amount of effort and no cost, and could produce the desired results.

Movie Ads

You get to the movies in plenty of time to grab a tub of popcorn and a drink. You find a seat and settle in, ready for the show to begin. If you are lucky, there will be previews of coming attractions. Imagine, now, in addition to clips of upcoming shows, your company's name on the screen, advertising job opportunities. This technique is gaining in popularity. Businesses are beginning to target captive, unsuspecting audiences with proactive recruiting ads during the previews at theater complexes. The amount of information is kept to a minimum: usually just the company name, an easy-to-remember telephone number (few movie-goers are prepared to write in a dark theater), and either a list of openings or a statement about job opportunities. Some employers try to link their promotions to specific movies and anticipated types of viewers; others go for the shotgun approach, and run their ads regardless of what is showing.

Company-Sponsored Social Affairs

If your organization goes in for huge social events on certain occasions, such as a big picnic to celebrate Independence Day, encourage employees to bring family and friends. Then set up a job opportunities table with a list of openings and brochures. This proactive form of recruitment requires an investment of only additional food and one or two employees willing to answer questions from interested applicants. It helps if the employees attending the affair have good things to say about you as an employer and pass their endorsement on to others.

Summary

This chapter began by exploring four key prerecruitment factors: how much money you have to spend, how quickly you need to fill an opening, whether you need to reach a wide audience, and the exemption level of the available position. The issue of proactive versus reactive recruitment was then discussed, followed by an assessment of two of the most popular forms of recruitment: employee referrals and advertising. Additionally, twenty-five other recruitment sources were explored, some of them traditional, others less conventional, but still viable. Table 3-1 summarizes the advantages and disadvantages of these sources.

With numerous recruitment sources available (including contingent workers, described in Chapter 1), you should never find yourself in the position of saying, "I can't find anyone to fill this job." Nor, out of desperation, should you ever feel pressured into taking the first person who applies for an opening. This often backfires when the new employee quits or is terminated for poor performance in a short period of time. You are then in a position of having to recruit all over again.

By using the array of sources described in this chapter, you can afford to be selective. The investment in time and money will pay off when you find the best candidate for the job.

Table 3-1. Advantages and disadvantages of various recruitment sources.

Recruitment Source	Primary Advantages	Primary Disadvantages	Level of Recruitment	Proactive or Reactive
Employee referrals	Inexpensive; expeditious; related bonus boosts morale	May result in charges of systemic discrimination if not used in conjunction with other recruitment sources	Nonexempt; exempt	Reactive
Newspaper and magazine advertising	Reaches a wide audience; can solicit responses via blind ads; magazine ads zero in on specific occupation categories	Can be very costly	Nonexempt; exempt	Proactive
Job posting	Creates openings at lower, easier-to-fill levels; saves time and money; boosts employee morale; reveals hidden talent	Managers feel they can no longer select persons of their choice; managers resent employees who want to post for jobs; time may be lost waiting for replacement	Nonexempt; exempt	Proactive
Employment agencies and search firms	Access to large labor pool; can help fill position quickly	Can be very costly; may refer unqualified applicants	Employment agencies: nonexempt; search firms: exempt	Reactive

(continued)

Table 3-1. (continued)

Recruitment Source	Primary Advantages	Primary Disadvantages	Level of Recruitment	Proactive or Reactive
HR files	No cost; good public relations	If on a manual system, can be time-consuming; poor notes taken by the previous interviewer may misrepresent applicant; outdated notes	Nonexempt; exempt	Proactive
Walk-ins, call-ins, write-ins	No cost; good public relations	Poorly monitored system can result in lost applications	Walk-ins: nonexempt; call-ins: nonexempt and exempt; write-ins: exempt	Reactive
School recruiting	Opportunity to groom and develop future management of a company; opportunity to select top graduates	Can be costly; difficult to evaluate potential	Exempt	Proactive
Job fairs	May fill many openings in a short period of time; opportunity to network with other recruiters	Can be costly; usually means working on weekends	Exempt	Proactive
Open house	Good public relations; may fill several openings at one time	Can be costly; time-consuming	Nonexempt; exempt	Proactive

Method	Advantages	Disadvantages	Exempt/Nonexempt	Reactive/Proactive
Government agencies	Cost free; can result in referral of many applicants; can help with affirmative action goals; can help fill positions quickly	May send unqualified applicants; may challenge reasons for rejection	Nonexempt	Reactive
Direct mail	Personalized form of recruitment; selective	Time-consuming; mail may not be opened	Exempt	Proactive
Radio and television	Reaches a wide audience; can reach prospects not actively looking for a job	Can be costly	Nonexempt	Reactive
Research firms	Allows for more involvement in the interviewing process	Services end upon contacting of candidates	Exempt	Proactive
Preemployment training	Creates trained workforce prepared for times when targeted jobs become available	Time-consuming; may not be cost-effective; no guarantee trained workers will not apply acquired skills to another company	Nonexempt	Proactive
Outplacement firms	Can result in referral of many applicants; can help fill openings quickly; can provide a thorough profile of applicants	Incomplete picture of intangible qualities	Exempt; sometimes nonexempt	Reactive
Billboard advertising	Can be eye-catching; visually creative	Can offer only a limited amount of information; may be missed entirely	Nonexempt	Proactive

(continued)

Table 3-1. (continued)

Recruitment Source	Primary Advantages	Primary Disadvantages	Level of Recruitment	Proactive or Reactive
Response cards	Personalized form of recruitment; selective	Time-consuming; can be costly	Exempt	Proactive
Military	Applicants with desirable intangible qualities; applicants with extensive hands-on experience	Applicants who lack general business knowledge	Nonexempt; exempt	Reactive (military recruiting firms; proactive (military career conferences and job fairs)
Newspaper inserts	Easily removed from the paper; less likely to be misplaced; eye-catching	Easily lost; easily overlooked; may not be taken seriously	Nonexempt; exempt	Proactive
Professional associations	Personal referrals; able to obtain resumés and information about applicants without direct solicitation; can be cost-effective	Time-consuming; can be supplied with applicants with no marketable skills; someone else's rejected applicants	Nonexempt; exempt	Proactive

On-site recruitment	Can reach a wide audience; can save time; good public relations	May not be taken seriously; may get lots of unqualified candidates	Nonexempt	Proactive
Bumper sticker advertisements	Eye-catching	May not be taken seriously	Nonexempt	Proactive
Clients and customers	Applicants come personally recommended	Could lead to strained relations with clients or customers	Nonexempt; exempt	Proactive
Banners and signs	Cost-effective	Requires location on heavily trafficked street	Nonexempt	Proactive
Voice ads	Easy; cost-effective	Time-consuming	Nonexempt; exempt	Proactive
Movie ads	Unique	Possible resentment by movie-goers	Nonexempt	Proactive
Company-sponsored social affairs	Cost-effective	Those attending a social function may resent a sales pitch	Nonexempt; exempt	Proactive

Chapter 4
Electronic Recruiting

If you are an HR specialist whose experience spans a decade or two, you no doubt remember receiving stacks of resumés sent by search firms, in response to newspaper ads, or by one of the other more traditional recruitment resources described in Chapter 3. Too busy to do them justice during a typical workday, you probably loaded these resumés into your briefcase and dutifully reviewed them during the commute home or after dinner in front of the TV (muted, of course). When you came across a resumé longer than two pages (one page, as the evening grew later), you groaned, fighting the temptation to file it for violating "the law against submitting a resumé that is too long for a tired HR professional to review at the end of a busy day."

Wow, have things changed! Increasingly, employers are using the Internet to recruit, either by developing Web pages of their own or by linking up with Web-based job search services. Applicants too are preparing and transmitting many more resumés electronically, thereby relieving recruiters from being inundated by thousands of paper resumés. The Internet is rapidly moving up in the ranks of recruitment resources, as greater numbers of applicants and employers communicate with one another, computer to computer.

Who Uses High-Tech Recruiting

Usually when charting the increase in the use of a particular recruitment tool (or anything else, for that matter), it takes several years to identify a notable pattern. It is rare to see a large increase in just one year, and rarer still to see a steady increase across the board in every main job category. Yet that is what has happened with online recruitment. In 1996, less than 20 percent of nontechnical jobs and only 40 percent of all computer openings were filled through Internet postings. Just one year later, those numbers had changed dramatically. In some categories, as much as 60 percent of all jobs were filled as a result of online recruitment, with computer jobs, not surprisingly, in the lead. Even the figures for the job category showing the smallest gain—accounting—were impressive, growing 7 percent in one year.

Let us take a closer look at those figures, reported in September 1997 in *HR Focus.* The computer field showed the greatest increase in the number of openings filled through Internet postings. In 1996, 40 percent of all computer jobs were posted and filled via online recruitment; in 1997, that figure jumped to 59 percent. Technical jobs followed, making a dramatic leap from a mere 8 percent in 1996 to 37 percent one year later. Next comes engineering, moving a more modest 13 percent, from 16 percent in 1996 to 29 percent in 1997. The category of consultants increased from 2 percent to 21 percent, marketing changed from 4 percent to 14 percent, and sales went up to 15 percent from 4 percent. Accounting moved from 3 percent to 10 percent.

Another survey of HR professionals nationwide, conducted by JWT Specialized Communications, and entitled, ''Net Working: A Research Study on Employment and the Internet,'' published in *Si Review* (fall 1996), reports the increased frequency of various positions advertised on the Internet. The percentage of management and senior-level technical jobs advertised is about the same—30 percent and 34 percent, respectively—while 42 percent of entry-level and professional technical openings appear on the Net. The figures for nontechnical jobs are somewhat lower: 27 percent for senior level, 32 percent for management positions, 33 percent for entry level and professional jobs, and 27 percent for clerical or administrative work.

Many of the applicants searching electronic postings for jobs are new graduates. In fact, says *HR Magazine* (August 1997), about 80 percent of new graduates use the Internet with complete ease, seeking out careers in computers, high technology, and other fields. Many college students seeking part-time employment also favor the Internet as a recruitment source.

The Internet has not replaced traditional recruitment methods, yet these figures demonstrate that businesses have a high level of confidence in the Internet as a recruitment tool. This reflects an about-face on the part of employers, who not long ago viewed online recruiting with skepticism. Now, according to an on-site survey conducted by Technometricia at the American Management Association's 1997 Annual Human Resources Conference and Exposition, many more recruiters are diving head first into the world of Web sites. Fifty-three percent of those surveyed are now posting job openings on the Internet, and 22 percent of the respondents list Internet postings as among their most valuable recruiting tools. Many "aware nonusers" cite lack of access as their main reason for not trying the Internet to date.

Advantages and Disadvantages of the Internet

The number one advantage Web users cited is its cost. Hands down, the Internet is more cost-effective than most other recruitment methods. Sources most commonly compared with the Internet are newspaper ads and trade magazines, in addition to search firms and employment agencies. For example, the cost of placing a large ad in a local newspaper in the Boston area runs between $1,200 and $1,500. Advertising on the Monster Board, one of many popular Net job centers (http:www.monster.com), costs about $150; the cost for job seekers is free. They can visit Web sites like the Monster Board, CareerMosaic (htpp://www.careermosaic.com), Careerpath (http://www.careerpath.com), and America's Job Bank (htpp://www.ajb.dni.us), at any time, searching through thousands of job openings each day according to geographic area, position, or specific company. While many job postings are for technical jobs, the rest are broadly diverse, including health care positions, business management jobs, food service openings, and clerical jobs.

Close behind cost as an advantage to using online recruiting is its speed. Applicants can submit resumés to employers advertising on the Internet and get responses within hours. Employers can bypass the several days it takes to submit a newspaper ad and post jobs with the click of a few keys on the computer. Resumés may start coming in immediately.

Another advantage to online recruiting is the reduction in paperwork. Resumés submitted in the traditional way can pile up in a hurry. This does not occur with resumés that are submitted and routed electronically. Online recruiting is essentially a paperless process.

Employers have access to a greater number of candidates when recruiting on the Internet. Not only does the Net target large numbers of people actively looking for jobs, but it also attracts passive applicants—those not necessarily looking but curious about employment opportunities. Since passive applicants are more likely to be interested in openings at specific companies, experts recommend that businesses set up their own Web sites. Employers also benefit from the advantage of posting an ad on the Internet and leaving it up for as long as it generates results.

There are some disadvantages in using the Internet to advertise job openings. The biggest drawback is the lack of breadth of reach. Despite their popularity, computers are not accessible to all job seekers. Furthermore, all computer users are not linked up with the Internet. So employers that limit their recruitment efforts to the Net will miss a large population of potential employees.

Employers also complain about drawing too many inappropriate or unqualified responses. Of course, this can also occur with other recruitment sources, such as newspaper ads.

Finally, companies may be deluged with Net-generated resumés and have trouble reviewing them. Setting up an internal mechanism to track the resumés and the application process will help to alleviate this problem. This so-called virtual recruiter, or automated system for storing resumés and applicant data, provides a way of transferring information from resumés into an applicant database and organizing the data into a format that recruiters can search. Resumés can be imported into the system by e-mail, fax, or scanning and are converted into text.

Cyberspace Resumés

Reading a cyberspace resumé requires some adjustment. While the focus remains the same—searching for information that reflects a person's ability to perform a job—the process is somewhat different. As one recruiter put it, "What pleases a computer is likely to bore a person."

An automated system provides a method of transferring information from resumés into an applicant database and organizing the data into a format that recruiters can search. The process scans resumés using optical character recognition technology for key words and phrases that describe the skills required for each job. Action words, indicating the nature and level of work accomplished, are less important than industry-specific language. The scanning process benefits applicants with the most measurable, tangible skills; applicants who exclude relevant terms and familiar industry acronyms are likely to be bypassed. The process can also search for years of experience, education, and other desired specifications. Employers can even assign weighted values to the various criteria.

Employers advertising on the Net are learning to accept cookie-cutter resumés. Increasingly, applicants are taking advantage of the many sites on the Web that offer electronic resumé writing forms. "Resumix Creating Your Resume" (http://www.resumix.com/resume/resumeindex.html) and "Intellimatch Power Resume Builder" (http://www.intellimatch.com/watson/owa/w3.html) are among the many services available. Some services offer a "one-size-fits-all" type of resumé format, while others walk the job hunter through a series of categories for a detailed, more personalized resumé. Most do not assist the applicant in organizing the resumé (e.g., chronologically or by function). That kind of guidance is offered by other services, such as Job Smart Resume Guide (http://jobsmart. org/tools/resume/index.htm). Tips on design are offered by yet another category of Net resume writing experts, such as The Riley Guide (http://www.jobtrak.com/jobguide/index.html).

Since paper resumés, neatly set on high-quality ecru paper, are being replaced by the Internet version—dull plain text that may never be printed out—practical advice on coping with the computer is the norm, rather than actual design tips. For example, highlighting key accomplishments with asterisks and capital letters is encouraged, but underlining is discouraged, since scanning can garble underlined words.

Even the classic guide to job hunting, *What Color Is Your Parachute*, by Richard Nelson Bolles, is now an electronic guide, listing a compendium of net resources ("What Color Is Your Parachute, Electronic Edition"; htpp://www.washingtonpost.com/wp-adv//classifieds/careerpost/parachute/parafram2.htm).

Cyberspace resumé-writing guides recommend including a cover letter. Recruiters are accustomed to reading a summary of the applicant's objectives and personal characteristics, so the contents of a cover page, electronic or paper, have remained much the same.

Employers should review many of these guides to ascertain what is appropriate and acceptable in the way of format and design for electronically transmitted resumés.

Web Sites

Employers interested in electronic recruiting have two basic choices: to list openings with a service such as America's Job Bank or put up their own Web page. Net job centers allow employers to link up with potential employees by providing online, searchable resumé databases. Although buying into one of these centers can result in filling many openings cost-effectively, the nature of the three-way relationship of the service, employer, and potential employee makes it more of a reactive form of recruitment (see Chapter 3). Companies that put up their own Web page, however, are recruiting proactively, increasing their chances of finding suitable employees. In one year alone, the number of companies with their own Web sites jumped 400 percent, according to the "Staffing" supplement to the August 1997 issue of *Workforce*. Hence, the focus in this segment will be on building home pages.

For companies that already have Web pages, adding a job opportunities section is simple and inexpensive. If your HR staff is unfamiliar with Internet recruiting, information systems (IS) experts may need to work with them initially. Postings may need to be updated through IS, but ultimately HR staff should be able to accomplish this work themselves. In some organizations, managers independently post job openings on the Internet without going through HR. At the very least, HR should be notified of what jobs have been posted since most resumés (paper and electronic) go through HR for an initial job match assessment.

Starting a Web Page

The first step in designing a Web page from scratch is to determine what you want to accomplish. It is tempting to answer, "to lure applicants," but any recruiter who has ever used a recruitment source that did not target applicants with the required credentials or skills knows that this answer is not really accurate. It is an awful thing to run an ad and get only a handful of responses; it is far worse to get inundated with responses from unqualified candidates. Every recruitment source must be properly directed, and cyberspace postings are no different. Think, then, about what your postings are to accomplish: attracting qualified candidates whose backgrounds and interests are compatible with the environment and offerings of your organization. That statement identifies your company as unique and immediately sets it apart; hence, your Web page should stand out.

Now you can focus on what users want from a Web page. Talk with competitors to determine who uses their Web pages and the kind of feedback they are receiving. (One company was the recipient of numerous e-mail messages chastising it for not changing job postings for several months.) Consult with your IS staff, other employees, and even external candidates about what they expect to find on a Web page. Information from these sources can supplement advice from outside Web experts.

Before making a commitment to outside consultants to set up your Web page, verify their effectiveness by talking with businesses, preferably ones similar to yours, that have used them. This process is not unlike conducting references checks on prospective employees. Here are some questions to ask previous clients of potential consultants:

- Do they have both technical expertise and design experience?
- How helpful were they in a set-up situation?
- How patient were they in explaining terms and processes to nontechnical HR people?
- Did they bother to find out what your company was all about, in terms of products, market, and direction?
- Did they acknowledge that you know your business best and therefore should either write the text for the page or at least contribute to it?
- Did they make suggestions as to the best format and design of your page?
- Did they advise you as to the appropriate equipment for high-speed access to the Internet?
- Did they try to start you off with more than you needed?
- Did they continue to offer support services after building your Web page?
- Did they recommend upgrades to your page after a probationary test run?

It does not help to ascertain how long a Web page consultant has been in business since this is such a new field. Prior business experience, however, preferably with much of it being computer related, is relevant.

Now determine how your page will be organized. It may be set up by job function, geographic location, or business unit. Perhaps you will offer generic information about the work environment, company missions, and benefits before listing actual job postings. Consider, too, providing the format for an instant electronic resume. A table of contents on the Web page will allow those browsing the site to locate topics of interest instantly. Experiment, asking for feedback from staff and consultants as to which format is likely to draw the greatest number of qualified candidates. Also, do not overlook the impact of visual design. Too much text is a turn-off; so are huge graphics that slow things down to a crawl and make viewers impatient. Few users are willing to wait more than thirty to sixty seconds for a page to load. (Some experts say this advice pertains to home pages only; second- and third-level pages can take longer to load since the person obviously wants to see the materials.) Strike a balance between smaller graphics that load quickly and meaningful text, to capture and retain the interest of job hunters.

If you decide to forgo the help of a consultant and create a Web page on your own, try one of many Web authoring programs, such as Microsoft Front Page, Assistant Pro, and Internet Design Shop. Many of these programs assist with content and visibility but not design. (Additional information on authoring software is available later in this chapter.)

Companies generally start with a Web "presence," a bare-bones home page that provides the company name, geographic locations, telephone and fax numbers, basic information about the company, such as a brief history and its primary product areas, and the person to contact. These pages are later upgraded, depending on requests received over the Internet for more information, as well as the company's own observations and advice from consultants. On average, start-up pages are upgraded two to three times in the first twelve to eighteen months.

Web Site Upkeep

An up-to-date Web site is the key to successful recruiting on the Internet. Job listings should rarely remain for more than thirty days; few things prove more irritating for Web browsers than sorting through old listings and outdated information. Add new postings every week and review electronically submitted resumés daily. Also, keep current with regard to new capabilities, such as colors, backgrounds, and effects. And give the site a face-lift every six months or so.

The issue of exposure is also critical. Even an inexpensive Web site is ineffective if it is not seen or accessed. Certainly employers need to display their Internet address, or uniform resource locator (URL), on business cards, brochures, advertisements, and even their letterhead, but that alone may not ensure sufficient exposure. Many companies, in addition, purchase hypertext links or hotlinks: buttons that lead directly into its server from other Internet services, such as Career Mosaic and the Online Career Center, both popular employment service sites. This allows Web surfers to jump from one site to another, ensuring easier access and greater exposure.

It is a good idea to track how often the site is being accessed and what pages are the most popular. Tracking the number of hits on each page can offer insights into how the Web site should be redesigned and what features should be revised or eliminated down the road.

Web Site Costs

Advertising on the Internet is relatively inexpensive when compared with search firms or newspaper ads. Using an outside consultant to create the original design for your site can cost as little as $500, and as much as $25,000 for a large corporate site. Annual upkeep and maintenance can cost an equivalent amount. For companies that pass on retaining the services of a consultant and do their own design and site maintenance, the savings can be substantial. Start-up fees may be as little as $1,000 for purchasing publishing and graphics software and approximately an additional $100 a month for an outside server. The monthly server fee can be eliminated if employers purchase a server outright for between $3,000 and $10,000.

A hidden cost often neglected when calculating Web site–related expenses is the training of staff. Having an impressive online recruiting system is not going to do you any good if your HR employees are unfamiliar with its operation. Training may be done in-house by IS employees who are technically competent as well as able to communicate the workings of a Web site effectively. Sometimes it is more desirable to bring in a consultant who can explain how the site works, in addition to the respective roles of HR staff, managers, and others involved.

Hypertext Markup Language

As long as you have a computer connected to the Internet and the software to manage a home page, job seekers browsing the Web can view whatever you post. The actual documents are ordinary text and graphics converted into a special programming language called hypertext markup language (HTML). New software makes HTML easier to use and eliminates the need for special coding. Once a Web page is created, you can view it using any one of a number of browsers, like Navigator or Microsoft Internet Explorer, regardless of your computer or operating system. HTML allows an organization to get its message across.

However, just as an effective newspaper ad cannot write itself, HTML cannot transform poorly organized data and unattractive graphics into outstanding Web sites. That requires expertise derived from understanding how HTML works in relation to the desired result.

You must choose between learning HTML or locating a program

that creates HTML files for you. Employers generally choose the latter.

Numerous HTML programs are available, ranging in capabilities. Some offer excellent editing capabilities, can import from virtually any word processing program, and provide customized templates. HoTMetaL Pro (http://www.sq.com) is one such program, allowing you to build a home page or an entire site from scratch. There is a catch with HoTMetaL, however: It requires a good deal of HTML expertise. Another program that is easier to use, but offers somewhat less in the way of services, is HTML Assistant Pro (http://Fox.NSTN.Ca:80/~harawitz). There are also tools that can simply convert word processing documents into HTML. Among them are Microsoft's Internet Assistant (http:/www.microsoft.com/moffice/freestuf/msword/download/ia/default/htm) and Web-Author for Word for Windows (htpp://www.qdeck.com).

Keep in mind that even the most sophisticated HTML program cannot create visually dazzling pages. That task falls to you or a design specialist.

Online Recruitment Guidelines

Recruiting online is a popular way of increasing the visibility of job openings at a reasonable cost. Assuming you have decided to establish a corporate Web site, here are guidelines for making your effort a success:

1. *Make searching for job openings easy.* A user-friendly Web site means making available an "employment" button in a prominent place on your home page and offering a resumé builder service or form that routes the data into your e-mail or database.

2. *Make the site navigable.* Broad appeal is an important ingredient to Web site success. For people who know exactly what they want, speed and easy access are crucial. Browsers, on the other hand, want to explore, interacting with stimulating graphics and interesting text.

3. *Be prepared to respond to applicants quickly.* In describing the recruitment capabilities of the Internet, a frequent user accurately noted that it "offers incredible new opportunities to disappoint." After applying for a position within only minutes, candidates will expect a quick response. If they do not get it, chances are they will lose interest and move on.

4. *Maintain an up-to-date employment opportunity database.* The importance of keeping a Web site current cannot be overemphasized. If you cannot manage this internally, hire the services of a company.

5. *Screen out unqualified candidates.* Does this sound idealistic? Maybe, but there is a technique that Texas Instruments Inc.(TI) has been using for years with success: a candidate profiler (www.ti.com/recruit/dosc/fitcheck.htm). Before applicants apply for a job opening, they take a "FitCheck," answering a series of questions designed to determine their qualifications and compatibility with TI's corporate culture. After reviewing the results of the FitCheck, they can decide whether to proceed with an application. The result is a pre-screened, interested, and qualified applicant pool.

6. *Balance content with design.* Maybe appearances should not matter to job seekers, but they do. As with display newspaper ads, visual appeal will draw candidates to your page, and the content will pique their interest.

7. *Keep it organized.* Job seekers want to focus on the relevant data right away. Although some may want to browse the entire site, taking it all in, most will zero in on what you have to offer, decide if they are interested, and apply. If this cannot be done with ease, chances are they will move on to another site.

8. *Take advantage of all the information you can learn about your Web visitors.* You will not hire every applicant expressing an interest in your company, but you can collect data about them that may prove useful to recruitment strategies later. One of the great things about electronic recruiting is that everything is measurable, so decide what you want to know. There is bound to be an Internet service that can provide it. For example, it may be helpful to ascertain which schools or organizations visited your Web site, or perhaps you are interested in what other pages were looked at. This kind of information can be valuable to the continual reevaluation of your approach to online recruiting.

9. *Make your address easy to remember.* This has been accomplished with license plates for years; it is no surprise that companies are custom designing their Web site addresses. For an additional $100 or so, you can register a unique, easy-to-remember URL.

10. *Do not say too much.* This last tip may be a tough one to follow. To many companies, more information is considered preferable. In fact, you need not put information on your site just because it is available. A Web site is not a laundry list of data. Be selective about the information you provide and the form in which it is offered.

Legal Compliance

Federal contractors and subcontractors must track applicant flow to comply with affirmative action regulations. When resumés are submitted directly to a company in response to a newspaper ad, there is no question that the person is a job applicant and must therefore be counted. The applicant status of people whose resumés are reviewed electronically is not as clear. Are they considered applicants for purposes of federal record keeping?

To date, the Labor Department advises treating resumés viewed through an online service in the same way as solicited resumés. According to Shirley J. Wilcher, the director of the Office of Federal Contract Compliance Programs (OFCCP), "Generally speaking, electronic applications are identical to traditional 'hard copy' applications for purposes of the Federal Contract Compliance Programs. . . . The concept of an applicant is that of a person who has indicated an interest in being considered for hiring, promotion, or other employment opportunities. . . . Individuals who place their resumés on electronic bulletin boards are indicating 'an interest in being considered for hiring' and are, therefore, to be included in the contractor's applicant flow data required by 41 CFR s60-2.12(m), when the use of such sources is part of the contractor's recruitment process" (*HR Magazine,* September 1995).

This statement defines anyone who expresses interest in a job as an applicant; therefore, until advised otherwise, federal contractors and subcontractors should keep records of all resumés they screen from online databases. Some HR specialists advocate new guidelines allowing companies merely to verify that they have used a particular database on a certain date rather than tracking individual resumés.

International Internet Recruitment

Web sites offer a global presence as an increasing number of companies are posting their job openings online in more than a hundred countries. Not surprisingly, most of these sites are produced in English. Since English is the most widely spoken language in the world, this may seem advantageous. However, for most people, English is a second language. They may be familiar with the basic structure of the language and able to converse in or read it. This does not mean, however, that they are aware of the nuances we so often use without regard to whether they constitute "proper English."

It is impractical, costly, and excessively time-consuming to prepare variations of each Web page in several different languages. You can, however, develop one site in one language that most people will be able to understand. This requires a focus on how you speak and read the English language. Here are some guidelines:

• *Avoid jargon, which can interfere with a clear, precise message.* Readers may be confused by its meaning, thereby slowing them down. Clearly, industry-unique buzzwords or acronyms are appropriate, but only if you are fairly certain that at least 90 percent of your readers will understand their precise meaning.

With terms that are ambiguous, provide a definition the first time the word or term appears in the text. It is also a good idea to review the document from the perspective of someone outside the culture of an American organization. If you have the least suspicion that readers will not share the meaning that is intended, either spell it out or make a clearer choice.

• *Select proper word usage.* The English language is full of words that are confused with one another. For example, do you know the difference between *assure, ensure,* and *insure; affect* and *effect; adapt* and *adopt; advise* and *inform;* or *accept* and *except?* We all probably learned the meanings of these words at some point in our education, but when it comes time to using them in a sentence, we often play a guessing game as to which one is correct. To people for whom English is a second language, correct word usage is very important. They probably know the difference between *continual* and *continuous* and would find disturbing text that confuses the two.

• *Use proper grammar, punctuation, and spelling.* Web writing is unique, in that spaces between many words are eliminated and "periods" appear in the middle of sentences. In spite of this, the actual text of your job offerings should consist of proper grammar, punctuation, and spelling. Again, people for whom English is a second language are more likely to be aware of rules of grammar and pick out errors. These errors could be viewed as a carelessness that is representative of your organization, influencing a candidate's decision to submit an application.

• *Do not avoid clichés.* If describing business writing, I would say the opposite; however, in writing Internet text for a population consisting largely of people for whom English is a second language, clichés can actually be helpful. Certain overused, stock phrases are probably familiar and more likely to convey your meaning.

• *Be careful about how you use numbers.* Something as simple as noting a resumé filing date can be incorrectly interpreted by someone from another country. For example, in Europe, the numbers are reversed; hence a filing date of 9/11/99 would be interpreted as meaning November 9, 1999.

• *Be careful about the colors you select for your graphics.* In many countries, colors have distinct, important, and sometimes religious meanings. Hence, misusing a color on the Web site can result in lost applicants. For example, in some cultures, purple is the color of royalty; in Brazil it is associated with death.

You may choose to have your current Web site translated, graphics included, into another language. Many translation companies will do this for a nominal sum of about $100 per page, depending on the content, number, and complexity of graphics. Such companies include Webtrans (Webtrans.com), Weblations (weblations.com), and International Communications (intl.com).

This seems reasonable in terms of cost and may appear to solve any potential problems associated with presenting your Web page in English, but there is an additional problem that comes with translation: The alphabets of other languages may have characters not found in English, so you may need a product like Alis Technologies (alis.com) or Accent Software (accentsoft.com) to create Web sites in multiple languages. If you decide to browse foreign-language Web sites, such services as Globalink (globalink.com) will translate those pages into English for a nominal fee.

Summary

The Internet is rapidly becoming one of the most popular forms of recruitment. Although it has not replaced traditional recruitment methods, applicants in computer and other technical and nontechnical fields (especially new graduates) are going online to find jobs; employers too are increasingly posting their openings electronically.

The primary reason employers are turning to the Internet for recruiting is its cost-effectiveness. They also appreciate its speed, the reduction in paperwork, and access to more potential employees—not only those actively looking for jobs but passive applicants as well. The greatest disadvantage employers cite is the lack of breadth of reach, since not all job seekers have access to a computer or, if they do, are not necessarily linked to the Internet. Employers also complain about drawing too many inappropriate or unqualified responses and not having enough time to review all electronically transmitted resumés.

Businesses that advertise on the Net are learning that cyberspace resumés look and read differently than traditional resumés do. They are advised to review many of the resumé-writing guides applicants use to determine what is considered proper format and design.

Employers advertising on the Internet can list openings with Net job centers that allow them to link up with potential employees through online, searchable resumé databases. Increasingly, however, companies are supplementing this reactive form of recruitment with the more proactive company Web page. Setting up a Web page requires a clear understanding of what both the organization and its users want to accomplish. The advice of internal information systems experts, as well as outside consultants, will help you in this regard. Deciding how the text of your page will be organized and what graphics to use is vital. Learning hypertext markup language (HTML) or locating a program that creates HTML files for you is an essential part of the process.

Once your Web page is set up, keep it current by removing old postings and adding new listings weekly. It is also a good idea to give your page an overall facelift every six months, introducing new colors and graphics.

Web sites need not be expensive to be effective, but even an inexpensive page is useless if no one sees it. Exposure, then, is critical to electronic recruitment success.

Until such time as the Labor Department issues guidelines to the contrary, employers should treat electronic applications the same as traditional paper resumés for the purposes of tracking applicant flow in compliance with affirmative action regulations.

Finally, since Web sites are making a global presence in increasing numbers, employers should exercise care when posting their job openings online in countries where English, if spoken, is a second language.

Chapter 5
Interview Preparation

A commonly held but erroneous belief is that interviewing does not require any degree of preparation. The perception is that an interview consists of two people sitting down together, having a conversation. As they talk, one person—the interviewer—asks questions, and the other—the applicant—answers the questions. Whether a job offer is extended depends on how well the applicant answers the questions.

Such an impression is largely based on observations of interviews being conducted by seasoned interviewers who certainly can make employment interviews seem like effortless conversation. It is, however, inaccurate because these interviewers have put a great deal of work behind this casual front by completing a number of preparatory steps before meeting the applicants.

Reviewing Job Specifications

The process of interview preparation begins with reviewing the specifications of a job every time it becomes available. This means reviewing the position's responsibilities, requirements, reporting relationships, environmental factors, exemption and union status, salary, benefits, and growth opportunities. This important task provides necessary answers to four key questions:

1. Am I thoroughly familiar with the qualities being sought in an applicant?
2. Are these qualities both job related and realistic?
3. Can I clearly communicate the duties and responsibilities of this position to applicants?
4. Am I prepared to provide additional relevant information about the job and the company to applicants?

Duties and Responsibilities

If you are an HR specialist, make a point of spending time in the department where openings exist. Observe and converse with incumbents as they perform various aspects of the job. Talk to supervisors for their perspective of the scope of work. If possible, seek out people who have previously held the position to see how the job may have evolved. Try to visit on more than one occasion so that you will be able to observe a typical day.

If a personal visit is not possible, have lengthy telephone conversations with several departmental representatives. Also, request a job description, and review its contents for a detailed description of the level and degree of responsibility. Job descriptions are an interviewer's most valuable tool. Guidelines for developing maximally effective job descriptions follow this section.

It is extremely important for HR specialists to learn as much as possible about the responsibilities of a particular job. Not only will it prepare them for the face-to-face interview, but it will also help to establish a rapport between the HR staff and individual departments. This is critical, since in many organizations there is some dispute as to who should recruit, interview, and select new employees: HR experts or department heads. The argument against HR grows stronger if the position in question is highly technical in nature. This is a difficult argument to resolve. On the one hand, it is quite true that HR experts do not have the in-depth knowledge of a particular job that someone in that field possesses. On the other hand, they have a wide range of overall interviewing skills, which enables them to ascertain the information needed to make appropriate hiring decisions.

The ideal arrangement is a partnership between the HR department and the department in which an opening exists. The HR specialist should screen the resumés and applications and conduct the initial interview to determine overall job suitability. Referrals may then be made to the department, where a more detailed, technical interview can be held. As a final step, representatives from both departments should compare notes and reach a joint final decision.

In reviewing the duties and responsibilities of an opening, determine if they are realistic in relation to other factors, such as previous experience and education. Determine, too, if they are relevant to the overall job function and if they overlap with the responsibilities of other jobs.

It is important to review the duties and responsibilities of a job opening each time a position becomes available. Even if an opening was filled six months ago and is now vacant again, assess the responsibilities of the job to make certain no major changes have occurred in the interim. This will ensure up-to-date job information and accuracy when discussing the position with potential employees.

Education and Prior Experience

Generally the department head in charge of the area where a specific opening exists will describe the qualifications needed for the job; HR specialists then comment on their appropriateness. Together, any educational and experience prerequisites are agreed on and established.

This process is most effective when managers and HR representatives ask these key questions:

- What skills and knowledge are needed to perform the primary duties and responsibilities of this job successfully?
- Why are these skills and knowledge necessary?
- Why couldn't someone without these skills and knowledge perform the primary duties of this job?
- Are the requirements consistent with the job duties and responsibilities?
- Are we being influenced by the background of the current or last incumbent?
- Are we subjectively considering our own personal expectations of the job?
- Are we compromising because we are in a hurry to fill the job?
- Are we unrealistically searching for the ideal candidate?
- Are we succumbing to pressure from senior management as to what are appropriate job requirements?
- Are the requirements in accordance with all applicable equal employment opportunity (EEO) laws and regulations?

Arbitrarily setting high minimum standards in the hope of filling a position with the most qualified person can backfire. Suppose that you are trying to fill a first-line supervisor's spot, and you decide on someone who not only has a great deal of hands-on experience but is also well rounded. To you, this translates into someone with at least five years of supervisory experience and a four-year college degree. If asked some of the questions just suggested, you would probably conclude that these requirements are too high for a first-line supervisory position. Also, for reasons of possible discrimination, you would have to modify them. But even if there were no applicable employment laws, there is a good reason for setting more flexible standards:

If you came across applicants falling short of this experience and educational profile but who met other intangible or nonconcrete requirements and came highly recommended, you would not be able to hire them. It would be difficult to justify hiring someone not meeting the minimum requirements of the job, especially if you also rejected candidates who exceeded them.

In addition to asking yourself these basic questions regarding experience and education, there is a way of setting requirements that does not paint you into a corner but still allows you to be highly selective. By using carefully worded terminology in the job description, you can choose the candidate who best combines concrete and intangible requirements. These phrases include the following:

- Demonstrated ability to _____ required.
- In-depth knowledge of _____ required.
- Extensive experience in _____ required.
- Knowledge of _____ would be an advantage.
- Proven ability to _____ required.
- We are looking for an effective _____.
- Proven track record of _____ needed.
- Substantial experience in _____ essential.
- Familiarity with _____ would be ideal.
- Degree relevant to _____ preferred.
- Degree in _____ preferred.
- Advanced degree a plus.
- College degree in _____ highly desirable.
- An equivalent combination of education and experience.

These sample phrases all provide the latitude to select someone who, for example, may be lacking in one area, such as education, but compensates with a great deal of experience. The use of such terms does not mean hiring standards are compromised; rather, it means that care is being taken to avoid setting requirements that cannot be justified by the specific duties of the job, while at the same time offering the widest range of choice among applicants.

Intangible Requirements

To balance the lack of specific educational or experiential requirements, intangible criteria can be helpful—for example:

- Ability to get along with coworkers, management, employees, clients, and customers
- Appearance

- Assertiveness
- Attitude
- Creativity and imagination
- Initiative
- Management style
- Maturity
- Personality
- Responsiveness
- Self-confidence
- Temperament

These factors can be significant, but only when examined in relation to the requirements of the opening. That is, in addition to determining any relevant education and experience prerequisites and examining the scope and degree of responsibilities, you should explore the question of what type of individual would be most compatible with the position. This may best be determined by learning as much as possible about such factors as the amount of stress involved, the amount of independent work (as opposed to closely supervised work), and the overall management style of the department. The combined information should translate into a profile of the ideal employee.

Keeping this profile in mind as candidates are considered can be helpful, particularly if two or more applicants meet the concrete requirements of the job. You can then compare intangible job-related criteria to help make the final decision. Intangibles can also be helpful in evaluating candidates for entry-level jobs for which there are few, if any, tangible educational and experience prerequisites.

Be careful when making comparisons based on intangibles, since the meaning of certain terms is highly subjective. For example, some of the more popular applicant evaluation phrases—saying that an applicant has a bad attitude, a winning personality, a nice appearance, or a mature approach to work—may not always translate the same way for everyone. Furthermore, such descriptions really do not tell anything substantive about what the person can contribute to a job. Hence, be careful not to weigh intangible elements too heavily or select someone solely on the basis of any of these factors. If considered at all, such factors should be job related, not based on personal bias.

Reporting Relationships

Another facet of the familiarization process has to do with reporting relationships. In this regard, ask yourself the following questions:

- What position will this job report to, both directly and indirectly?
- Where does this job appear on the department's organizational chart?
- What positions, if any, report directly and indirectly to this job?
- What is the relationship between this job and other jobs in the department in terms of level and scope of responsibility?
- What is the relationship between this job and other jobs in the organization?

These questions pertain to positions, as opposed to specific individuals. This precludes the possibility of the answers being influenced by the personality or skill of a particular employee.

Work Environment

A job's work environment consists of four distinct areas. A work environment checklist appears in Appendix D.

Physical Working Conditions

This encompasses such factors as sitting or standing for long periods of time, working in areas that may not be well ventilated, exposure to chemicals or toxic fumes, working in cramped quarters, working in a very noisy location, and working with video display terminals for long periods of time. If the working conditions are ideal, few interviewers will hesitate to inform prospective employees of this. After all, this helps sell the company and the job, perhaps even compensating for areas that are less ideal—perhaps the starting salary is not up to par with that of a competitor, or the benefits package is not as comprehensive. However, if the working conditions leave something to be desired, the tendency is to omit reference to them when discussing the job, in the hope that once employees begin work and discover the flaw in the work environment, they will adjust rather than leave. Unfortunately, what frequently occurs is that new employees resent the deception and either quit or develop poor work habits.

The problems of high turnover and low morale as they relate to unsatisfactory working conditions can easily be prevented. First, accurately describe existing working conditions to prospective employees. If an unpleasant condition is temporary, by all means say so, but do not make anything up. Be sure to ask candidates whether they have ever worked under similar conditions before and for how long.

Also determine how they feel about being asked to work under these circumstances. When they respond, it is as important to watch as it is to listen to their answers. Often there is a contradiction between an applicant's verbal and nonverbal responses. Your skill as an interviewer will in part be determined by how well you incorporate and evaluate each type of response to reach a decision. Chapter 9 deals with the issues of actively listening and nonverbal communication more fully. For now, suffice it to say that if a candidate states that he does not mind standing seven hours a day, but you sense some resistance in his body language, you must pursue the subject until you are more certain of his true reaction.

Another accurate way to assess potential employees' responses to uncomfortable working conditions is to show them where they would be working. Unless this is logistically impractical, a quick trip to the job site should be part of the interview. This way there will be no surprises and a new employee knows exactly what to expect when reporting to work for the first time.

Geographic Location of the Job

If at all possible show potential employees where they would be working. If recruiting from a central office for positions in satellite branches, be specific in the description of the job site, and offer videos, CD-ROMs, or brochures illustrating the location where an opening exists.

Sometimes a position will call for rotation from one location to another. If this is the case, be prepared to describe the working conditions of each location and how long each assignment is likely to last. Be sure to solicit a reaction to the idea of job rotation. Many employees prefer to settle into a work routine where they are familiar with the environment, the commute, and the other workers. On the other hand, some people like the variety offered by a rotational position.

Travel

Be sure to discuss the geographic span and the expected frequency of job-related travel. Tell applicants, too, how much advance notice they can generally expect to receive before having to leave. In the case of local travel, applicants will want to know whether they will be expected to provide their own transportation. They will also want to know how reimbursement for job-related travel expenses is handled.

Specific Schedule

This is especially important for clerical and entry-level positions, where employees need to be told what days of the week they are expected to work, when to report to work each day, and when they may leave. If alternative work arrangements are available (e.g., flextime and the other possibilities discussed in Chapter 1), applicants need to know their options.

Also, be sure your know how much time is allotted for meals, as well as other scheduled breaks throughout the day. Conveying this information to applicants can avoid disciplinary problems after they become employees.

Exemption Status

The Fair Labor Standards Act (FLSA) defines the term *exempt* literally to mean "exempt from overtime compensation"; that is, an employer is not required to pay exempt employees for time worked beyond their regularly scheduled workweek. Although this generally pertains to executives, managers, and some supervisors, the act does not prohibit companies from paying managerial staff for overtime. However, with the exception of strikes and other work-related emergencies, this is rarely done.

The term *nonexempt* literally means "not exempt from overtime compensation." Nonexempt employees, such as clerical workers, must be paid for any time worked beyond their regularly scheduled workweek.

The actual work performed by employees, not their job titles, determines exemption status. With most positions, there is no question as to the exemption status. However, some jobs fall into a gray area and are not as easily categorized. To assist with exemption classification, the Department of Labor offers a series of requirements that must be met before classifying someone as exempt. These requirements appear in both a short and long test that help evaluate the four employee classifications recognized by the FLSA: executive, administrative, professional, and outside salespersons. The tests include minimum salary requirements that are not frequently revised. Therefore, these should not be relied upon for determining exemption status. A more reliable gauge is the specific duties performed and level of a job's responsibility. Degree of independent judgment required and extent of managerial authority are two additional key criteria.

A copy of the Department of Labor's guidelines may be obtained by writing to the Employment Standards Administration, Wage and Hour Division, Washington, D.C. 20210.

Union Status

The National Labor Relations Act (Wagner Act) clearly states, "Employees shall have the right to self-organization, to form, join, or assist labor organizations, to bargain collectively, through representatives of their own choosing, and to engage in other concerted activities, for the purpose of collective bargaining or other mutual aid or protection."

Union membership has been in a steady decline since the early 1980s, but union organizing activities are now on the upswing. Organizing efforts target primarily small, public sector establishments with large numbers of women and younger employees, as well as private sector companies with under a hundred employees. Industries experiencing the greatest amount of organizing are nursing homes and other care facilities, and computer manufacturers.

Most organizing activity is taking place in the Northeast and Midwest, where labor unions have traditionally had a strong presence.

That being said, interviewers should be prepared to tell applicants whether they will be required to join a union, which union it is, information relative to initiation fees or required dues, and what being a union member entails. Exercise caution when discussing this subject. Do not express your personal opinions regarding unions or try to bias applicants, either for or against unions. Also, avoid inquiries regarding their present views toward unions or questions about past union involvement. Your job is to be informative and descriptive only.

Salary Ranges

Whether this information is disclosed to an applicant at the initial interview is a matter of company policy, but interviewers should certainly know what a job pays so they can determine if a candidate warrants further consideration. If, for example, there is an opening for an administrative assistant paying an annual salary of from $35,000 to $47,500 and an applicant is currently earning an annual salary of $37,750, there is no problem. If, on the other hand, a managerial position becomes available offering a salary range of from $50,000 to $68,000 and an applicant is currently making $67,000, there are some areas of concern. What is your company's policy regarding starting a new employee at the maximum of the salary range? If you offer the maximum, will this person accept an increase of just $1,000 a year? What about subsequent salary increases? Does your company "red circle" employees at the ceiling of the range so that they remain frozen there until either the salary structure is reevaluated or the position is reclassified?

Other salary-related issues may arise. Applicants may be earning considerably less than your minimum salary for what may be considered comparable work. It could be that they are currently underpaid or not being altogether forthright about the actual duties and responsibilities they perform. This situation calls for a more thorough line of questioning during the interview regarding the level and scope of tasks currently being performed.

Applicants sometimes indicate that they are earning considerably more than the maximum for an available position. Do not automatically assume that this translates into overqualification or that the person will not remain on the job. There are a number of explanations as to why someone would be willing to take a reduction in pay, including the opportunity to work for a specific company, the desire to learn new skills or enter a new field, or an inability to find suitable work in one's own profession.

Related to the issue of salary is the "sign-on" or "hiring" bonus. Previously reserved for executive-level candidates and highly specialized, hard-to-fill positions, the bonus is now becoming an increasingly popular means for attracting top college graduates. It generally amounts to up to 10 percent of salary not surpassing $100,000, and between 15 and 20 percent for salaries over $100,000. Depending on how difficult it may be to fill a job or how desirable it is to attract a particular individual, the bonus may reach as high as 25 percent.

The sign-on bonus enables employers to attract top-quality employees without disturbing the company's salary structure. Problems relating to salary increases in subsequent years may arise if the person's new salary is the same or only slightly greater than the combined starting salary and bonus.

Note that the need for acquiring a job candidate's salary history is increasingly being challenged as concerns about pay inequities for men and women prevail (this is discussed further on in this chapter).

Benefits

Describing your company's benefits package can be an excellent selling point, especially for hard-to-fill positions. Interviewers are advised to prepare a forty-five- to sixty-second summary of company benefits, such as medical and disability insurance, dental coverage, life insurance, profit-sharing plans, stock bonus programs, vacation days, personal days, leaves of absence, holidays, and tuition reimbursement.

Be careful not to give the impression that a discussion of your company's benefits means an applicant is being seriously considered for a job. Make it clear that providing this information is part of the interview process and that the selected applicant will receive more comprehensive benefits information at the time of hire.

Growth Opportunities

Generally applicants are interested in whether they will be able to move up in an organization. It is therefore helpful to know about the frequency of performance appraisals, salary reviews, and increases; policies regarding promotions; relationship of a position's level and scope of responsibilities to that of others within a job family; policies governing internal job posting; likelihood of advancement; tuition reimbursement plans; and training.

It is important to provide an accurate account of growth opportunities to preclude the possibility that morale problems will develop. For example, if an applicant is applying for a position that is one step removed from the top position in a job family and that position has been occupied by the same person for the past ten years, the opportunity for growth by way of promotion is unlikely. There may be other ways to grow, such as an expansion of responsibilities, which could lead to the creation of a new job classification.

Preparing Job Descriptions

At first glance, reviewing a job's specifications may seem like an overwhelming task. However, there is a single tool that can provide all the information needed: a job description—a formalized document of factual and concise information identifying the job, its responsibilities, and the work it entails. This multipurpose tool can be used in virtually every aspect of the employment process:

Recruitment	Performance appraisals
Interviewing	Promotions
Selection	Transfers
Job postings	Disciplinary actions
Training	Demotions

Grievance proceedings
Employee orientations
Work flow analyses
Salary structuring

Clarifying relationships
 between jobs and work
 assignments
Exit interviews
Outplacement

Since job descriptions can be used for many different purposes, employers should take care to write them as comprehensively as possible. Initially this will require a fair amount of time, but it will prove well worth the effort.

The task begins with a thorough job analysis. This is the process of gathering data that will later be used for preparing the actual job description. There are many ways to collect the required data. Following are some of the most successful methods:

• *Distributing questionnaires to incumbents, their managers, and anyone whose work is directly affected by the available position.* Questionnaires are considered especially helpful for identifying distinct categories of responsibilities and should be as job specific as possible.

• *Asking incumbents and their managers to maintain logs over a period of time.* Work logs are effective tools for determining the frequency of time spent on different activities.

• *Directly observing incumbents as they work.* This method can be useful as long as the workers are not made to feel uncomfortable.

• *Interviewing incumbents, their managers, and others who interact with the incumbents.* Ask similar questions of everyone involved, focusing on what the job entails, as opposed to how they think it should be accomplished.

Once the job analysis stage is satisfactorily completed, it is time to prepare the written job descriptions. Job descriptions come in two different formats: generic and specific. Generic job descriptions are written in broad, general terms and may be used for several similar positions in different departments of the same organization. When preparing generic job descriptions, take care to combine only those duties that all positions of the same title have in common. Specific job descriptions define the duties and tasks of one particular position. They are written when a given position requires the performance of unique or distinct responsibilities, thereby separating it from other jobs.

Here are fifteen guidelines for writing effective job descriptions:

1. *Arrange duties and responsibilities in a logical, sequential order.* Begin with the task requiring the greatest amount of time or carrying the greatest responsibility.

2. *State separate duties clearly and concisely.* This way anyone can glance at the description and easily identify each duty.

3. *Try to avoid generalizations or ambiguous words.* Use specific language and be exact in your meaning. To illustrate, "Handles mail" might be better expressed as "Sorts mail" or "Distributes mail."

4. *Do not try to list every task.* Use the phrase, "primary duties and responsibilities include . . ." at the beginning of your job description and proceed from there. You may also choose to close with the phrase, "Performs other related duties and responsibilities, as required."

5. *Include specific examples of duties wherever possible.* This will enable the reader more fully to understand the scope of responsibility involved.

6. *Use nontechnical language.* A good job description explains the responsibilities of a job in terms that are understandable to everyone using it.

7. *Indicate the frequency of occurrence of each duty.* One popular way of doing this is to have a column on the left of the list of tasks with corresponding percentages that represent the estimated amount of time devoted to each primary duty.

8. *List duties individually and concisely rather than using narrative paragraph form.* A job description is not an English composition.

9. *Do not refer to specific people.* Instead, refer to titles and positions. Incumbents are likely to change positions long before the positions themselves are revamped or eliminated.

10. *Use the present tense.* It reads more smoothly.

11. *Be objective and accurate in describing the job.* Be careful not to describe the incumbent, yourself when you held that particular job, someone who may have just been fired for poor performance, or someone who was recently promoted for outstanding job performance. Describe the job as it should be performed—not as you would like to see it performed.

12. *Stress what the incumbent does instead of explaining a procedure that is used.* To illustrate, use "records appointments" rather than "a record of appointments must be kept."

13. *Be certain that all requirements are job related and are in accordance with equal employment opportunity laws and regulations.* This will preclude the likelihood of legal problems developing later on.

14. *Eliminate unnecessary articles,* such as *a* and *the*. Do not make the description too wordy. Most job descriptions can be completed in one or two pages. The length of a job description does not increase the importance of the job.

15. *Use action words.* This means any word that describes a specific function, such as *organizes*. Action words do not leave room for confusion. Within a sentence, one word should stand out as most descriptive—a word that could really stand alone. This action word also conveys to the reader a degree of responsibility. For example, compare "directs" to "under the direction of. . . ." Try to begin each sentence with an action word; the first word used should introduce the function being described.

Here is a list of 125 sample action words that employers can refer to when writing job descriptions:

accepts	corrects	generates
acts	correlates	guides
administers	counsels	identifies
advises	creates	implements
allocates	delegates	informs
analyzes	deletes	initiates
anticipates	designs	inputs
approves	determines	inspects
arranges	develops	instructs
ascertains	devises	interprets
assigns	directs	interviews
assists	disseminates	investigates
audits	documents	issues
authorizes	drafts	itemizes
balances	edits	lists
batches	ensures	locates
calculates	establishes	maintains
circulates	evaluates	manages
classifies	examines	measures
codes	facilitates	modifies
collects	figures	monitors
compiles	files	negotiates
conducts	fills in	notifies
consolidates	fines	observes
constructs	follows up	obtains
consults	formulates	operates
coordinates	furnishes	organizes

originates	records	specifies
outlines	refers	studies
oversees	renders	submits
participates	reports	summarizes
performs	represents	supervises
plans	requests	tabulates
prepares	researches	trains
processes	reviews	transcribes
proposes	revises	transposes
provides	routes	troubleshoots
pursues	schedules	types
rates	screens	utilizes
receives	selects	verifies
recommends	signs	writes

Considering certain issues before actually writing the job description can be helpful:

• Does the job holder supervise the work of others? If so, give job titles and a brief description of the responsibilities of those supervised.

• What duties does the job holder perform regularly, periodically, and infrequently? List these in order of importance.

• What degree of supervision is exercised over the job holder?

• To what extent are instructions necessary in assigning work to the job holder?

• How much decision-making authority or judgment is allowed to the job holder in the performance of the required duties?

• What are the working conditions?

• What skills are required for the successful performance of the job?

• What authority does the job holder have in such matters as training other people or directing the workforce?

• At what stage of its completion is the work of the job holder reviewed by someone else?

• What machines or equipment is the job holder responsible for operating? Describe the equipment's complexity.

• What would be the cost to management of serious mistakes or errors that the job holder might make in the regular performance of the required duties?

• What employees within the organization and customers or clients outside the organization will the job holder interact with on a regular basis?

The exact contents of a job description will be dictated by the specific environment and needs of an organization. What follows provides the basic categories of job information required for most positions:

1. Date
2. Job analyst or preparer
3. Job title
4. Division and department
5. Reporting relationship
6. Location of the job
7. Exemption status
8. Salary grade and range
9. Work schedule
10. Job summary
11. Duties and responsibilities, including extent of authority and degree of independent judgment required
12. Job requirements, including education, prior work experience, and specialized skill and knowledge
13. Physical environment and working conditions
14. Equipment and machinery to be used
15. Other relevant factors, such as degree of contact with the public or customers and access to confidential information

A job description form containing these categories appears in Appendix E.

Once a job description is written, review it once or twice each year to make certain the nature of the job has not changed substantially.

Reviewing the Employment Application and Resumé

Never conduct an interview without first reviewing the candidate's completed application and/or resumé, for two main reasons. First, you will become familiar with the person's credentials, background, and qualifications as they relate to the requirements and responsibilities of the job; second, you can identify areas for discussion during the interview.

Each organization should have an application form that reflects its own environment. For example, the application form for a highly technical company will differ from one used by a nonprofit organization. Some companies have more than one form: one for professional or exempt positions, another for nonexempt positions.

Appendix F contains a sample job application form with categories that might be used in most organizations. Review its contents with your organization in mind, modifying it as required.

When designing an application form, remember that all categories must be relevant and job related. This is critical from the standpoint of compliance with EEO laws and regulations. In this regard, familiarity with federal laws is not sufficient, since many state laws are more stringent. Therefore, even if you are in compliance with federal regulations, you could still be in violation of state regulations. Where there is a difference, the stricter laws prevails. Oversight or ignorance of the law does not provide immunity.

Resumés differ from applications in that people start with a blank piece of paper (or screen, in the case of electronic resumés, described in Chapter 4) as opposed to a form with specific questions. Consequently applicants offer whatever data they choose on a resumé. Generally the same basic information should appear on a resumé as appears on an application form—for example, work history (employer, location, duration, duties, and special accomplishments), educational degrees, and scholastic achievements. Career objectives may also be cited.

Following are ten key areas to focus on when reviewing an application or resumé. Remember these are guidelines only. Deviation from any one of the standards should not, in and of itself, result in the rejection of a candidate. Nor should a specific standard in this list be considered at all if it is not relevant to the responsibilities of the position in question:

1. *Scan the overall appearance of the application or resumé.* Check to see that it is neat and easy to read. The handwriting on applications should be legible, paper resumés should be typed and printed, and electronic-generated resumés should reflect cyberspace resumé-writing guidelines in terms of organizing the information and highlighting key accomplishments. The contents of applications and resumés should be grammatically correct and the language easy to understand. Paper resumés are generally one to two pages in length and should be professional in appearance. Although they are not essential, cover letters usually accompany resumés and show added interest on the part of the applicant.

2. *Look for any blanks or omissions.* This is easy with an application form; with a resumé, check to see that basic information (work and education) has not been excluded. Make note of any missing information so that you can ask the applicant about it. Some employment application forms are poorly designed, as are some electronic resumé formats, and candidates may inadvertently overlook certain questions or categories. Or it may be that an applicant purposely omitted certain information. If this is the case, it is up to you to find out why and to determine the importance of the missing data during the interview.

3. *Review the applicant's work history and make a note of any time gaps between jobs.* If an applicant indicates that he or she took some time off between jobs to travel throughout Europe, make a note of it. Be careful that you do not pass judgment, deciding that this was a frivolous and irresponsible pursuit. Fill in the gaps and worry about drawing conclusions after the interview process is completed.

4. *Consider any overlaps in time.* For example, the dates on an application may show that the candidate was attending school and working at the same time. Of course, this is possible, but not if the school happens to be in California and the job was in New York (unless it was a correspondence school). Even if the locations are consistent, you need to verify the accuracy of the dates.

5. *Make a note of any other inconsistencies.* To illustrate, say there is an applicant with an extensive educational background who has been employed in a series of nonexempt jobs. This may be because she has degrees in a highly specialized field and cannot find suitable work, or it may be that she has misrepresented her educational credentials. It is up to you to find out.

6. *Consider the frequency of job changes.* People voluntarily leave jobs for many reasons, including an inaccurate description of the work at the time of hire, an improper job match, personality conflicts on the job, inadequate salary increases, limited growth opportunities, and unkept promises. Some employees who know that they are doing poorly voluntarily terminate their employment just prior to a scheduled performance evaluation. Then there are instances when an employee is let go. This may occur when a company shuts down for economic reasons, when major organizational changes cause the deletion of several positions, or when a contingent assignment has been completed and there is no additional work to be done. Of course, employees are also terminated for poor performance.

When reviewing a candidate's employment record, do not draw premature, negative conclusions regarding the frequency of job changes. To determine what constitutes a frequent change is highly subjective. Too often interviewers set arbitrary guidelines, sometimes patterned after their own work history. You may decide that changing jobs more often than once every two years is too frequent and that this translates into unreliability. However, at this stage of the interview process, you simply do not have enough information to make such a decision. After all, you have not even met the applicant yet. Make a note that you want to discuss the pattern of job changes, and move on to the next category.

7. *Be objective when evaluating a person's salary requirements.* A common assumption in our society is that everyone wants and needs to make more money. Indeed, it is one of the most commonly cited reasons for changing jobs. However, you will undoubtedly come across applicants who are willing to take a job at a lower salary than they were making previously or are earning now. The reasons vary. Sometimes an individual wants to move from one area of specialization to another and recognizes that a lack of expertise in the field will mean less money. Perhaps an applicant wants to work for a particular company and is willing to earn less in order to do so. Some people view job satisfaction of paramount importance. For those who have been unemployed for a long time and cannot find work at their old rate of pay, any job is seen as an opportunity. The message here is, Do not draw conclusions.

It is significant to note that, while not apparently illegal, requesting that applicants provide information relevant to salaries earned in past positions may be a violation of the Equal Pay Act of 1963, which prohibits paying women less than men for performing substantially equal work (see Chapter 6). This could occur where an employer learns that a woman applicant has been earning considerably less in previous jobs than has a male candidate with a comparable background of skill and experience. If both are hired for the same type of job, will be performing substantially equal work, are offered starting salaries that are, say, $5,000 above their previous salaries, and perform at comparable levels of effectiveness during their respective terms of employment, the pay differential between the two will widen that much more.

Consider, for example, a male candidate hired at a starting annual salary of $50,000 and a woman who is hired to perform comparable work at a salary of $45,000. Both receive an "above-average" evaluation at the time of their first performance evaluation, resulting in a 7 percent increase. The original $5,000 gap between their respective salaries has just increased to $5,350; the male employee's annual earnings rise to $53,500, and the woman employee's salary increases to only $48,150. If their performance levels remain comparable at the time of their next review, warranting another 7 percent raise, the gap will increase to $5,994.50, since the man will now be earning $57,245 and the woman will be making only $51,250.50 (little more than the man was offered at the time of hire). Such a pay difference that is based on past earnings could be a violation of the Equal Pay Act because it is, in effect, a differential based on sex.

For this reason, reference to salaries in past positions does not appear in the sample application form in Appendixes F and G.

8. *Carefully review the candidate's reasons for leaving previous jobs.* Look for a pattern. For example, if the reason given for leaving several jobs in a row is "no room for growth," it may be that this person's job expectations are unrealistic. This explanation could be perfectly legitimate, or it could be a cover-up for other, less acceptable, reasons. This is a key area to explore in the face-to-face interview.

9. *If the person's duties are not clearly described on the application or resumé, make a note to ask for elaboration.* Job titles may also require explanation. Some titles are not functional or descriptive and therefore do not reveal the general realm of responsibility. Examples of such titles include "administrative assistant" and "vice president." Sometimes titles sound very grand, but upon probing, you discover that they carry few substantive responsibilities.

10. *Review the application or resumé for red-flag areas*—any information that does not seem to make sense or that leaves you with an uneasy feeling. A classic example is the response to the category "Reason for Leaving Last Job." The popular answer "personal" should alert you to a possible problem. Many interviewers assume that they have no right to pursue this further—that to do so would be an invasion of the person's privacy. This is not true. You have an obligation to ask the applicant to be more specific. If people begin to volunteer truly personal information about their home life and personal relationships, then you must interrupt and ask them to focus on job-related incidents that may have contributed to their decision to leave. Also note that "personal" is frequently a cover-up for "fired."

Screening Applicants by Telephone

With the exception of applicants who come through a third-party employment agency or search firm, internal job posting, school recruiting, job fairs, and open houses, telephone screening is appropriate in virtually every instance. In particular, telephone screening is considered an essential preinterview activity for professional candidates who will be traveling some distance, usually for a series of face-to-face interviews taking up the better part of a day.

Telephone screening is intended to accomplish one of two objectives: to establish continued interest in a job candidate and result in the scheduling of an appointment to meet in person for an in-depth interview, or to determine that a candidate's qualifications do not sufficiently meet the job's specifications. Under no circumstances should telephone screening be viewed as a substitute for the face-to-face interview.

Successful telephone screening depends on establishing and following a certain format. It is usually wise to contact candidates at their home during nonworking hours. Identify yourself and explain the purpose of your call. Also, confirm the individual's interest in the specific job. Suggest that the candidate allot approximately fifteen to forty-five minutes for the call, with fifteen to twenty minutes being considered sufficient for a nonexempt-level candidate and thirty to forty-five minutes being set aside for a professional candidate.

When the specified time arrives, be prepared to describe the available position, being careful not to identify the qualities being sought in the desired candidate. Encourage the applicant to ask questions related to the specific opening or the company. Have ready a series of questions to assist you in determining whether continued interest is warranted. Some questions to ask nonexempt-level applicants are:

- Why they are leaving their current (or last) employer
- What they do (or did) in a typical day
- What they like (or liked) most and least about their present (or last) job
- Why they are applying for this particular position

In addition, ask questions relative to any significant aspects of the job. For example, if it requires standing for long periods of time, ask applicants to describe jobs where they have had to do this. In addition, describe a typical situation that is likely to occur with this job, and ask the candidates to describe how they have handled similar situations in the past.

Appropriate questions to ask exempt-level applicants include the following:

- Why they are leaving their current (or last) employer and why they are applying for this particular position

- What they know about your organization
- What they have contributed in past positions
- What contributions they anticipate being able to make in this position
- What they expect from your company
- How this position fits into their long-term goals

Then, based on the particulars of the job, ask a series of questions regarding how they have handled certain situations in past positions.

As candidates respond, remind yourself of the purpose of the call: You are deciding whether a face-to-face interview is in order, not whether they should be hired. Take notes as they talk. If the conversation itself is not determinative, reviewing their responses after the call can help you decide whether to schedule an interview. If you do decide to bring them in, the notes can be used as a point of reference and comparison as you repeat some of the questions asked on the telephone, seeking more in-depth information.

Be careful not to judge the quality of a candidate's telephone presentation if effective verbal communication skills are not a job-related criterion. On the other hand, some people, especially those in sales or marketing, do very well communicating on the telephone; consequently, you must be able to separate style from substance.

Before concluding the conversation, go over a brief checklist:

- Does the applicant understand the job?
- Did you ask questions that will enable you to determine whether further interest is warranted?
- Did the applicant ask pertinent questions?
- Has the applicant expressed interest in the job?
- Does the applicant meet the basic qualifications for the job?
- Is there consistency between the information on the resumé or application and what the applicant has told you?

If there is no doubt in your mind that the person should be invited in for an interview, do so before the conversation is completed. If you are not certain and want to review your notes before making a decision, thank the candidate for her time, describe the next step, and estimate when she may expect to hear from you. If you are absolutely certain that the candidate is not suitable for the job, you have one or two choices: Be honest and say that her qualifications are not suitable or that there is a lack of specific expertise or knowledge necessary for the job, or say that you will be reviewing the results of your conversations with all the candidates before taking any further action. If you do reject the candidate outright, explain your policy on keeping applications and resumés on file and encourage her to apply again in the future for other openings. If you have handled the situation tactfully, the person can hang up feeling good, even though no job interview is forthcoming.

Telephone screening offers numerous benefits. The process enables you to weed out candidates who are not qualified, thereby allowing more time to devote to viable potential employees. It is also an impartial process; that is, neither party can be influenced or distracted by such visual factors as appearance, clothing, or grooming. These can be important job-related intangibles (discussed later in this chapter), but they are irrelevant at this screening stage.

Allowing Sufficient Time for the Interview

When determining how much time to allot for each interview, think about the entire process, not just the portion devoted to the face-to-face meeting. Time is needed before the interview to review the application and resumé; during the interview for both you and the applicant to ask questions and for you to provide information about the job and company; and after the interview to write up your notes, reflect on what took place, set up additional appointments, and check references. Additional time may also be required before or after the interview for testing.

Considering all that must be done, just how much time should be set aside for each interview? Much depends on the nature of the job, that is, whether it is nonexempt or exempt. Generally more time is needed for interviewing professionals—usually 90 to 120 minutes. This amount of time should be sufficient for you to ascertain the necessary information about a candidate's qualifications and get a good idea of job suitability and applicant interest. If the actual face-to-face interview runs much beyond 90 minutes, it becomes tiresome for both the applicant and the interviewer. A 90-minute interview leaves approximately 30 minutes to be divided between the pre- and postinterview activities previously mentioned.

In the case of interviews for nonexempt positions, approximately 45 to 75 minutes should be allotted, with 30 to 45 minutes for the face-to-face meeting. More concrete areas are usually probed at this level: specific job duties, attendance records, and the like. These take less time to explore than do the numerous intangible areas examined at the exempt level, such as management style, level of creativity, and initiative.

These time frames are guidelines only. Be flexible in the amount of time allotted, but also be aware of these general parameters because they can help you ascertain sufficient information and avoid discussing irrelevant factors. For example, if you find that your interviews are over within fifteen minutes, you may not be phrasing your questions properly; that is, you are asking yes-no questions as opposed to behavioral or open-ended questions (see Chapters 7 and 8). It may also be that you are not adequately probing suspicious areas, or perhaps simply do not know what questions to ask. If, on the other hand, your interviews last much beyond forty-five minutes for a non-exempt position or ninety minutes for an exempt position, it is likely that the applicant has taken control of the interview. When this occurs, interviewers often find themselves describing their own career with the company at some length. They may also find themselves discussing the contents of books on their shelves or explaining photos on their desks. It is not unusual for inexperienced applicants to try to steer interviewers away from questions regarding their job suitability. By diverting the interviewer's attention and talking a blue streak about irrelevant matters, applicants hope to cloud the real issue of whether they are qualified for the job. Of course, some people simply like to talk a lot and do not intend to be devious. Regardless of the motive, however, interviewers are cautioned against allowing applicants to take control of the interview. This is less likely to happen if you are aware of the appropriate time frame for an interview.

To help maximize the time set aside for meeting applicants, consider the three scheduling guidelines that follow:

1. *Interview only during the time of day when your "biological clock" is at its peak—that is, when you are most alert.* If you tend to slow down around midmorning but then pick up again around 1 P.M., schedule interviews during the afternoon hours. If you are at your best first thing in the morning, late-afternoon appointments would be unwise.

2. *When you have a number of positions to fill and several candidates remain to be seen, try to take a ten-minute break between interviews.* Use the time to take a short walk, get a drink of water, stretch, make a few short phone calls, or do other work. The break will help you feel more in control of your interview schedule and also allow you to focus more clearly on your next applicant.

3. *Try not to conduct more than four or five interviews in one workday.* Obviously this may not always be possible, particularly when you have a number of openings to fill. But if you can space your interviews with other work, you will find that your attention level during the interviews and as well as the other work is likely to improve.

Planning an Appropriate Environment

If applicants are expected to talk freely, they must be assured that what they are saying cannot be overheard by others. This is particularly important when discussing sensitive matters, such as why they are being asked to leave their current jobs. Hence, interviewers must ensure privacy. Not everyone has a private office, but everyone does have access to privacy. This may mean borrowing someone else's office when it is not being used, using the company cafeteria or dining room during off-hours, or sitting in a portion of the lobby that is set apart from areas receiving the most traffic. Such options may be preferable if your own office has partial partitions instead of full floor-to-ceiling walls. Sounds can easily carry over and around partitions; depending on their height, people can also easily peer over the top.

Interviewers should ensure a minimum number of distractions. More obvious distractions include your telephone ringing without someone answering it for you, people walking into your office during the interview, or papers requiring attention left exposed on top of your desk. Some interviewers claim that such distractions are actually beneficial in that they allow for an assessment of how the applicant handles interruptions. This is unlikely. Distractions and interruptions waste valuable time for both the applicant and the interviewer. Moreover, the applicant may be left with an unfavorable impression of the interviewer in particular, and possibly the organization overall.

A more subtle distraction, but one that can interfere as much as a telephone ringing or someone barging in during the interview, is the interviewer's own thoughts. Thinking about all the work that needs to be done may not only prevent you from focusing fully on the applicant but may even result in resentment for keeping you from it. To guard against this, remind yourself just prior to meeting an applicant that interviewing is an important part of your work. It might also help if you cleared off your desk before the applicant enters.

Interviewers should make certain that the applicant is comfortable. It is a simple fact that if the applicant feels comfortable, you will be assured of a more productive interview. Comfort level is not determined by how much furniture there is in your office, whether you have rugs on the floor, or a scenic view. It is your behavior and general approach to the interview that will largely determine the comfort level of the applicant. If you come across as friendly, appear genuinely interested in what the applicant has to say, and have made an effort to ensure privacy and prevent interruptions, what the inter-view surroundings look like is not going to matter a great deal. If you can offer the applicant a choice of seats, that's fine. If, however, space is limited, and there is only one chair in addition to yours, that is all right too. What matters is that the applicant feel welcome.

Following are the most common office seating arrangements be-tween an interviewer and an applicant:

- The applicant and interviewer seated on either side of a desk
- The applicant's chair on the side of the desk
- The applicant and the interviewer sitting across from one an-other, away from the desk
- The applicant and the interviewer seated at a table, either next to each other or across from each other
- The applicant and the interviewer seated at opposite ends of a sofa
- The applicant or interviewer seated on a sofa with the other person seated on a chair across from or next to the sofa

There is no one proper relationship between your seat and the applicant's seat. Some interviewers feel that desks create barriers be-tween themselves and the applicant. If this is how you feel, then desks do indeed become barriers. Also, some interviewers want to see as much of the applicant as possible so they can better assess nonverbal communication. However, if you are comfortable seated behind your desk, then by all means sit there. The applicant is likely to feel comfortable at the other side of the desk in this instance.

Bear in mind that whatever seating arrangement you choose, the applicant should be between a distance of from two to five feet from you.

Planning Basic Questions

In addition to reviewing the completed application or resumé for areas to be explored, plan a handful of general questions. These will serve as the foundation for your interview. The job description is an excellent source for this. By reviewing the job description, you can easily identify the required skills. Then proceed to formulate the questions you will need to ask in order to determine whether the applicants possess these skills and are capable of performing the re-quired duties and responsibilities. Hypothetical situations can also be developed and presented to candidates, enabling them to demonstrate their potential.

Be careful not to list too many questions or become very specific during this stage of preparation. If you have an extensive list of detailed questions, the tendency will be to read from that list during the interview. This will result in a stiff, formalized session, which could make the applicant feel ill at ease. In addition, with a lengthy list of questions, interviewers feel compelled to cover the entire list and often end up being redundant. Again, this can result in the applicant's feeling uncomfortable and wondering whether you are really listening to the responses.

Limit yourself to about a half-dozen general questions. Once you get into the interview, the other questions that need to be asked will follow as offshoots of the applicant's answers. In fact, if your first question is a good, open-ended question, the applicant's response should provide additional questions to ask. An example of an effective first question might be, "Would you please describe your activities during a typical day at your current [or most recent] job?" As you listen to the applicant's response, note any areas mentioned that you want to pursue further during the interview.

This one question alone will yield enough information to fill an entire interview if you listen closely to the applicant's answer and use portions of it as the basis for additional questions. Consider, for example, the applicant who is currently working as a customer service representative. Upon asking her the question, "Would you please describe your activities during a typical day at your present job?" the applicant provides a rather scant response: "Well, let's see. Each day is really kind of different since I deal with customers and you never know what they're going to call about; but basically my job is to handle the customer hot line, research any questions, and process complaints."

If you were to leave this answer and go on to another question, you would be overlooking a wealth of information. The applicant has handed you four valuable pieces of data worthy of exploration:

1. Her job requires dealing with a variety of people and situations.
2. She "handles" a customer hot line.
3. She "researches" questions.
4. She "processes" complaints.

Here are some of the questions that may now be asked based on these data:

"What is the nature of some of the situations with which you are asked to deal?"

"Who are the people who call you?"

"What is the process that someone with a complaint is supposed to follow?"

"What is your role in this process?"

"Exactly what is the customer hot line?"

"When you say that you 'handle' the hot line, exactly what do you mean?"

"What do you say to a customer who calls on the hot line?"

"What do you say to a customer who calls with a specific question?"

"Has there ever been a time when you did not have the answer being sought by a customer? What did you do?"

"What do you do when a customer is not satisfied with the answer you have given? Give me a specific example of when this has happened."

"Tell me about a time when a customer was extremely angry. What happened?"

"Tell me about a time when a customer demanded to speak to someone else."

"Describe a time when you had to handle several demanding customers at the same time."

"Describe a situation in which a customer repeatedly called, claiming his problem had still not been resolved. How did you handle it?"

"How much of your time is devoted to researching questions?"

"Describe the research process, including the resources you use."

"How do you prepare for each day, knowing that you will probably have to listen to several people complaining about a variety of problems?"

These are just some of the questions triggered by the applicant's response to one broad, open-ended question. Each of these is also likely to result in additional answers and further inquiries, which ultimately will provide you with a clear picture of the level and scope of this individual's current responsibilities.

This one question is so comprehensive that it alone could suffice as the only prepared question you have before beginning the interview. However, most interviewers feel better prepared if they have additional questions planned; furthermore, applicants not having any prior work experience cannot provide information about a typical workday. Here, then, are some questions that may be prepared prior to the interview. Note that all are broad enough so that the answers will result in additional questions; there will then be no need to prepare more than a few:

For Applicants With Prior Work Experience

"What (do/did) you like most and least about your (current/most recent) job?"

"Describe a situation in your (current/most recent) job involving _____. How did you handle it?"

"What (are/were) some of the duties in your (current/most recent) job that you (find/found) to be difficult and easy? Why?"

"Why (do/did) you want to leave your (current/most recent) job?"

"How do you generally approach tasks you dislike? Please give me a specific example relative to your (current/most recent) job."

For Applicants With Formal Education But
No Prior Work Experience

"What were your favorite and least favorite subjects in (high school/college/other)? Why?"

"Describe your study habits."

"Why did you major in _____?"

"How do you feel your studies in _____ prepared you for this job?"

For Applicants Without Formal Education or Work Experience

"Here are a series of hypothetical situations that are likely to occur on the job. How would you handle them?"

"What has prepared you for this job?"

Understanding the Role of Perception

One additional area of interview preparation is the role of perception. This is a critical phase in the objective evaluation of job candidates. Before meeting an applicant, interviewers should briefly review the five primary ways in which we formulate our perceptions and ideas about people.

First Impressions

This is the most prevalent and often the most damaging way of formulating our ideas about people, since we often form first impressions without even realizing it. Interviewers unaware of the importance of perception frequently boast, "The minute he walked in the door, I could tell he was right for the job."

This is a mistake. You cannot determine job suitability by sizing people up in a split second based on their appearance. Of course, appearance, which consists of many components including clothing, colors, and grooming, does play a role in the selection process. After all, employees represent an organization, and therefore the image that they project is a direct reflection on that company. The problem is that interviewers have a tendency to form preconceived notions of how employees in certain job classifications should look. An accountant, for example, conjures up a different image than does a mechanic. If a person applying for a mechanic's opening came to an interview dressed in a suit, you would be surprised but probably not turned off. However, if an accountant appeared in your office wearing overalls, it is far more likely that you would form a negative first impression. This is true because we tend to have very specific ideas of how an employee in a particular job category should look.

First impressions should play a role in your decision-making process, but not to the exclusion of all the other factors to be examined. Do not allow them to act as a substitute for judgment. Try not to form a complete impression until after you have conducted the interview. You may find that the applicant's attire or grooming is the only problem. The person's job skills may be superior to those of all other candidates. At this point, you can talk to the applicant about the desired image of your organization. Then schedule a brief follow-up interview to see if your message was clearly received.

Information From Others

An applicant who comes highly recommended by someone for whom you have high regard can elicit a positive response from you prior to the actual face-to-face meeting. On the other hand, someone you dislike may make a referral to you, automatically creating a negative bias toward the person being recommended. In both instances you are allowing yourself to be influenced by information from others. Instead of assessing the applicant on her own merits, you are assessing the person making the recommendation, thereby transferring your opinion from the referral source to the applicant. As with first impressions, information from others does play a role in the decision-making process. Anything that might supplement the data on an application or resumé can be helpful, but it is premature to make an evaluation based on this highly subjective aspect of perception at this stage of the employment process.

Single Statements

Suppose an applicant's response to one of your questions rubs you the wrong way. If you are not aware of the impact that a single statement can have, it could bother you to the extent that you eliminate the person from further consideration. This might occur even though the comment does not constitute a valid reason for rejection. You must be particularly careful if this should happen during the initial stage of the interview, when you are trying to put the applicant at ease and establish rapport. This is commonly accomplished through a few minutes of small talk (see Chapter 9). During this portion of the interview, you might comment about some political news that caught you eye in the morning newspaper. The applicant might then express his views on the subject, which happen to be contrary to yours. If you are not careful, this difference could influence your objectivity in assessing the applicant's job suitability. You will then have let a single statement—one that is totally irrelevant to the decision-making process—affect your judgment.

Even single statements that are job related must be weighed in relation to other qualifying factors. Keep in mind that it is usually a combination of factors that results in the rejection of a candidate.

Nonverbal Communication

Nonverbal communication, commonly referred to as body language, is a vital aspect of the employment process. Often an interviewer can learn as much about applicants through their nonverbal messages as can be learned from verbal ones. This topic will be additionally explored in Chapter 9. However, it is important at this point to recognize body language as one of the components of perception. Nonverbal messages that are misinterpreted by the interviewer can result in poor selection or rejection decisions. This usually occurs when body language is interpreted according to the interviewer's own gestures or expressions. For example, just because you have a tendency to avoid eye contact when you are hiding something does not mean that the applicant is avoiding your eyes for the same reason. It may very well be a sign that she is deep in thought.

Each of us has our own pattern of nonverbal expression, attributable to a combination of cultural and environmental factors. These factors influence such elements of body language as gesture, posture, touching, and the distance we maintain from one another. With regard to the last, referred to as proxemics, our culture recognizes from two to five feet as being an appropriate distance between interviewer and applicant. A candidate from a culture that regards this as too much distance might immediately pull his chair up much closer to the interviewer. The interviewer might interpret this as a violation of space or as an act of aggression or intimacy, leaving him with feelings of discomfort, hostility, or intimidation. Some interviewers may go so far as to move their chairs back or get up during instances of excessive proximity.

Another aspect of nonverbal communication, chronemics, has to do with the amount of time that passes between verbal exchanges. In our culture, we expect people to respond to questions immediately. In other cultures, people deliberately wait before answering. An applicant who does this might be perceived by her interviewer as being bored, inattentive, confused, or nervous.

Be careful not to draw conclusions too early in the interview process based on an applicant's nonverbal messages. Allow time for the individual's patterns to emerge, and then relate these patterns to the other factors involved in making a selection.

Ethnocentrism

This means that we use our values, standards, and beliefs to judge or evaluate others. Overall, this is a perfectly natural result of the cultural conditioning process that we are all exposed to. In our early years, we are taught by well-intentioned parents, teachers, and religious leaders to think and act according to certain standards and values. At the age of five or six, few of us questioned the validity of these standards. Unfortunately, many people grow up believing that these are the only acceptable standards. This results in stereotypical thinking. Consequently, we assign specific attributes and roles to others, based on surface characteristics, such as sex, age, or ethnic origin.

Other factors come into play. For example, the interviewer sees from a resumé that the applicant graduated from the same college that she attended. On the basis of the interviewer's fond memories and high regard for the school, certain positive qualities about this candidate may erroneously be assumed. Or perhaps the resumé shows that the applicant attended Harvard. The interviewer's general assumptions about Harvard graduates could lead her to conclude hastily that the person would be an asset to the company.

Negative reactions may also occur. For instance, a candidate may be working for an organization from which your brother was recently fired. This negative association could bias your assessment of the applicant's job suitability. When perceptions are based on ethnocentric thinking, objectivity falls by the wayside. The chances for open, effective communication are blocked whenever an applicant's response or nonverbal messages deviate from the interviewer's preconceived notions. Keep in mind that ethnocentrism does not pertain to work-related standards established by the company; rather, it comes into play in the intangible areas of an individual's style and approach. It is in direct opposition to objectivity, which is an interviewer's number one obligation.

These five aspects of perception—first impressions, information from others, single statements, body language, and ethnocentrism—together form a valuable tool in the preparation stage of interviewing. Briefly reviewing them just prior to meeting with an applicant can help you avoid hasty hiring or rejection decisions based on nonfactual, subjective factors.

Summary

Even the most seasoned interviewer prepares prior to meeting with an applicant. The process begins with a review of the job's specifications, most effectively summarized in a job description. This is followed with a thorough review of the candidate's application and/or resumé so that the interviewer can become familiar with the person's credentials, background, and qualifications as they relate to the requirements and responsibilities of the job. It also enables the interviewer to identify areas to discuss during the interview.

Whenever possible, conduct telephone screening interviews. This allows you to establish continued interest and schedule an appointment to meet in person for an in-depth meeting, or to determine that a candidate's qualifications do not sufficiently meet the job's specifications. Under no circumstances should telephone screening be viewed as a substitute for the face-to-face interview.

Interviewers are advised to allow a total of about 90 to 120 minutes for the interview process concerning professional candidates, with 60 to 90 minutes for the actual face-to-face meeting; approximately 45 to 75 minutes should be allocated for nonexempt positions, with 30 to 45 minutes for the interview. The remaining time is for reviewing the application and/or resumé, testing, writing up notes, reflecting on what took place, setting up additional appointments, and checking references.

Employers should provide a private and comfortable environment for interviews. They should also prepare a half-dozen or so questions in advance, to serve as the foundation for the interview.

Finally, understanding the role of perception will enable interviewers to evaluate applicants objectively.

Chapter 6
Employment and the Law

Equal employment opportunity (EEO) and affirmative action laws and regulations exist to ensure all individuals the right to compete for all work opportunities without bias because of their race, color, religion, sex, national origin, age, or disability. Non-HR specialists should not skip over this chapter thinking that EEO and affirmative action are not their concern. Anyone having anything to do with any aspect of the employment process is expected to have a basic knowledge of EEO. Unintentional violations caused by ignorance of the law are not excusable.

The information contained in this chapter is not intended to represent legal advice and is current as of this writing.

Federal Legislation

The following fair employment laws and categories of discrimination represent federal statutes, rules, and regulations. Employers are urged to obtain a copy of each of these laws. Unless otherwise noted, copies of the laws may be obtained from:

Equal Employment Opportunity Commission (EEOC)
Department of Labor
1801 L Street, Northwest
Washington, D.C. 20507
202/663-4900

In some instances, booklets outlining highlights of these laws, employer responsibilities, and employee rights are also available.

State and local laws may differ and should also be considered. Failure to comply with these laws could result in costly litigation.

Readers are urged to consult with counsel in all equal employment matters.

Civil Rights Act of 1866

Many people are surprised to learn that employment-related laws have been around for nearly 135 years. One of the earliest and most significant pieces of legislation was the Civil Rights Act of 1866. The most relevant portion for today's employers is Section 1981, Title 42, which ensures all people the same "equal rights under the law . . . as is enjoyed by white citizens . . . to . . . make and enforce" contracts.

Essentially, this has been interpreted to mean that discrimination against nonwhites in the making of written or implied contracts relevant to hiring and promotions is illegal. This law was originally intended to support charges of race discrimination and was expanded in 1982 to include national origin discrimination. It applies to all employers regardless of the number of employees.

Over the years, this early civil rights act has been a significant weapon against employers. It permits the person suing to seek punitive damages, in addition to compensatory damages such as back pay. Moreover, it provides for a jury trial.

Although the awards for violation of this act can be substantial, the claimant must establish *intent* to discriminate on the part of the employer. That is, it is necessary to prove that the employer deliberately denied an individual an opportunity for employment or promotion on the basis of his race or national origin. This is to be distinguished from establishing *effect*, which means that although one or more representatives of an organization did not intend to deny someone equal employment opportunity on the basis of his race or national origin, the effect of a certain employment practice, such as exclusively using employee referrals as a recruitment source, was discriminatory. It is usually more difficult to establish intent to discriminate than it is to show effect.

Civil Rights Act of 1964

This is probably the best-known piece of civil rights legislation and the most widely used; it protects several classes of people and pertains to many employment situations. Title VII of this act prohibits discrimination on the basis of race, color, religion, sex, or national origin in all matters of employment, from recruitment through discharge. The criteria for coverage under Title VII include any company doing business in the United States that has fifteen or more employees. Title VII does not regulate the employment practices of U.S. companies employing American citizens outside the United States. Violations are monitored by the EEOC.

Violators of Title VII are generally required to "make whole." This includes providing reinstatement, if relevant, and back pay. Jury trials are not allowed.

Plaintiffs in Title VII suits generally need not prove intent; rather, they may challenge apparently neutral employment policies having a discriminatory effect.

Employers will find it significant that many claimants sue for violations of both Section 1981 and Title VII.

The EEOC's 1980 guidelines on sexual harassment have become an important aspect of the Civil Rights Act of 1964. Sexual harassment is defined as "unwelcome sexual advances, requests for sexual favors, or other unwanted verbal or physical conduct of a sexual nature that is made a term and condition of employment, or used as the basis for making employment decisions; or which creates a hostile, intimidating or otherwise offensive work environment."

There are two types of sexual harassment. Quid pro quo harassment involves rewards or threats; sex is made a condition of employment. Hostile environment harassment involves regular and repeated offensive conduct that interferes with an employee's ability to work. Examples of hostile environment conduct include offensive jokes, vulgar language or gestures, sexual slurs and innuendo, suggestive comments, unwanted physical contact, leering, stalking, sexual pictures, and graffiti.

Men or women may be victims of sexual harassment; consequently members of both sexes may sue for violation of Title VII.

The courts originally applied the "reasonable person" standard of behavior in sexual harassment matters: that is, the judicial construct of an individual who thinks and responds like an ordinary person. This was later replaced by the "reasonable woman" standard, reflecting judicial recognition that men and women tend to view sexual matters differently. What may be trivial to a reasonable man may be viewed as quite serious to a reasonable female.

The EEOC guidelines state that employers are absolutely liable for acts of sexual harassment if they are committed by a supervisor or manager. If the acts are committed by rank-and-file employees or nonemployees, such as customers or vendors, employers are liable only if they know or should have known about the situation and failed to take action. Corporate officials, supervisors and managers, HR professionals, individuals who falsely claim sexual harassment, and other employees who spread unproved allegations or gossip may face personal liability.

Following the Civil Rights Act of 1964, acts of discrimination continued. The excuse most commonly offered by employers was that although there was certainly no intention to discriminate, they simply could not find women and minorities to fill job openings. The result of this frequently repeated statement was a revamping of recruitment sources. Up to this point, the most popular, cost-effective means of recruitment was word of mouth. The inherent problem with this method was that whenever there was an opening at a supervisory or managerial level—the level at which women and minorities were so few in number—the existing managers, predominately white males, spread the word among close friends and colleagues: other white males. Not surprisingly, the candidates referred were more white males. Therefore, the word-of-mouth system was inherently discriminatory when it was the only method of recruitment used. Recruitment sources were subsequently expanded to include many of those identified in Chapters 3 and 4.

Even after recruitment sources were expanded, discrimination continued. Employers no longer claimed an inability to find women and minorities to hire; the problem now claimed was that they could not find *qualified* women and minorities. A close examination of most educational and experiential requirements revealed unrealistic standards that were not necessary for successful performance of the job. It was also true that because of the limited educational and employment opportunities afforded women and minorities, few individuals falling into these two categories possessed the stipulated qualifications.

The result of this close examination of position qualifications was a revamping of job requirements. An employer could no longer arbitrarily decide that a degree was necessary for a given position. It now had to be shown that a person without a degree could not do the job. Individuals with an equivalent combination of education and experience had to be considered. Similarly, an arbitrarily set number of years of prior experience was eliminated and replaced with more realistic requirements.

Affirmative Action

Because Title VII did not immediately have the desired effect against discrimination, a series of executive orders was issued by the federal government, first by President Kennedy in 1961, and later strengthened by President Johnson in 1965. The best known, EO

11246, contained an EEO clause that required companies doing business with the federal government to make a series of commitments. Three of the most significant commitments are as follows:

1. *Practice nondiscrimination in employment.* When a company does business with the federal government, it is on the basis of a contract. Should the company discriminate in employment practices, it would effectively be violating its contract. The ramifications could be severe, including contract cancellation and debarment, meaning that the government would no longer do business with that company.

2. *Obey the rules and regulations of the Department of Labor.* This agreement extends to allowing periodic checking of its premises by labor representatives to ensure compliance with the other two commitments listed here.

3. *Attain affirmative action goals.* This commits a company to hiring, training, and promoting a certain percentage of qualified women and minorities. The actual percentage is based on the number of women and minorities in a specific geographic location, referred to as a Standard Metropolitan Statistical Area (SMSA). Employers should contact the Office of Federal Contract Compliance Programs (OFCCP) to determine the most recent requirements for separate affirmative action plans pertaining to different establishments.

Increasingly, employers are adopting formal, written affirmative action plans, even where these are not required, in an effort to correct racial and gender imbalances in the workplace. (Currently, the OFCCP requires federal contractors to develop written affirmative action programs where fifty or more workers are employed and the employer does $50,000 in business annually with the federal government.) In the absence of a written plan, it is more difficult to provide credible evidence that the employer is making a bona-fide effort to correct real or perceived problems. Minimally, these written plans should encompass seven key elements:

1. A policy statement
2. Internal dissemination of the policy
3. External dissemination of the policy
4. Positive utilization efforts
5. A review of internal procedures
6. Implementation, development, and execution
7. The establishment of a complaint procedure

In addition, any plan should be temporary only, to be abandoned and replaced by a diversity-driven work environment once workplace equity has been achieved (see Chapter 2).

Affirmative action guidelines may be obtained by contacting the United States Department of Labor:

OFCCP
200 Constitution Avenue, Northwest
Washington, D.C. 20210
202/219-6666

The OFCCP has also published a compliance manual that outlines the specific steps its field staff follows in reviewing and monitoring affirmative action plans.

Equal Pay Act of 1963

The Equal Pay Act of 1963 requires equal pay for men and women performing substantially equal work. The work must be of comparable skill, effort, and responsibility, performed under similar working conditions. Coverage applies to all aspects of the employment process, including starting salaries, annual increases, and promotions. This law protects women only. Others who feel they are being discriminated against in matters of pay may claim violation of Title VII. The criterion for coverage is at least two employees.

Unequal pay for equal work is permitted in certain instances, for example, when wage differences are based on superior educational credentials or extensive prior experience. However, this pay difference should diminish and ultimately disappear after a number of years on the job.

An important issue related to equal pay is *comparable worth*. Several states have implemented programs for comparable worth pay whereby employers are required to compare completely different job categories. Those held predominantly by women (e.g., nursing and secretarial) must be compared with those occupied predominantly by men (e.g., truck driving and warehouse work). Point systems determine the level of skill involved in the job, as well as the economic value of each position. If the female-dominated jobs are deemed comparable, pay adjustments are made to reduce the difference in wages.

The important distinction between comparable worth and equal pay is that in order to claim violation of the Equal Pay Act, identical job classifications must be compared. Therefore, if a woman accountant believes that she is not receiving an equal rate of pay to that of her male counterpart—a male accountant performing substantially equal work—she may have sufficient cause to claim violation of the Equal Pay Act. On the other hand, comparable worth compares different job categories. For example, if a clerk-typist believes that her work is of comparable worth to that of a male custodian working for the same employer, she might sue on the basis of sex discrimination. Since there is no federal law that deals specifically with comparable worth, she would sue for violation of Title VII.

Companies are urged to assess their hiring practices and work toward minimizing designated female or male categories.

Age Discrimination in Employment Act of 1967

The federal Age Discrimination in Employment Act of 1967 (ADEA), as originally written, protected workers from ages forty to seventy. A 1978 amendment permitted jury trials, which gave claimants more power. Effective January 1, 1987, Congress unanimously approved, and President Reagan signed into law, H.R. 4154, amending ADEA by extending its protection to workers beyond the age of seventy. Now, most private sector and federal, state, and local government employees cannot be discriminated against in matters of pay, benefits, or continued employment regardless of how old they may be. The act also pertains to employees of employment agencies and labor organizations, as well as to U.S. citizens working outside the United States.

ADEA contains an exemption for bona-fide executives or high-level policymakers who may be retired as early as age sixty-five, if they have been employed at that level for the preceding two years and meet certain criteria, including exercising discretionary powers on a regular basis; the authority to hire, promote, and terminate employees; and a primary duty to manage an entire organization, department, or subdivision. (Contact the EEOC for detailed guidelines.)

The general criterion for coverage under ADEA is employment of at least twenty employees. Labor organizations employing at least twenty-five workers are required to comply. Part-time employees are included when calculating coverage.

The following guidelines should help you avoid age discrimination suits:

• Language in HR policies and procedures manuals, employee handbooks, orientation publications, and any other company-issued written material should be age neutral.

• Employment application forms should not require applicants to provide their date of birth.

• Some state laws prohibit listing of graduation dates on the application form.

• Interviewers should ask only age-neutral questions.

• Apply the same salary guidelines when hiring older workers as you would when hiring anyone else. Do not try to justify a lower salary because an older worker is receiving a pension or social security.

• Do not deny older workers training, promotional, or transfer opportunities.

• Make certain that poor work performance, supported by comprehensive written performance appraisals and documentation or other "good cause"—and not age—is the basis for all disciplinary action, including termination.

Rehabilitation Act of 1973

Section 501 of this federal law prohibits discrimination against persons with disabilities by contractors doing business with the federal government totaling $2,500 or more per year. Those employers who are government contractors, do business totaling $50,000 or more per year, and have fifty or more employees must prepare an affirmative action plan to comply with the act, although hiring and promotion goals and timetables are not required under this plan. Section 504 requires employers receiving federal financial assistance to take affirmative action in hiring and promoting qualified workers with disabilities.

The act protects "any person who (1) has a physical or mental impairment that substantially limits one or more of the person's major life activities, (2) has a record of such an impairment, or (3) is regarded as having such an impairment." Included in this definition are former drug addicts and recovering alcoholics. Current drug or alcohol users are not protected. Victims of acquired immune deficiency syndrome (AIDS) and AIDS-related conditions are also covered by this act.

An employer's obligation extends to making a reasonable effort to accommodate the person's disability as long as such accommodation does not create an undue hardship. Undue hardships are determined by considering such factors as the size of the organization, the type of work, and the nature and cost of such accommodation. For example, job restructuring might be required if the person with the disability can perform the essential functions of the job but requires assistance with one remaining aspect of the work, such as heavy lifting. Others aspects of job restructuring may be modification of procedures, providing readers or interpreters, or modification of equipment. Any adjustment, including alternations to facilities, that does not create an undue hardship may be required.

Many resources are available to assist in modifying facilities and equipment to accommodate workers with disabilities, such as the Job Accommodation Network (West Virginia University; 918 Chestnut Ridge Road; Suite 1; PO Box 6080; Morgantown, WV 26506-6080 [800/526-7234]).

With regard to positions requiring tests (see Chapter 11 for detailed information), generally if an applicant cannot take a required test because of a disability, he must be allowed to demonstrate the ability to perform the essential functions of the job through alternative means.

Also relevant to the subject of disabilities is the issue of preemployment physicals. Generally if your organization has been conducting preemployment physicals as a matter of past practice, then there is no problem with continuing. However, if this has not been the case and you start requiring physicals, you must prove necessity. In addition, physicals must be required for everyone. Furthermore, the physical cannot be the first step in the application process. Either it may be the last factor evaluated or required only after a conditional job offer is made.

An individual's physical fitness for work must be determined by a qualified physician. Any negative findings should be phrased in specific, objective, job-related terms. The results of the examination must be shared with the applicant. If the applicant can perform the job that she is interviewing for, the fear that employment will aggravate an existing condition is a weak basis for denying that person employment. You are on stronger ground if the condition is degenerative. If the applicant can do the job but probably not the next job in the promotional chain, employment may be denied if you can document that promotion is the normal pattern in that particular job family.

Americans With Disabilities Act of 1990

In July 1990, President Bush signed landmark legislation prohibiting all employers, including privately owned businesses and local governments, from discriminating against employees or job candidates with disabilities. Exempt are the federal government, government-owned corporations, Native American tribes, and bona-fide tax-exempt private membership clubs. Religious organizations are permitted to give preference to the employment of their own members. In addition, the law requires every kind of establishment to be accessible to and usable by persons with disabilities. This legislation, entitled the Americans with Disabilities Act of 1990 (ADA), pertains to employers with fifteen or more employees and is monitored by the EEOC.

Under the ADA, the term *disability* is defined the same as in the Rehabilitation Act of 1973, that is, as a physical or mental impairment that substantially limits an individual's major life activities. The definition also encompasses the history of an impairment and the perception of having an impairment. Examples of disabilities that are covered include impaired sight and hearing; muscular conditions such as cerebral palsy and muscular dystrophy; diseases like cancer, AIDS, diabetes, and epilepsy; cosmetic disfigurements; emotional disturbances; stuttering; smoke sensitivity; tension; and depression. In fact, over one thousand different impairments are covered by this act. Current users of illegal drugs or alcohol are not protected by the ADA. Also, people with contagious diseases or those posing a direct threat to the health or safety or others are not covered. In addition, ADA specifically excludes homosexuals, bisexuals, transvestites, transsexuals, individuals with sexual behavior disorders, compulsive gamblers, kleptomaniacs, and pyromaniacs.

Under the ADA, employers are required to make a "reasonable accommodation" for applicants or employees able to perform the "essential" functions of the job with reasonable proficiency. Reasonable accommodation includes job restructuring, allowing part-time or modified work schedules, reassignments, hiring additional workers to aid employees with disabilities in the performance of their jobs, and installing new equipment or modifying existing equipment. An accommodation is considered unreasonable only where undue physical or financial hardship is placed on the employer. Such hardship is determined according to the overall size of an organization in relation to the size of its workforce, its budget, and the nature and cost of the required accommodation.

Essential functions are loosely defined as tasks that are "fundamental and not marginal," according to the Senate report on the ADA. Employers are encouraged to conduct a detailed review of each job to determine just which functions are essential. This should include an assessment of the amount of time devoted to each task.

The ADA also refers to what an employer may require in the way of preemployment physical examinations. According to the act, employers cannot single out individuals with disabilities for medical exams. If they are shown to be job related and consistent with the requirements of the business, medical examinations are permitted after an offer of employment has been made, prior to the start of work. In this instance, an employer may condition an offer of employment on the results of the exam.

Vietnam Era Veterans Readjustment Act of 1974

This act requires federal contractors and subcontractors doing at least $10,000 in business annually with the federal government to take affirmative action to hire and promote veterans, including veterans of the Vietnam era, who incurred a disability or had a disability aggravated in the line of duty. Employers with fifty or more employees and a federal contract of at least $50,000 annually are required to prepare a written affirmative action program to improve the hiring and advancement of veterans, although no goals or timetables are required. Depending on the nature and extent of the disability, reasonable accommodations might be required.

Pregnancy Discrimination Act of 1978

The Pregnancy Discrimination Act (PDA) of 1978 recognizes pregnancy as a temporary disability and prohibits sex discrimination based on pregnancy, childbirth, or related conditions. Women must be permitted to work as long as they are capable of performing the essential functions of their current job. Similarly, pregnant applicants may not be denied equal employment opportunities if they are able to perform the essential functions of the available job. The act prohibits mandatory pregnancy leaves of any duration unless a similar requirement is imposed on male employees with disabilities that impair their job performance. If an employer insists on establishing special rules for pregnancy, such rules must be dictated by business necessity or related to issues of health or safety. The PDA further mandates that an employer permit an employee on maternity leave to return to her job on the same basis as other employees returning after an illness or disability leave.

An important concern related to pregnancy discrimination has to do with fetal protection. Whether an employer may bar women of childbearing age from jobs that involve toxic substances, X-rays, lead exposure, or the like is an issue that has been addressed by the EEOC in a series of fetal protection guidelines. The guidelines require employers to determine first if there is substantial risk of harm to an employee's potential offspring from exposure to a workplace hazard. To accomplish this, employers should rely on scientific evidence of the risk of fetal or reproductive harm from exposure and the minimum period of time required for exposure to cause harm. Then the employer should assess its policy and determine whether there is a reasonable alternative that would be less discriminatory than exclusion, such as a temporary transfer to another (nontoxic) job or wearing a personal protection device.

Religious Discrimination Guidelines

The EEOC guidelines define religion and religious practices as "moral or ethical beliefs as to what is right and wrong which are sincerely held with the strength of traditional religious views." In 1972 Congress amended that portion of Title VII pertaining to religion in the workplace by expanding the definition to include an individual's right to "all aspects of religious observance and practice, as well as belief, unless an employer demonstrates that he is unable to reasonably accommodate an employee's or prospective employee's religious observance or practice without undue hardship on the conduct of the employer's business." This amendment placed the burden on employers to prove their inability reasonably to accommodate an individual's religious practices.

The issue of religion may come up during an employment interview, often in conjunction with a requirement to work on Saturdays or Sundays. All preemployment inquiries concerning availability on these or any other days must be job related, dictated by business necessity, and worded in such a way that availability is stressed, as opposed to specific questions about religion. Therefore, if a position requires working on Sunday, you might phrase your inquiry in this way: "This job requires working on Sundays. Will you be able to meet this job requirement?" Even if the applicant responds, "No, I cannot work on Sundays because of my religion," document the response as, "Applicant is unable to meet the job requirement of working on Sundays." Do not make any reference to the reason given.

Your next step is to make a reasonable effort to accommodate this person's religious practices as long as they do not create an undue hardship—for example:

- Finding voluntary substitutes for the period of time when this individual would be unavailable
- Flexible scheduling of hours so that her religion could be accommodated

- Consideration of another position with comparable salary, responsibilities, working conditions, location, and growth opportunities
- Hiring a contingent employee to cover the person's duties during the time when she would be unable to work.

As with accommodating persons with disabilities, what would constitute an undue hardship depends on a number of factors, including prohibitive cost. Undue hardship must be provable.

In some cases, employees able to meet a job's work schedule at the time of hire may subsequently become involved with particular religious practice and, as a result, are no longer able to do so. In such instances, employers should make good-faith attempts to accommodate religious-based scheduling requests. Such accommodation might include adjusting work schedules, implementing flexible working hours, or responding to other viable employee suggestions that will integrate the employee's religious needs with the needs of the company.

Certain work assignments might also require some adjustment if an employee raises a religious objection. For example, a foreign work assignment to a country whose prevailing religious practices conflict with the beliefs of an individual might be the basis for that individual's request to work at a different location. Every effort should be made to accommodate such a request.

Balancing an employee's religious beliefs with an organization's dress and grooming practices may also become an issue. When the safety of the employee or others is at stake, the employee may be required to conform to company policy in spite of any religious convictions. If safety is not a factor, the employer should make a reasonable effort to accommodate religious-based attire and grooming.

Religion and work should be kept separate, meaning that employers have the right to require "quiet and unobtrusive" observance.

National Origin Discrimination Guidelines

The EEOC's Guidelines on Discrimination Because of National Origin preclude denial of equal employment opportunity because of an individual's ancestry; place of origin; or physical, cultural, or linguistic characteristics. There are four main areas pertaining to employment:

1. Citizenship requirements may not be valid if they have the purpose or effect of discrimination on the basis of national origin.

2. Selection criteria that appear to be neutral at first glance may have an adverse impact on certain national groups.
3. Speak-English-only rules may be considered discriminatory when applied at all times.
4. Ethnic slurs may be considered national origin discrimination and must not be tolerated.

Immigration Reform and Control Act of 1986

IRCA makes the employment of illegal aliens unlawful and establishes requirements for the employer to determine an applicant's authorization to work in the United States. The act applies to employers with four or more workers.

The Immigration and Naturalization Service (INS) determines what constitutes an acceptable document proving work eligibility and identity. Some of the documents that establish both identity and employment eligibility are a U.S. passport certificate of U.S. citizenship or naturalization, alien registration receipt card ("green card"), and temporary resident card. If applicants do not have a single document that satisfies both needs, they must produce a document establishing identity, such as a driver's license, in addition to a document establishing employment eligibility, such as a social security card or a birth certificate. Employers face penalties for hiring unauthorized employees and for failure to complete and maintain the required I-9 forms.

The question of whether it is legal to hire a U.S. citizen over an equally qualified authorized alien is frequently asked. The answer, according to the INS, is, "On an individual basis, the employer may prefer a United States citizen or national over an equally qualified alien." This is not to say, however, that employers may practice bias against qualified aliens, or that charges of national origin discrimination may not result if a hiring decision is based on factors other than job qualifications. The U.S. Justice Department's Office of Special Counsel for Immigration Related Unfair Employment Practices handles charges of discrimination on the basis of national origin or citizenship status (800/255-7688). The EEOC may also have jurisdiction over some cases.

Employee Polygraph Protection Act

With few exceptions, this act prohibits the use of polygraph tests (commonly known as lie detectors) and other mechanical or electrical testing mechanism by private employers. The ban has its greatest implications in pre- and employment situations, where polygraphs may no longer be routinely used as a screening device for job applicants. Additional information on polygraphs appears in Chapter 11.

Drugfree Workplace Act of 1988

Employers holding contracts with or receiving grants from the federal government of $25,000 or more must meet certain posting and record-keeping requirements and must develop policies prohibiting the unlawful manufacture, distribution, possession, or use of controlled substances in the workplace. The act does not make a definitive statement about drug testing.

Civil Rights Act of 1991

The Civil Rights Act of 1991 went well beyond the Civil Rights Act of 1964's Title VII, "make-whole" remedies of back pay, reinstatement, and some attorneys' fees:

• Coverage has been extended to U.S. citizens employed at a U.S. company's foreign site.

• The burden of proof is placed on employers to show lack of discrimination.

• Jury trials are permitted.

• Awards of compensatory and punitive damages are permitted in cases of intentional discrimination.

• Victims of intentional sex discrimination are permitted to seek compensatory and punitive damages up to $300,000.

• Victims of race discrimination are permitted to seek unlimited damages. (This has prompted some companies to require nonunion employees to submit discrimination claims to binding arbitration. Companies may also request that job applicants give up the right to sue as a condition of employment.)

• A "glass ceiling" commission has been established to develop policies for the removal of barriers to women and minorities seeking advancement.

• "Race norming," or the practice of adjusting test scores by race, is banned.

Overall, then, the Civil Rights Act of 1991 seems to favor employees over employers.

Family and Medical Leave Act of 1993

The FMLA provides eligible employees with up to a total of twelve weeks leave during any twelve-month period for the birth of a child, placement of a child for adoption or foster care, an employee's serious health condition or caring for a spouse, child, or parent with a serious health condition. To qualify, employees must have worked for at least twelve months and not fewer than 1,250 hours in the past year, and must give thirty days' notice of the leave, when practical. Employers may require a doctor's certification to substantiate the employee's request to tend to family medical problems. (These forms are available from the Department of Labor.) Employees may also be required to use up all of their accrued vacation, personal, or sick leave before taking unpaid leave. Employers may deny leave to salaried employees within the highest-paid 10 percent of the workforce, if such leave would create undue hardship for the company. Upon returning to work, employees are entitled to the same job or one that is equal in status and pay, as well as continued health and other benefits.

The FMLA covers private businesses with fifty or more employees, state and federal employees, public agencies, and private elementary and secondary schools. The act may not interfere with collective bargaining agreements, more generous company policies, or less restrictive state or local laws.

The Department of Labor offers the Fact Sheet on Family and Medical Leave Act and Compliance Guide to Family and Medical Leave Act for additional information.

Reverse Discrimination

Charges of reverse discrimination by nonminorities are usually brought by white males, who maintain that they have been denied equal employment opportunities because of favoritism shown to minorities and women. Such claims are often the result of affirmative action plans that inherently limit employment, promotional, and training opportunities for nonminorities.

Employers are afforded a certain degree of protection against charges of reverse discrimination by the EEOC. According to 1979 guidelines, employers demonstrating that they have conducted a reasonable self-analysis and have developed a sound basis for concluding that affirmative action is appropriate may be immunized from reverse discrimination complaints filed with that agency.

Federal Record-Keeping Requirements

Many of the laws just described carry specific record-keeping requirements. Some of these are summarized as follows:

• *Age Discrimination in Employment Act.* Covered employers must keep payroll or any other records containing the name, address, birthdate, occupation, rate of pay, and weekly compensation for each employee for three years.

• *Americans with Disabilities Act.* Employers governed by the ADA must retain all HR records involving a person with a disability, whether the person was hired or not. Keep requests for reasonable accommodation, applications for the job, and records concerning hiring, promotion, demotion, transfer, layoff, termination, pay rates, compensation, training, and apprenticeships. All records must be kept for one year from the date the record was made or an employment action is taken, whichever is later. If you have fired someone, all of the person's records must be kept for one year from the date of termination. Medical records must be kept in a separate, confidential file, with access limited to designated company officials.

• *Executive Order 11246.* Covered employers must keep affirmative action programs, utilization analyses, and information on all applicants, including data on race, gender, disability, veteran status, and requested position. The retention period is unspecified, but experts recommend a minimum of three years. Employers need not retain unsolicited applications for unadvertised jobs.

• *Equal Pay Act.* Employers must retain FLSA-required records, as well as wage payments, wage rates, job evaluations, job descriptions, merit or seniority systems, bargaining agreements, and descriptions of wage differentials for employees of both genders for an unspecified period of time.

• *Family and Medical Leave Act.* FMLA requires covered employers to keep basic payroll and employee records, including name, address, occupation, rate of pay, terms of compensation, daily and weekly hours worked per pay period, and additions to and deductions from wages. Additionally, you are expected to keep notes on the dates that an FMLA leave is taken or the hours of leave if less than a full day, as well as copies of employee notices of leave furnished to you, and of general and specific notices given to employees under the act. Maintain documents describing employee benefits or employer practices and policies regarding leaves, records reflecting premium payments of employee benefits, and records of any dispute between employee and employer regarding designation of the leave. Documentation related to medical certificates or histories about employees or family members must be kept in a separate file. Keep FMLA-related records for three years, separate from the employee's other HR files, and accessible only to designated officials.

    • *Immigration Reform and Control Act.* I-9 forms must be kept for three years or one year after termination, whichever is later.

    • *Rehabilitation Act of 1973.* Federal contractors and subcontractors must keep employment records for applicants and employees who have disabilities for one year. Also, keep a record of complaints and actions taken under the act.

    • *Title VII of the Civil Rights Act of 1964.* Title VII requires covered employers to maintain records that would be relevant to any discrimination charge brought by any agency or individual. Such records would include all HR documents about the complainant, as well as documents about other employees in similar positions, application forms, and test papers completed by applicants for the same position. These documents must be retained for one year after the record was made or the action taken, or, if a charge is made, until it is resolved. Employers are also required to keep records of selection for apprenticeship programs for two years from the date of application for the program or for the apprenticeship period, whichever is longer.

The Impact of EEO and Affirmative Action Legislation on the Employment Process

Let us now look at how these EEO and affirmative action laws affect recruitment, hiring, and selection. As an employer you have the right to select whomever you determine is best qualified to perform the duties and responsibilities of a given job. You are not required to select the *most* qualified person; rather, you are required to select someone meeting the minimum requirements of the job.

    Your responsibility does not end there, however; other factors must be considered. First, make certain that you are not denying anyone equal employment opportunity, either inadvertently or because of personal bias. Second, check your employment practices for possible systemic discrimination. Third, make certain that your requirements are job related and not arbitrarily set. With regard to education, this means ensuring that there is valid, objective documentation for job criteria. If high school is required, it must be relevant to the job. The same holds true for college degrees. However, since degrees are usually required for higher-level positions with fewer tangible requirements, the guidelines are also less tangible. For example, degree requirements are permitted when the consequences of employing an unqualified person are grave, especially when public health or safety is involved. Positions demanding a great deal of judgment often have degree requirements, as well as those demanding knowledge of technical or professional subject matter.

Although requiring a college degree for a higher-level position is relatively safe, the burden of proof may still be on employers to show job relatedness. The less tangible the reason is, the more difficult this will be. It is often wiser to state "degree preferred" or "degree highly desirable." Even better, spell out exactly what knowledge and skill level you are seeking. That way, applicants who have additional years of experience or have attended college without receiving a degree will not be locked out of consideration. You are helping yourself, as well as such candidates, by broadening the field of choice.

Be careful about changing educational requirements. If you have an opening with specific requirements and find someone for the job who does not quite meet them, do not lower the requirements or hire the applicant. You are leaving yourself wide open to discrimination charges by other applicants. Also, if the opening has a set of educational requirements and an applicant meets them, but in retrospect the requirements are not deemed stringent enough, you are asking for trouble. If you want to change them once set, reevaluate the entire job in relation to the specific duties. Only then can you properly determine whether the education requirements warrant adjustment.

As with education, requirements for previous work experience should be job related. The standards should never be arbitrary, artificial, or unnecessary. The more complex the job, the more reasonable it is to have experience requirements. However, if you have not required specific experience in the past and the job has not changed substantially in its level of responsibility or specific duties, do not start now. The new requirements may have a greater negative impact on women and minorities than on white males. The greater this disparity is between past and current job requirements, the greater the burden will be on you to prove the necessity for the requirements.

Be careful, too, about asking for a specific number of years of experience. It is difficult to prove that four years' experience is not adequate but that five years is. It is also difficult to justify preference for someone with a little more experience as opposed to just enough. As with degrees, then, it is best to say that five years' experience is preferred, not required. Not only is it unwise from an EEO standpoint to ask for a specific number of years of experience, but you may also preclude yourself from hiring the best candidate when measured by other criteria.

Finally, be aware of your organization's affirmative action goals and take them into consideration when weighing the qualifications of women and minorities versus white males. Full compliance with affirmative action goals is your objective, and every effort should be made to achieve this end whenever you have an opening.

If, after considering all of these factors and assessing both the tangible and intangible qualifications of the candidates, you determine that the most suitable person for the job is someone who happens to be a white male, go ahead and make that person a job offer. However, if the credentials of two candidates—one a white male and the other a minority member or a woman—are essentially the same, and your affirmative action goals have not been adequately met, you are urged to hire the minority member or the woman.

Bona-Fide Occupational Qualifications

Occasionally the requirements of a position seem to be discriminatory in nature. For instance, jobs that stipulate only male or female appear to be discriminatory. However, upon closer investigation, it becomes evident that the EEO concept of bona-fide occupational qualification (BFOQ) prevails. By definition, a BFOQ is a criterion that appears to be discriminatory but can be justified by business necessity. For example, an employer may have an opening for a model to show a new line of designer dresses. In this instance, being female would be a BFOQ. An example of an unacceptable BFOQ would be a position requiring heavy lifting where only male applicants were considered. The requirement of lifting may be tested. All applicants, male and female, could be asked to lift the weight normally required on the job. Those unable to perform this task would not be considered. Women able to lift the weight must be given an equal opportunity for the job.

BFOQs may apply to religion, gender, age and national origin, but never to race. Furthermore, general company preference does not constitute a legitimate BFOQ. The most valid BFOQ or business necessity defense is safety.

When there is doubt, the following business necessity guidelines should be applied:

- Document the business necessity.
- Explore alternative practices.

- Ensure across-the-board administration of the practice.
- Be sure that the business necessity is not based on stereotypical thinking, arbitrary standards, or tradition.

There are very few instances in which BFOQ applies. If you believe that your requirements qualify, check with your company's EEO officer before proceeding.

Avoiding Discrimination Charges

Typically it costs more than $100,000 just to go to court to defend yourself against charges of employment discrimination. Even if you "win," you are not likely to recover any of that money. Also, there are lost time, productivity, employee morale, and customer perception to consider.

According to a survey on employment litigation, conducted jointly by the Society for Human Resource Management (SHRM) and the law firm Jackson Lewis, approximately six out of ten respondents indicated that their organizations have had to defend at least one employment-related lawsuit in the past five years. The bulk of these lawsuits were related to discrimination issues: Race or national origin discrimination accounted for 15 percent of the suits, age discrimination represented 14 percent, 11 percent concerned gender-related salary issues, and 2 percent involved religious discrimination. Another 14 percent alleged sexual harassment. Twenty-three percent of the survey participants responded that individuals at their businesses had been sued personally, according to *Mosaics* (July–August 1997).

It doesn't take much for a lawsuit to get started. All a complainant must prove is that a job existed, she is a member of a protected group, she is qualified for the job, but she was rejected in spite of those qualifications, and the employer continued to look for someone else to fill the job.

With litigation so easy to initiate, your goal should be to prevent lawsuits, not win them. There is no sure-fire way of preventing applicants or employees from charging your organization with discrimination, but there are guidelines you can follow to help minimize the chances.

• *Make certain your hiring criteria are objective, uniformly applied, and consistent in effect.* By applying job criteria across the board that do not have a greater negative impact on any one group, you are demonstrating fair employment practices.

• *Show job relatedness.* Every criterion you set, each question you ask, and every decision you make should be job related.

• *Focus on making sound hiring decisions that properly match an applicant's skills, knowledge, and interests with a job's duties and responsibilities.* This should lead to fewer terminations since firing is the act that triggers many lawsuits.

• *Pay attention to red-flag areas on a candidate's application or resumé* (discussed in Chapter 5). Do not proceed with the employment process until you are satisfied that they have been thoroughly explored.

• *Conduct education and employment reference checks.* This is not always easy or even possible to do (see Chapter 12), but making the effort may reveal important information that can influence your decision to extend a job offer.

• *Think like a juror.* To avoid actions that generate lawsuits, think about how a juror would interpret your actions—for example, did the employee know what the employer expected of her? Did the employer follow policies and procedures known to the employee? Did the employer treat all employees consistently, reasonably, and fairly?

• *Treat all employees equally.* Most lawsuits alleging any form of discrimination are based on failure to treat employees equally. This includes overt discrimination and other more subtle forms of discrimination, such as stereotyping, patronizing, and favoritism. Note that "equal treatment" does not mean "same treatment." It does mean ensuring that each employee has the same opportunity for consideration as every other employee

• *Respect an employee's legal rights.* These include:
  —Civil rights
  —The right to a safe workplace
  —The right to refuse to perform illegal acts without fear of retaliation
  —The right not to be defamed
  —The right to nonharassing treatment
  —The right to participate in certain union activities
  —The right to compensation according to the Fair Labor Standards Act
  —The right to certain benefits under the Employee Retirement and Income Security Act (ERISA)

Some employees may have additional rights as a result of written or implied contracts (e.g., based on the language in employee handbooks).

• *Honestly appraise employees.* Negative performance appraisals are difficult to write, but they can save you a lot of trouble later. It is hard to justify termination on the basis of poor performance with a file filled with glowing reviews (and do not even think about back-documentation). If an employee exhibits performance problems, identify them and together set goals for improvement. If you ultimately end up terminating the employee, an unjust termination lawsuit will be difficult to sustain.

• *Take allegations seriously and act promptly.* Whether allegations are of sexual harassment or other forms of misconduct or illegal acts, responding quickly and appropriately will often defuse a situation and preclude a lawsuit.

Responding to Discrimination Charges

In spite of your best efforts and intentions, you may find yourself involved in an employment-related lawsuit. Even frivolous lawsuits require a response to the allegations. According to the SHRM White Paper, there are several steps employers should take immediately after being sued:

1. *Review the charge for procedural flaws.* When plaintiffs fail to follow procedures properly, the charges are often dismissed.

2. *Ensure that the complainant's HR file is kept intact.* Be sure all records relating to the lawsuit are kept until the complaint is resolved.

3. *Guard against retaliatory action.* Employees are protected by law against retaliation when filing discrimination lawsuits.

4. *Conduct your own investigation.* Go on a fact-finding mission to ferret out all relevant facts.

5. *Conduct an honest appraisal of the facts.* You may decide to settle rather than defend yourself against the charge.

6. *Prepare an official response.* This "statement of position" is used by the EEOC to evaluate the employee's claim. However, it may also be used against the employer later on.

7. *Prepare for the mediation conference.* New EEOC procedures encourage an investigator to mediate a settlement between the parties wherever possible.

8. *Anticipate an EEOC on-site investigation.* The EEOC often conducts an on-site fact-finding investigation, including interviewing witnesses.

9. *Anticipate settlement negotiations.* If no settlement has been reached by the time of the EEOC investigation, the EEOC investigator will probably initiate negotiations.

10. *Identify relevant policies and procedures.* Isolate policies and procedures that are the source of the charge and will help in your defense.

11. *Identify relevant training.* Assuming a discriminatory act did occur, determine if training will ensure that it does not continue and is not repeated.

For a copy of the full text of SHRM's White Paper, "Eleven Tips for Effectively Handling and Responding to a Charge of Discrimination," by Edmund D. Cooke, Jr. and John R. Ates, visit the SMRM home page at http://www.shrm.org/docs/whitepapers/sveeck.html.

Preemployment Questions

In general, the categories to steer clear of during the employment interview relate to race, religion, sex, national origin, and age. Some questions, however, have traditionally been considered acceptable during an interview, yet they are discriminatory in nature.

Asking such questions is not, in and of itself, illegal. Rather, once the information is ascertained, you may be charged with illegal use of it. For example, asking a woman applicant if she has children is not illegal. However, if the applicant is not hired because she answers affirmatively and consequently you anticipate excessive absenteeism, a charge of discrimination may result.

Bear in mind that just because you do not directly ask an applicant, on the application form or verbally, for specific information, she may offer it. If this occurs, you are equally liable if a question of illegal use arises. Suppose you inform an applicant that the available position requires travel. You then ask if she foresees any problem in leaving for a business trip with very little advance notice. She responds, "Oh, that will be no problem at all. My mother has been baby-sitting for my three kids ever since my divorce last year." The applicant has just volunteered information regarding two categories that are not job related: children and marital status. If she is rejected, she might claim discrimination on the basis of this information, even though you did not solicit it.

Should a candidate provide information that you should not have, make certain of three things:

1. Do not, under any circumstances, write it down.
2. Do not pursue the subject with the applicant.
3. Tell the applicant that the information is not job related and that you want to return to discussing her qualifications in relation to the job opening.

Table 6-1 identifies the most common categories and questions to avoid during the employment interview, both verbally and via the application form. Related recommended questions are also shown. Many of the recommended inquiries appear on the application form in Appendix F. Generally, the relevant aspects of a candidate's education and work experience should be the focus of every employment interview. Certain categories, such as security-sensitive jobs, may make BFOQs of some of the inquiries that are not generally recommended.

Remember, a great deal of information that should not be acquired during the employment interview may be requested for benefits purposes once an individual is hired.

Employment and Termination-at-Will

By definition, "employment and termination-at-will" is the right of an employer to terminate, at any time, for any reason, with or without cause, the employment of an individual who does not have a written contract defining the terms of employment. In exercising this employment and termination-at-will right, the employer, under previous case law, incurred no legal liability.

The employment and termination-at-will doctrine has been seriously eroded, however, by legislation such as Title VII, ADEA, the ADA, and other laws described earlier in this chapter. Such legislation prohibits employers from denying equal employment opportunities to all individuals and further prevents them from discharging an employee for non-job-related factors.

Employees now have additional rights protecting them from arbitrary acts of termination-at-will. The broadest form of protection, implied covenants of good faith and fair dealing, requires employers to prove "just cause" before terminating an employee. Public policy rights may also protect employees from being fired for exercising rights such as "whistle-blowing"—public disclosure of illegal actions taken by one's company—or for refusing to perform illegal acts on behalf of an employer. Moreover, the issue of implied contract rights may arise when the protection provided by statements on the em-

(text continues on page 157)

Table 6-1. Preemployment questions.

Subject	Questions Not Recommended	Recommended Questions
Name	What is your maiden name? Have you ever used any other name? Have you ever worked under another name? Have you ever changed your name?	Have you ever worked for this company under a different name? Is additional information relative to a change in name, use of an assumed name, or nickname necessary for us to check your work record? If yes, please explain.
Address	Do you own or rent your home? How long have you lived at this address?	What is your address? Where do you live?
Age	How old are you? What is your date of birth? Are you between eighteen and twenty-four, twenty-five and thirty-four, etc.?	Are you above the minimum working age of _____?
Physical appearance	How tall are you? How much do you weigh? What is the color of your eyes and hair?	None
Citizenship and national origin	Of what country are you a citizen? Where were you born? Where were your parents born? Are you a naturalized or a native-born citizen? What is your nationality? What kind of name is _____?	Are you a citizen of the United States? If you are not a U.S. citizen, do you have the legal right to remain permanently in the United States?
Marital status	What is your marital status? Have you ever been married? Divorced? Do you wish to be addressed as Mrs., Miss, or Ms.?	None

Children	Do you have any children? How many children do you have? What child care arrangements have you made? Do you intend to have children? When do you plan to have children? If you have children, will you return to work?	None
Police records	Have you ever been arrested?	Have you ever been convicted of a [crime? felony? crime greater than a misdemeanor?] Please explain. (Note: Applicants may not be denied employment because of a conviction record unless there is a direct correlation between the offense and the job, or unless hiring would constitute an unreasonable risk (Correction Law Article 22-A Sec. 754).
Religion	What is your religious background? What religious holidays do you observe? Is there anything in your religious beliefs that would prevent you from working the required schedule?	None
Disabilities	Do you have any disabilities? Have you ever been treated for any of the following [list of diseases and illnesses]? Do you now have, or have you ever had, a drug or alcohol addiction? Do you have physical, mental, or medical impediments that would interfere with your ability to perform the job for which you are applying? Are there any positions or duties for which you should not be considered because of existing physical, mental, or medical disabilities?	Can you perform the tasks required to carry out the job for which you have applied with or without accommodation?

(continued)

Table 6-1. (continued)

Subject	Questions Not Recommended	Recommended Questions
Photographs	Any question requiring that a photo be supplied before hire.	None
Languages	What is your native language? How did you learn to speak _____?	What is the degree of fluency with which you speak/write any language, including English? (Ask only if job related.)
Military experience	Have you ever served in the armed forces of any country? What kind of discharge did you receive?	What is your military experience in the armed forces of the United States?
Organizations	What clubs, organizations, or associations do you belong to?	What clubs, organizations, or associations, relative to the position for which you are applying, do you belong to?
References	A requirement that a reference be supplied by a particular kind of person, such as a religious leader.	Please provide the names, titles, addresses, and phone numbers of business references who are not related to you, other than your current or former employers.
Finances	Do you have any overdue bills?	None
Education	Are you a high school or college graduate? When did you attend high school or college?	Questions about the applicant's academic, vocational, or professional education, including the names and locations of the schools, the number of years completed, honors, diplomas and degrees received, and the major courses of study.
Experience	Any question regarding experience unrelated to the job.	Any questions regarding relevant work experience.

ployment application form, in employee handbooks, or in other company documents is interpreted as a binding contract. In this regard, employers are advised to develop at-will policies for inclusion in these documents. The ten guidelines that follow should be applied when developing a company's at-will policy:

1. *State the at-will principle.* It is important to declare that your company's handbook or manual is neither an employment contract nor a guarantee of employment. Consider the following sample from an employee handbook:

> This handbook has been designed to serve as a general summary of our current policies, procedures, and benefits for general information purposes. It provides guidance with regard to what you may expect from us and what we expect from you. We will make every effort to recognize the privileges described herein, unless doing so would impair the operation of business or expose the company to legal liability or financial loss. No provision of this handbook is to be construed as a guarantee of employment.

This simple disclaimer may not be enough, however, since courts have also examined actual practices. Make certain to consult with an attorney for appropriate language that precludes this problem.

2. *Do not make statements regarding job security.* Avoid phrases such as, "As long as your performance is satisfactory, you are guaranteed employment," or, "As an employee of [company name], you can look forward to a long and rewarding future," or "We treat employees of [company name] like members of our family and look forward to having you with us for a long time."

3. *Preserve the right to alter policies.* Clearly state that, at the discretion of the employer, certain policies and procedures may be amended, deleted, or replaced as deemed appropriate by management.

4. *Avoid naming a prospective employee's salary in yearly numbers when extending a written job offer.* A statement of annual salary may imply a one-year employment contract. Instead, use weekly, biweekly, or monthly numbers.

5. *Avoid using the word* fair. The term is subject to interpretation. Instead, use the word *consistent.*

6. *Avoid attempting a list that is all-inclusive,* particularly with respect to acts considered cause for disciplinary action.

7. *Avoid using the term probationary period.* It implies that, once a given period of time is over, the employee is there to stay. Also, avoid the term *permanent employee;* instead, substitute *regular employee.*

8. *Include employment-at-will statements on tuition reimbursement forms.* This will help safeguard against possible claims that the granting of tuition reimbursement implies a certain degree of job security.

9. *Apply sound, consistent management practices and principles to termination decisions.* Avoid arbitrary, artificial, or non-job-related reasons for termination; apply EEO guidelines; document reasons leading up to termination; and terminate for cause only.

10. *Ask employees to acknowledge having read and understood the contents of the company's at-will policy by signing a statement so indicating*—for example, "I understand that the handbook and all other written and oral material provided to me are intended for informational purposes only. Neither it, company practices, nor other communications create an employment contract."

Employers can also minimize the possibility of wrongful discharge allegations and can put the company in a better position to successfully defend against such action by implementing additional safeguards:

1. Advise prospective employees in writing, at the beginning of the application process that, if hired, they will be at-will employees. This is best accomplished by an at-will statement on the application form. A sample at-will statement appears as part of the application form in Appendix F.

2. Application forms should be in full compliance with applicable EEO laws.

3. Train managers and supervisors in effective and legal interviewing skills.

4. Ensure that applicants clearly understand the position they are being considered for prior to extending a job offer.

5. Ensure that all employees clearly understand what their jobs entail, in terms of both content and scope of responsibility.

6. Make certain job descriptions are accurate and job standards consistent with what is required.

7. Give all employees an up-to-date copy of the company's employee handbook, making it clear that the handbook does not constitute an employment contract.

8. Establish and follow a consistent method of evaluating job performance.

9. Grant salary increases according to an individual's skills and knowledge as they relate to a specific job.

10. Ensure that managers and supervisors are skilled at coaching and counseling.

11. Ensure that managers and supervisors are familiar with pertinent EEO and affirmative action laws, rules, and regulations.

12. Establish and follow a progressive disciplinary system.

13. Establish and follow grievance procedures for employees who are dissatisfied with working terms or conditions.

14. Ensure that managers and supervisors understand and practice effective documentation principles and techniques.

15. Grant all terminating employees exit interviews.

16. Handle all terminations consistently so employees will be less inclined to bring a suit against the company for wrongful dismissal.

A relatively new aspect of employment and termination-at-will is the development of noncompete agreements. Also known as "nonsolicitation agreements" or "restrict covenants," these agreements are designed to protect an employer's trade secrets, customer and marketing lists, and confidential knowledge about the employer picked up by an employee while on the job. Noncompete agreements, common in the computer industry, some professional partnerships, high-tech industries, and engineering environments, are usually presented for signature when a professional employee is hired or when a worker is promoted to a sensitive position. These agreements are intended to take effect upon termination, at which time employees may be restricted from working for a competitor for a specified period of time, often one to two years; working at the same or a comparable job in the same industry; or working in a defined geographical area for a competitor.

The current trend is toward protection of employees by placing limitations on the extent to which an employer can restrict a former employee's "right to work." There are no federal laws dealing directly with noncompete agreements, but there are some state laws.

Because the legal issues involving employment and termination-at-will are evolving, employers are advised to have all written materials pertaining to the employment process reviewed by counsel annually.

Negligent Hiring and Retention

Negligent hiring and retention may occur when employers fail to exercise reasonable care in hiring or retaining employees. Increasingly, employers are being held liable for the acts of their employees in the workplace and away from it. Named in such lawsuits are usually the employer, the employee who caused the injury, and the person directly responsible for hiring. Findings of personal liability are not uncommon. Negligent hiring actions have been brought by employees as well as by innocent third parties, such as customers, visitors, and clients injured by the criminal, violent, or negligent acts of an employee.

Plaintiffs must prove that the employee causing the injury was unfit for hiring or retention, that the employer's hiring or retention of that employee was the cause of the plaintiff's injuries, and that the employer knew or should have known of the employee's unfit condition. Generally, the deciding factor is whether an employer can establish that he exercised reasonable care in ensuring the safety of others. Reasonable care may include conducting preemployment testing, checking references, investigating gaps in an applicant's employment history, verifying academic achievements, conducting a criminal investigation, checking an applicant's credit history, or verifying the individual's driving record. The type of position an employee is hired for often plays a role in how extensive the investigation should be. For example, unsupervised positions in which the employee has a great deal of contact with customers, clients, visitors, or other employees may require more in-depth preemployment investigation than will jobs that are highly supervised.

Juries may not be sympathetic to the difficulties an employer might encounter in obtaining relevant background information on which to base a hiring decision. Employers in court because of negligent hiring or retention charges report that juries generally find for the plaintiff. The trial of such actions may involve the examination of a number of issues, including what the employer actually knew about the employee, as opposed to what it tried to ascertain; whether the potential risk to others could have been reasonably discovered through a reference or background check; and whether the risk to others was greater because of the nature of the job. Consideration of these questions may implicate the employer in an act of negligent hiring or retention. Employers should note that such lawsuits may prove more costly than typical employee litigation because of potentially higher awards of punitive damages.

From all that has been said, it is apparent that preventive measures are an employer's best defense against charges of negligent hiring or retention. In this regard, employers are advised to do the following:

- Conduct comprehensive employment interviews.
- Investigate gaps in employment.
- Conduct job-related preemployment tests.
- Conduct thorough reference checks.
- Keep written notes of information received when checking references.
- Decide whether a criminal investigation is warranted, based on information received.
- Immediately investigate any allegations of employee misconduct.
- Consult with legal counsel when in doubt as to what course of action to take.

Summary

Every HR specialist and manager having anything whatsoever to do with the employment process is responsible for a knowledge of key federal EEO and affirmative action laws and regulations as well as relevant record-keeping requirements. In addition, they should understand how the laws affect interviewing and hiring. Although no employer can avoid discrimination charges altogether, there are ways of minimizing and effectively dealing with such charges. Knowing what preemployment questions to avoid can also reduce discrimination charges.

The issue of employment and termination-at-will was also explored, focusing on the importance of at-will statements. Finally, we examined negligent hiring and retention as a form of liability that should encourage employers to scrutinize an individual's suitability for hire.

Chapter 7

A Competency-Based Approach to Employment Interviewing

Not long ago, I was invited to speak at a workshop on legal and effective interviewing skills. Although my particular segment on sexual harassment was scheduled for late in the afternoon, I arrived early, intrigued by the preceding topic, described as "the most comprehensive, legally sound approach to employment interviewing." It turned out to be what I would describe as a "cookie cutter, hit-or-miss approach." The speaker assured his audience of new HR specialists and managers that the most productive and litigation-free approach to interviewing was to prepare a lengthy list of about fifty questions, most of which were generic and open-ended, some close-ended, and a few "what would you do if . . . ?" questions. Then, he advised asking these questions—the same questions—of every applicant for every job. To be fair, he did have a separate list for nonexempt and exempt jobs. But that was it: two lists of questions for every job opening. His reasoning was that if you develop a series of legal questions that are work related and ask them of every candidate, you cannot possibly be accused of discrimination.

On the surface, this makes sense. However, after reading the preceding chapter on employment and the law, you know, at least in part, why this approach is risky. True, questions must be asked across the board to be nondiscriminatory. In addition, however, they must be consistent in effect; that is, questions should not have a greater negative impact on any one group. Also, simply because you avoid illegal questions does not preclude the applicant from volunteering information you have no business knowing. If such information is used, you are just as liable in those instances as if the illegal questions were asked directly.

More significant and to the point of this chapter, to be effective, questions must be *job specific,* not just overall work related. And although open-ended questions supplemented by close-ended and hypothetical questions are generally appropriate for most positions, these are only some of the questions that will yield valuable information about a candidate's job suitability. The most effective types of questions assess an applicant's demonstrated abilities as they relate to the requirements and responsibilities of a particular job. The questions stem from an understanding of the job's specifications derived from the job description and a review of each candidate's background by means of his application and resumé. This is a *competency-based* approach to employment interviewing.

Key Competency Categories

For our purposes, a competency is defined as a skill, trait, quality, or characteristic that contributes to a person's ability to perform the duties and responsibilities of a job effectively. Competencies are the gauges for job success. Identifying job-specific competencies enables you to assess how effective a person has been in the past and therefore how effectively she is likely to perform in your organization. Although every job requires different competencies, there are four primary categories:

1. Tangible or measurable skills
2. Knowledge
3. Behavior
4. Interpersonal skills

Most jobs emphasize the need for one category over the others, but every employee should be able to demonstrate competencies to some extent in all four categories.

For many jobs today, concrete, tangible, or measurable skill is critical to success. Measurable competencies demonstrate what applicants have done in past jobs. A sampling of competencies for a technical job includes having overall technical know-how, tailoring technical information to different audiences, applying technical expertise to solve business problems, staying technologically current, understanding the technologies of the organization, optimizing technology, balancing multiple projects, and communicating project status.

Although these competencies are indisputably necessary and should certainly be explored while interviewing for a technical job, the other three categories need to be examined as well. The reason is simple: a person brings much more than technical skill to a job. Complex beings that we all are, we also bring an array of knowledge, behaviors and interpersonal skills, all of which contribute to our success or failure on the job. This is true regardless of the job or grade level.

Consider this situation: two openings for the same type of job with two people hired, both of them technically competent. One of them (let's call him Paul) has slightly more experience than the other (Justine), but both possess outstanding technical know-how. After one year Justine's performance review reveals that she is doing above-average work, while Paul's indicates borderline, barely adequate performance. Why? Paul has trouble focusing on the key elements of a project and does not interact well with customers. In addition, while Justine responds well to feedback, Paul views suggestions as criticism. His poor performance evaluation derives from a number of nontechnical issues. What went wrong?

Looking back, the interviewer in this scenario focused all of his questions on the candidates' technical capabilities, erroneously assuming that inquiries relating to the other competencies were irrelevant for a technical job. Had he asked questions about how Paul interacted with customers in past jobs or asked for examples of how Paul handled past projects, he might not have extended a job offer, in spite of Paul's technical expertise.

The second competency, knowledge, concerns what candidates know and how they think. Included in this category are project management skills, problem-solving abilities, decision-making skills, the ability to focus on key elements of a project, time management, and the ability to use resources effectively. These are considered intangible qualities: more difficult to measure and quantify than concrete skills but no less important. Every job, regardless of level, requires a certain degree of knowledge. Even an entry-level position demands some degree of decision making or problem solving. Interviewers should ask knowledge-related questions appropriate to the level and nature of a job to determine not only what candidates know but how they think. This is especially important when jobs do not require previous measurable experience, thereby precluding your ability to draw from past job-related experiences.

The third competency concerns a candidate's key behaviors, or how she acts under certain conditions. Suppose the position calls for a high level of client satisfaction. In past client-oriented jobs, was this applicant committed to developing lasting partnerships with clients? Did she keep clients informed of key developments? Did she follow up to ensure client satisfaction? If she worked as part of or led a team, did she help team members focus on client requirements? Did she incorporate client views in decision making? There are numerous questions you can ask candidates with regard to job-specific behaviors that will reveal whether they will function effectively in your company's environment to meet client needs.

The fourth and final competency category involves interpersonal skills—that is, how applicants interact with others. Do they actively listen? Can they exercise self-control when upset? Are they able to motivate and work effectively with a wide range of people? Do they respect the views and ideas of others? Are they receptive to feedback? Can they manage conflict effectively? Every job requires some degree of interaction with others. Regardless of how competent job holders may be at what they can do, what they know, and how they behave, if they are unable to interact effectively with their managers, coworkers, employees, or clients, then their work and the work of others will suffer. Interviewers must ask questions that focus on how the applicants interacted in past jobs in situations similar to those that are likely to occur in your organization.

It is not too much of a stretch to comprehend how focusing on one set of competencies, at the expense of the other three, can have a negative impact on your role as a manager or HR representative. You operate as an agent for your organization; if the applicants you hire exhibit problems, this reflects on your judgment and abilities. It also makes your day-to-day job more difficult, creating possible production, morale, and motivational problems. And, of course, hiring the wrong people can be costly.

On the positive side of the ledger, by hiring all-around qualified candidates, you get more out of a person. These people are also more likely to enjoy their work and remain with your organization, with a positive impact on turnover rates and recruitment expenses. Productivity is also likely to improve, as will levels of customer and client satisfaction.

Job-Specific Competencies

Each job thus requires competencies from all four categories of tangible or technical skills, knowledge, behavior, and interpersonal skills.

It also necessitates a different set of *job-specific* competencies, which depend on the particular responsibilities involved.

Several sources will determine which competencies are relevant for each opening. Information about the job is generated primarily by the position description (discussed in Chapter 5). Additional information may be gleaned from a job requisition and postings. Also, talk with department heads, managers, and supervisors having an in-depth understanding of the opening. They will be most helpful with the tangible and knowledge proficiencies. Incumbents can prove helpful, too, since they can probably provide helpful information regarding the behaviors and interpersonal skills needed for the job.

Once you have gathered information about the job, isolate job-specific competencies. This is a two-step procedure: (1) make a list of all the required competencies, and (2) identify each competency according to its category. By example, consider a programmer analyst. Here is a partial list of competencies needed to perform this job successfully, as determined by examining an HR department–generated job description and posting, and conversations with a manager and two incumbents. Note that the list consists of both responsibilities and requirements:

- Designs applications, significant subsystems, and/or complete individual programs
- Identifies alternative implementations or strategies and weighs the impact of each
- Estimates time requirements for a set of modules with internal and external dependencies
- Experienced in real-time, multiprocessing systems within an event-driven architecture
- Experienced in C + + /UNIX
- Must be able to work as a member of a team
- Capable of learning new ideas quickly
- Able to develop software of the highest quality in a high-pressure environment with other team members
- Able to meet deadlines
- Experienced with complex modules/systems

Now you are ready to identify each competency according to its category. Review what each of the competencies represents: "Tangible" or "technical" reflects what candidates can do; "knowledge" refers to what they know and how they think; "behaviors" reveal how they act; and "interpersonal skills" indicate how they interact. Return to your list and mark each one with a **T** for technical or tangible, **K** for knowledge, **B** for behavior and **I** for interpersonal skills. Note that a competency can reflect more than one category:

T/K	Designs applications, significant subsystems, and/or complete individual programs
T/K	Identifies alternative implementations or strategies and weighs the impact of each
T/K	Estimates time requirements for a set of modules with internal and external dependencies
T/K	Experienced in real-time, multiprocessing systems within an event driven architecture
T/K	Experienced in C++/UNIX
B/I	Must be able to work as a member of a team
K	Capable of learning new ideas quickly
T/I	Able to develop software of the highest quality in a high-pressure environment with other team members
B	Able to meet deadlines
T	Experienced with complex modules/systems

Now go back over your list to ensure that all four categories are represented. You will no doubt see a greater emphasis of some competencies over others (in the case of a programmer-analyst, the emphasis is technical). Also, where competencies are paired, tangible and knowledge generally fall together, as do behaviors and interpersonal skills. That's fine, as long as all four areas are represented. If they are not, go back and seek out additional information. This is a critical step that interviewers should perform before meeting a candidate to ensure that they will probe all relevant areas during the interview.

Having isolated job-specific competencies, you are ready to correlate what the job requires with what the applicant has to offer. Information about the applicant can come from several sources. Two of the most comprehensive are the completed employment application form and a resumé. The two are *not* interchangeable. The application requires candidates to answer specific questions. The categories on the form direct them, seeking specific information. It is immediately evident if candidates leave some categories blank or give vague or partial answers. The information provided on a paper resumé, on the other hand, is entirely up to the applicants (cyberspace resumés may follow a specific format). They decide what is provided or concealed, and it is up to a savvy interviewer to zero in on missing, incomplete, or inaccurate information. The verbiage on a resumé, more narrative than any answer to a question on an application, can also dazzle or misguide an interviewer who is easily influenced by important-sounding titles and fancy phrases.

It is a good idea, then, to require an application from everyone submitting a resumé. It should be completed on company premises to preclude the possibility of outside assistance, and applicants should be instructed to answer all the questions, precluding the use of "see resumé" in response to some questions.

Applicant-related information can also be gleaned from referrals. If candidates come to you as a result of staff word-of-mouth recruiting, the referring employee can provide helpful job-related information. Perhaps they worked together as programmer analysts in the past. That could yield information about an applicant's technical, knowledge, and behavior competencies. Maybe your employee supervised the referral in a past job; important information about interpersonal skills could be discerned from that relationship.

When considering data from a referral, do not be influenced by irrelevant factors. For example, if the referral comes from a colleague for whom you have a high regard, do not assume that the candidate will elicit the same response. Similarly, if you hold little regard for the person making a recommendation, you could be biased against the applicant before even meeting him. Avoid this trap by adhering to job-related competencies, derived from the four primary categories.

References (discussed in detail in Chapter 12) can also provide valuable information about a candidate. Try to contact at least three former employers to establish a pattern. If one former manager indicates that the candidate was trouble from the outset and was glad when she resigned, but two others say she was outstanding, it's probable that there are others issues affecting the first reference. Additional probing is needed to get a clearer, more consistent picture.

Once you have identified the job-specific competencies and have information about the candidate, you are ready to proceed with the next step in a competency-based interview.

Characteristics of Competency-Based Questions

Competency-based questions focus on relating past job performance to probable future on-the-job behavior. The questions are based on information relevant to specific job-related skills, abilities and traits; the answers reveal the likelihood of similar future performance. The process works because past behavior is an indicator of future behavior. Be careful not to translate this last statement as reading, "Past behavior predicts future behavior," or "Future behavior is the same as past behavior." Proponents of the competency-based approach to employment interviewing clearly point out that past behavior is an indicator only. No one can predict with absolute certainty how someone will behave in a job. There are too many variables that can affect a person's performance, among them:

- A significant change in the work environment
- The approach, attitude, or personality of a supervisor or manager
- Difficulties in an employee's personal life
- A long-term or degenerative illness or disability
- A department's dramatic departure from established procedures
- The introduction of a new organizational philosophy
- What is perceived as being an unfair performance appraisal or salary increase
- Being bypassed for a promotion

Any of these alone can alter how an employee approaches work, and even the most compatible, conscientious, dedicated workers can be affected. Since interviewers cannot anticipate these influences when first meeting a candidate, they must develop a line of questioning that will project, as accurately as possible, how an employee is likely to behave. This is best accomplished by asking the applicant to draw from the past.

Suppose you have an opening that is known for its emergency projects and unreasonable deadlines. You can find out if a person is up to the challenge by asking about similar experiences in the past. Here is how you might phrase the question: "Tell me about a time in your last job when you were given an emergency project with what you believed to be an unrealistic deadline. What did you do?" Suppose the applicant's response indicates a firm grasp of how to handle this type of situation. You still need to know if the applicant was required to interrupt her normal workload frequently to tend to emergencies or only occasionally. In addition, you will want to know if the rest of her work suffered while she tended to the emergency project. Some follow-up competency-based questions would be:

"How many times, in a typical month, did this sort of emergency occur?"
"Describe the system you had for effectively dealing with these emergencies and the impact it had on the rest of your work."
"Who else was involved in meeting these deadlines?"

"What was your role in relation to theirs?"
"Was there ever been a time when you felt the deadline could not be met? What did you do?"

Competency-based questions seek specific examples. These examples will allow you to project how a candidate is likely to perform in your organization. If the environment, conditions, and circumstances are essentially the same in the person's current or previous company as in yours, then your task has been made simple. Of course, this is rarely the case. That's why you need to extract information about all four competency categories. You need to know not only if the candidate knew what to do and how to think, but also how to act and interact. Answers to the follow-up questions will reveal how proficient the candidate is in all four categories when confronted with demanding emergency projects.

Competency-based interviews, then, allow you to make hiring decisions based on facts. They are structured, job specific, and focused on relevant concrete and intangible competencies. In addition, they are legally defensible. Interviewers should note that competency-based interviews do not consist entirely of competency-based questions. Chapter 8 will discuss additional employment interview questioning techniques. Nevertheless, competency-based questions should represent about 70 percent of any interview, supplemented by other types of questions. They will improve the interview in these ways:

- Identifying the skills and characteristics needed to succeed in a specific work environment
- Isolating the competencies required for a given job
- Earmarking relevant experiences necessary to have acquired these competencies
- Clarifying what candidates have learned from their experiences
- Determining whether candidates can apply what they have learned to a given job and work environment

Competency-Based Lead-Ins

When preparing competency-based questions, remember two things: They require specific examples concerning what the applicant has done in the past, and they should tie in directly with job-specific competencies.

That said, competency-based questions are among the easiest to formulate. If the job requires the ability to oversee a project, you would ask the candidate:

> "Tell me about a time when you had to oversee a project. What did the task require?"
> "Who else was involved?"
> "What steps did you take to accomplish your goal?"

Or perhaps the job involves working extensively as a member of a team. Then the questions might include:

> "How frequently do you work as a member of a team?"
> "Describe a specific time when you worked as a member of a team. What was the nature of the project?"
> "What was your role?"
> "Who else was involved?"
> "What was your relationship to the other people on the team?"
> "Describe the process."
> "What was the outcome?"
> "Were there instances when you made suggestions that were not acted upon?
> Please give me specific examples."

Each of these competency-based questions is introduced by a lead-in phrase that alerts the applicant to an important fact: that you want specific examples. Here is a sampling of lead-ins:

> "Describe a time when you . . ."
>
> "Give an example of a time in which you . . ."
>
> "Tell me about a time when you . . ."
>
> "Tell me about a specific job experience in which you . . ."
>
> "Give me an example of a specific occasion when you . . ."
>
> "Describe a situation in which you were called upon to . . ."
>
> "Describe the most significant . . ."
>
> "What did you do in your last job in order to . . ."
>
> "How often in the last year were you called upon to . . ."
>
> "Tell me about a time when you didn't want to _____. What happened?"

"Describe a situation in which you felt _____. What was the result?"

By the time you have asked the third or fourth competency-based question, applicants will realize that they must respond with specifics whenever you begin with a lead-in phrase.

When to Ask Competency-Based Questions

Effective competency-based employment interviews are structured to ensure control by the interviewer and coverage of the four key competencies. They are also legally defensible. For maximum effectiveness, the interviews should consist of five stages: rapport building, introductory, core, confirmation, and closing. Each has a specific purpose and should take up a designated percentage of the interview. Competency-based questions are highly effective in some stages, minimally effective in others, and completely useless in another.

1. *Rapport building.* This is the stage during which applicants are encouraged to relax and feel at ease with the interviewer. Non-job-related topics are discussed, such as the weather or the applicant's commute. It should represent approximately 2 percent of the interview. The effectiveness of asking competency-based questions in the rapport-building stage is none.

2. *Introductory.* The initial questions an interviewer poses are intended to help still-nervous applicants feel at ease. These questions should encourage the applicant to talk about a familiar topic, such as her current or most recent job. In addition, the first few questions should be broad enough to generate additional questions, as well as allowing the interviewer to begin assessing the candidate's relevant verbal and organizational skills. This stage should represent about 3 percent of the interview. The effectiveness of asking competency-based questions in the introductory stage is minimal.

3. *Core:* During this segment, interviewers gather information about specific technical skills, knowledge, behavior, and interpersonal skills. It allows for an examination of the applicant's past job performance and projects future performance based on specific job-related examples. Interviewers can ultimately make hiring decisions based on facts, as opposed to intuitive feelings or bias. The core stage should represent approximately 85 percent of the interview, with as much as 65 percent of it devoted to competency-based questions. The

effectiveness of asking competency-based questions in the core stage is high.

4. *Confirmation.* During this stage, interviewers can verify what they learned about job-specific competencies during the core stage. Topics of discussion should be limited to those aspects of work experience and education already discussed during the core segment. The confirmation stage should represent approximately 5 percent of the interview. The effectiveness of asking competency-based questions in the confirmation stage is minimal.

5. *Closing.* This final stage is the interviewer's opportunity to ensure that she has covered all relevant competencies needed to make an effective hiring decision. It is also the applicant's last chance to sell himself—to say how and why he would be an asset to the organization. The closing stage should represent approximately 5 percent of the interview, with most to all of it taken up with competency-based questions. The effectiveness of asking these questions at this point is high.

Developing Competency-Based Questions

The information you have gathered through job descriptions and other sources as the basis for an interview, combined with the applicant's background, will yield a great deal of data about a possible job match—if you know how to phrase your questions properly. Since nearly three-quarters of an interview involves asking for specific examples related to past job performance, employers must convert topics about which they seek information into competency-based questions. Note that it is not always necessary to ask questions in the interrogative form. Statements can often be just as effective.

This is best accomplished by first listing the primary duties and responsibilities of the job. Let's assume there is an opening for an assistant to the director of human resources. A partial list of tasks reads as follows:

• Recruits and interviews applicants for nonexempt positions; refers qualified candidates to appropriate department managers.

• Performs reference checks on potential employees.

• Helps director of human resources plan and conduct each month's organizational orientation program.

• Assists in the implementation of policies and procedures; may be required to explain or interpret certain policies.

• Assists in the development and maintenance of up-to-date job descriptions for nonexempt positions throughout the company.

• Assists in the maintenance and administration of the organization's compensation program; monitors salary increase recommendations as they are received to ensure compliance with merit increase guidelines.

Now isolate the first task: "Recruits and interviews applicants for nonexempt positions; refers qualified candidates to appropriate department managers." Refer to the competency-based question lead-ins listed previously in this chapter and attach them to components of this task. Here is what you will get with very little effort:

> *"Describe a time when you* had a nonexempt position open for an unusually long period of time. How did you eventually fill it?"
>
> *"Give an example of a time in which you* referred an applicant whom you believed should have been hired to a department manager, but the referral was rejected. How did you resolve your differences with that manager?"
>
> *"Tell me about a time when you* had more applicants than you could handle."
>
> *"Tell me about a specific job experience in which you* hired someone who later didn't work out."
>
> *"Give me an example of a specific occasion when you* and a department head didn't agree on the requirements for a nonexempt opening."
>
> *"Describe a situation in which you were called upon to* fill several openings in one department at one time."
>
> *"Describe the most significant* recruiting experience you have had to date."
>
> *"What did you do in your last job in order to* convince a department head to hire someone?"
>
> *"How often in the last year were you called upon to* recruit for especially hard-to-fill openings? Tell me about the openings."
>
> *"Tell me about a time when you didn't want to* continue using a long-time recruiting source. *What happened?"*
>
> *"Describe a situation in which you felt* uneasy with the answers given by a particular applicant. *What was the result?"*

Of course, you do not have to use all the lead-ins, and you can substitute others of your own. This is exemplified with the remaining tasks, beginning with, *"Performs reference checks on potential employees."*

"Describe your process for conducting references. How did you follow up with former employers who failed to respond to your phone calls or letters?"

"Describe a time when you received negative references on a candidate that the department manager wanted to hire anyway. What happened?"

"Tell me about a time when you went back to a candidate with a negative reference and asked if he could explain why he felt the former employer had given the poor reference."

"Tell me about a reference that sounded too good to be true and later turned out to be just that."

"Tell me how you go about obtaining references with former employers who will only verify dates of employment."

"Tell me some of the questions you ask former employers to determine job suitability."

"Describe a situation in which you received conflicting references from two of an applicant's former employers. What did you do?"

"Tell me about a time when you called the former manager of an applicant your company was interested in hiring and she referred you to the HR department."

"How have you handled verification of school records? Please be specific."

"Tell me about a time when an applicant apparently falsified educational credentials. What did you do?"

"Tell me about a time when you received negative references on an applicant after she had already started work. What happened?"

The next task is, *"Helps director of human resources plan and conduct each month's organizational orientation program."* Here are some questions:

"Describe your role in your organization's orientation program?"

"What percentage of your time is taken up with preparing for and conducting your company's orientation program?"

"What is your favorite part of the orientation process? Why? What about your least favorite part?"

"Tell me about a time when you were asked questions to which you did not have answers."

"Have you ever had a situation when speakers you had lined up as part of orientation did not show up, printed materials were not ready, or something went wrong with the audiovisual equipment? What did you do?"

"Tell me some of the things you did in preparation for your first orientation that you no longer do."

"Describe the relationship between you and the other orientation developers and participants."

"How do you follow up with orientation attendees who are required to complete and return forms they received during the session?"

"Tell me about some ideas you might have for making the orientation experience more meaningful and more helpful to new employees."

The next area to probe is, *"Assists in the implementation of policies and procedures; may be required to explain or interpret certain policies."* Some useful questions include:

"Tell me about your role in implementing and interpreting HR policies and procedures for employees."

"How often do employees call you regarding policies and procedures?"

"Give me some examples of the nature of these calls."

"Describe a situation in which an employee required an explanation of an HR policy and became upset with the explanation. What did you do?"

"Has there ever been a time when an employee challenged the accuracy of a policy or procedure?"

"Give me an example of specific occasion when a long-time policy was revised."

"Describe a company policy or procedure that generates the most questions or concerns. Why do you think that is?"

For *"Assists in the development and maintenance of up-to-date job descriptions for nonexempt positions throughout the company,"* the following questions will be helpful:

"Describe your responsibilities when it comes to developing job descriptions."

"Tell me about some of the job categories for which you are responsible."

"Describe how you gather information for the job descriptions."

"Tell me about a time when you had difficulty developing a job description. Why do you think that was?"

"Have you ever been in a situation where the incumbents described a job differently than their managers did? What was the outcome?"

"How do you ensure that the job descriptions remain up-to-date?"

"Give me an example of a specific occasion when a job's responsibilities, its corresponding grade, and salary range did not seem to coincide. What happened?"

"What did you do in order to be more proficient in developing and maintaining accurate job descriptions?"

The final area is, *"Assists in the maintenance and administration of the organization's compensation program; monitors salary increase recommendations as they are received to ensure compliance with merit increase guidelines."* Consider asking:

"Describe your responsibilities in relation to your organization's compensation program."

"Tell me how performance appraisals relate to salary increases."

"Tell me about a time when you received a salary increase recommendation from a department head for an employee whose performance was below average."

"Describe the most challenging aspect of your compensation responsibilities."

"Give me a specific example of a time when an employee objected to the amount of his recommended increase. What was your role in resolving the dispute?"

"Describe a time when an employee was already at the top of her range, but whose performance warranted a raise. What happened?"

These six tasks alone resulted in more than fifty questions that will yield a great deal of job-related information, reflecting all four competency categories. Additionally, by practicing active listening skills (see Chapter 9), you are likely to come up with even more job-specific questions as a result of the applicant's answers.

With the half-dozen or so preplanned questions described in Chapter 5 and information contained in the job description and the candidate's application and resumé, competency-based questions should flow freely during the interview.

The process of asking these questions, is painless and highly productive, ultimately enabling you to make an effective hiring decision.

Summary

A competency-based approach to employment interviewing assesses a person's demonstrated abilities as they relate to the requirements and responsibilities of a particular job. There are four primary competency categories: tangible or technical skills, knowledge, behavior, and interpersonal skills. Most jobs emphasize the need for one category over the others, but every employee should be able to demonstrate competencies to some extent in all four categories. Every job also has a set of specific competencies, based on its individual requirements and responsibilities.

Competency-based questions seek specific examples from past job-related experiences. These examples allow you to project how a candidate is likely to perform in your organization.

Competency-based interviews are structured, job specific, allow you to make hiring decisions based on fact, and are legally defensible.

Chapter 8
Additional Employment Interview Questioning Techniques

Any thought can be expressed in a number of different ways. The wording you choose will determine how much information you receive and how useful that information is in making a hiring decision.

Competency-based questions should constitute approximately 70 percent of the employment interview. The remainder of time should be spent asking one of four other types of questions: open-ended; hypothetical, probing, and close-ended. Like competency-based questions, each of these works best at various stages of the interview.

There are also three questioning techniques to avoid: trait, multiple choice, and forced choice. These types of questions usually result in meaningless or misleading information.

Open-Ended Questions

By definition, open-ended questions require full, multiple-word responses. The answers generally lend themselves to discussion and result in information on which the interviewer can build additional questions. Open-ended questions encourage candidates to talk, thereby allowing the interviewer an opportunity to actively listen to responses, assess verbal communication skills, and observe the applicant's pattern of nonverbal communication. They also allow the interviewer time to plan subsequent questions. Open-ended questions are especially helpful in encouraging shy or otherwise quiet applicants to talk without the pressure that can accompany a competency-based question which requires the recollection of specific examples.

The partial interview with a customer representative candidate in Chapter 5 illustrates these points. Her answer to the open-ended question, "Would you please describe your activities during a typical day at your present job?" was vague: "Well, let's see. Each day is really kind of different since I deal with customers and you never know what they're going to call about; but basically, my job is to handle the customer hot line, research any questions, and process complaints." However, it yielded four categories for additional questions:

1. Her job requires dealing with a variety of people and situations.
2. She "handles" a customer hot line.
3. She "researches" questions.
4. She "processes" complaints.

Many of the follow-up questions were open-ended:

"What is the nature of some of the situations with which you are asked to deal?"
"Who are the people who call you?"
"What is the process that someone with a complaint is supposed to follow?"
"What is your role in this process?"
"Exactly what is the customer hot line?"
"When you say that you 'handle' the hot line, exactly what do you mean?"
"What do you say to a customer who calls on the hot line?"
"What do you say to a customer who calls with a specific question?"
"What do you do when a customer is not satisfied with the answer you have given him?"
"How do you prepare for each day, knowing that you will probably have to listen to several people complaining about a variety of problems?"

Bear in mind that asking open-ended questions such as these allows applicants to control the answers. Such inquiries are most helpful, then, when used to form a foundation for competency-based questions that direct a candidate to provide specific responses supplemented by examples. Take one of the open-ended questions just listed: "What do you do when a customer is not satisfied with the answer you have given him?" That's a perfectly legitimate question, relative to the responsibilities of a customer service representative. The applicant may reply, "I tell him I'm sorry he is dissatisfied with my answer and that I wish I could be more helpful." That generic answer tells you very little about how this candidate interacts with customers—the essence of her job. Now is the time to follow up with a competency-based question: "Give me a specific example of when this happened." The applicant must now draw from a real situation involving her interaction with a customer; the information her answer yields will help you evaluate a critical job-related skill.

Open-ended questions, then, can result in descriptive monologues, lacking substance or verifiable information. Without further probing, such responses are not very useful in painting an accurate picture of a candidate's job suitability.

Any open-ended question can be made more substantive by converting it into a competency-based question. For example, "How would you describe your ability to deal with difficult customers?" is open-ended. The competency-based version reads, "Describe a situation in which an irate customer held you responsible for something that was not your fault. What did you do?"

There may be two additional problems with open-ended questions. The applicant's response may include information that is irrelevant or that violates equal employment opportunity (EEO) laws. As soon as this occurs, the interviewer must bring the applicant back to the focus of the question. One way to do this is to say: "Excuse me, but we seem to have strayed from the original question of why you left your last job. I would like to get back to that." Another effective response might be, "Excuse me, but that information is not job related. Let's get back to your description of a typical day at the office." This is especially appropriate if information being volunteered has the potential for illegal use (as discussed in Chapter 6).

Another concern is that open-ended questions may be too broad in scope. The classic request, "Tell me about yourself," illustrates this point. Questions that require applicants to summarize many years in a single response are also ineffective. An example is, "Describe your work history," when you are addressing an applicant who has worked for over thirty years. Instead say, "Please describe your work experience over the past two years." This is still open-ended, but it establishes useful boundaries.

Following are further examples of generic, work-related, open-ended questions (note that the effectiveness of many of these would be enhanced if followed up with a competency-based question):

"What is your description of the ideal manager? Employee? Co-worker? Work environment? Work schedule?"

"How would you describe yourself as an employee? Co-worker?"

"What kind of people do you find it difficult [easy] to work with? Why?"

"What do you feel an employer owes an employee? How about what an employee owes an employer?"

"What were some of the duties of your last job that you found to be difficult?"

"How do you feel about the progress that you have made in your career to date?"

"How does your current job differ from the one you had before it?"

"Of all the jobs you have had, which did you find the most [least] rewarding?"

"In what ways do you feel your current job has prepared you to assume additional responsibilities?"

"What has been the most rewarding [frustrating] situation you have encountered in your career to date?"

"What does the prospect of this job offer you that your last job did not?"

"Why do you want to leave your current job?"

"What are you looking for in a company?"

"How does your experience in the military relate to your chosen field?"

"What immediate and long-term goals have you set for yourself?"

"What would you like to avoid in future jobs?"

"What do you consider to be your greatest strength?"

"What are the areas in which you require improvement? How would you go about making these improvements?"

"What aspects of your work give you the greatest satisfaction?"

"How do you approach tasks that you dislike?"

"How do you manage your time?"

"How do you go about making a decision?"

"What have past employers complimented [criticized] you for?"

"What types of work-related situations make you feel most comfortable [uneasy]?"

"What is the most difficult [rewarding] aspect of being a _____?"

"If you were asked to perform a task that was not in your job description, how would you respond?"

"How would you go about discussing job dissatisfaction with your boss?"

"What could your previous employers have done to convince you not to leave?"

Here are some additional open-ended questions, this time dealing with education:

"What were your favorite and least favorite subjects in high school [college]? Why?"

"What subjects did you do best in? Poorest in?"

"Why did you decide to major in _____?"

"Why did you decide to attend _____?"

"What career plans did you have at the beginning of college? How did they change?"

"How did high school [college] prepare you for the 'real world'?"

"What did you gain by attending high school [college]?"

"If you had the opportunity to attend school all over again, what, if anything, would you do differently?"

"How do you feel your studies in _____ have prepared you for this job?"

"Describe your study habits."

"Describe any part-time jobs you had while attending high school [college]."

"Which of your part-time jobs did you find most [least] interesting?"

"What advice would you give to someone who wanted to work and attend school at the same time?"

"What did you find to be most difficult about working and attending school at the same time?"

"What could the department head of the course you majored in have done to make the curriculum more interesting?"

"How did you handle required courses that were not of particular interest to you?"

"Describe what you consider to be characteristics of the ideal teacher."

Hypothetical Questions

Such questions are based on anticipated or known job-related tasks for the available opening, phrased in the form of problems and presented to the applicant for solutions. The questions are generally introduced with words and phrases like the following:

> "What would you do if . . ."
> "How would you handle . . ."
> "How would you solve . . ."
> "In the event that . . ."
> "If . . ."
> "Assuming . . ."
> "How would you avoid . . ."
> "Consider this scenario . . ."
> "What would you say . . ."
> "Suppose . . ."
> "How would you go about . . ."

Hypothetical questions allow for the evaluation of reasoning abilities, thought processes, values, attitudes, creativity, work style, and approach to different tasks.

Although the answers to hypothetical questions can produce important information about the applicant's reasoning ability and thought processes, interviewers are cautioned against expecting "right" answers. Without familiarity with the organization, applicants can offer responses based only on their previous experiences. Such answers, then, are based on how they think rather than what they know.

An important distinction between hypothetical and competency-based questions is that hypotheticals ask applicants to project what they might do in a fictitious (albeit realistic) scenario, whereas competency-based questions draw from the actual experiences of the applicant. The first is based on conjecture, the latter on fact.

Consider the distinction between two differently worded questions on the subject of unreasonable work demands. The first example is worded as a hypothetical question:

> "If you were a manager, and your team complained about having to meet some rather unreasonable demands presented by one of the company's top clients, how would you go about satisfying both the client and your staff?"

Now let's reword the question to be competency based:

> "Tell me about a time when, as a manager, your team complained about having to meet some rather unreasonable de-

mands presented by one of the company's top clients. How did you go about satisfying both the client and your staff?"

The first wording directs the applicant into the realm of possibilities. She is likely to answer using words like, "I would" or "I could." There is no way of knowing if she is providing you what she believes is a good answer and the one you want to hear, or if this is actually what she would do. In the second version, however, she must draw from a real situation and describe what happened. Could she make something up? Sure, but applicants cannot be certain about what you already know or what can be verified. It is more difficult to lie about something that can be referenced than it is to speculate about something that has not yet happened.

Naturally, the competency-based version requires a similar experience to draw from. If, after reviewing the applicant's resumé, you are unclear as to whether the candidate has experienced a similar situation in the past, word the question this way:

"As a manager, have you ever been in a situation where your team complained about having to meet some rather unreasonable demands presented by one of the company's top clients? If so, how did you go about satisfying both the client and your staff? If not, draw from your expertise as a manager, and imagine such a scenario. What would you do to satisfy both the client and your staff?"

Here are additional samples of hypothetical questions:

"How would you handle an employee who was consistently tardy?"

"How would you go about discussing job dissatisfaction with your boss?"

"How would you handle a long-term employee whose performance has always been outstanding, but who recently has started to make a number of mistakes in his work?"

"What would you say to an employee who challenged your authority?"

"What would you do if an employee went over your head?"

"Consider this scenario: You have just given a presentation and are asked a series of questions to which you do not know the answers. What would you do?"

"Suppose you are a member of a team and disagree with the

way the others want to approach a project. How would you go about changing their minds?"

"How would you solve the problem of an employee whose personal problems are interfering with her work performance?"

"If you were given a task that created an undue amount of pressure, what would you do?"

"How would you avoid conflict with coworkers? Your employees? Your manager? Clients?"

Hypothetical questions are also applicable for applicants with limited or no work experience.

Probing Questions

Probing questions enable the interviewer to delve more deeply for additional information. Best thought of as follow-up questions, they are usually short and simply worded. There are three types of probing questions:

1. *Rational probes* request reasons, using short questions such as: "Why?" "How?" "When?" "How often?" and "Who?"

2. *Clarifier probes* are used to qualify or expand on information provided in a previous response, using questions such as: "What caused that to happen?" "Who else was involved in that decision?" "What happened next?" and "What were the circumstances that resulted in that happening?"

3. *Verifier probes* check out the honesty of a statement—for example: "You state on your resumé that you currently work closely with the officers from your customers' firms. Name three of these officers. Then tell me about their areas of responsibility and exactly what you have done for them."

Applicants who have trouble providing full answers usually appreciate the extra help that comes from a probing question. These also show the applicant you are interested in what she is saying and want to learn more.

Interviewers are cautioned against asking too many probing questions consecutively, as they tend to make applicants feel defensive. In addition, your accompanying body language should express interest but not accusation: maintain eye contact, but avoid staring; periodically nod and smile; avoid raising your eyebrows. Body language is discussed more fully in Chapter 9.

Here are additional examples of rational probing questions:

"What kind of people do you find it difficult [easy] to work with? *Why?*"

"Do you take over for your manager when she is away? *How often?*"

"What motivates you? *Why?*"

"What is the greatest accomplishment of your career to date? *Why?*"

These further illustrate clarifier probes:

"Who or what has influenced you with regard to your career goals? *In what way?*"

"You said earlier that your team failed to meet the last deadline. *What caused that to happen?*"

"Before you said that you were part of the decision to revamp your company's compensation structure. *Who else was involved in that decision?*"

"You've described part of what took place when your company downsized. *What happened next?*"

"What are some of the problems you encountered in your last job? *How did you resolve them?*"

"Please give me an example of a project that did not turn out the way you planned. *What happened?*"

"What is your definition of company loyalty? *How far does it extend?*"

Additional examples of verifier probing questions include these:

"What would your former manager say about how you handled the Grisham deal?"

"How would your former employees describe your management style?"

"What would your coworkers say about your contributions to the last team project you participated in?"

"Earlier you stated that you led a team from your company that had linked up with a team from World Energies, Inc. to work on developing a new communications device. Tell me about three specific members from World Energies. What were their roles and responsibilities?"

Close-Ended Questions

These are questions that may be answered with a single word—generally yes or no. Close-ended questions can be helpful in a number of ways: They give the interviewer greater control, put certain applicants at ease, are useful when seeking clarification, are helpful when you need to verify information, and usually result in concise responses. Also, if there is a single issue that could terminate the interview, such as the absence of an important job requirement, then asking about it up front in a direct, close-ended way can disclose what you need to know quickly and succinctly.

Interviewers should avoid relying on close-ended questions for the bulk of their information on a candidate's job suitability. Answers to close-ended questions provide limited information, resulting in an incomplete picture of the person's abilities and experiences. Also, you will be unable to assess the applicant's verbal communication skills, if relevant.

Ask close-ended questions to serve the functions described above, but not as a substitute for open-ended or competency-based questions. Any questions that can be answered by a single word can be converted into an open-ended question. For example, "Did you like your last job?" can easily be changed to, "What did you like about your last job?" The open-ended version usually will yield more valuable information.

Close-ended questions can also be converted into competency-based questions. Asking, "Have you done a good amount of public speaking?" will result in a single-word answer and reveal little about the applicant's experience with public speaking. The open-ended version of this question is better, but still does not tell you much: "What is your experience with public speaking?" However, making this a competency-based question will provide a job-related, detailed response: "Tell me about a time when you had to address a large audience. How did you prepare for it?"

Here are examples of functional close-ended questions:

"How often do you travel in your current job?"
"Are you aware that the starting salary for this job is $525 per week?"
"Based on what you have told me so far, can I assume that you prefer working independently rather than as part of a team?"
"How many times did you step in for your manager in the past three months?"

"Earlier you said that the most challenging part of your job is conducting new employee orientations. Just before, you indicated you favor conducting interviews. Am I to understand that you consider the two areas to be equally rewarding?"

"What subject in school did you do best in? Poorest in?"

"What did you major in? Minor in?"

"How many hours a weeks did you work while carrying a full credit load in college?"

"What was your grade point average in your favorite subject? Least favorite subject?"

How to Relate the Questioning Techniques to Interview Stages

Chapter 7 identified the five stages of a competency-based interview as rapport building, introductory, core, confirmation, and closing. Competency-based questions comprise as much as 65 percent of the core stage and all 5 percent of the closing. The remaining 30 percent of the interview is divided among open-ended, hypothetical, probing, and close-ended questions.

Rapport Building

This stage, representing a scant but important 2 percent of the interview, sets the tone for the rest of the meeting. The purpose is to put applicants at ease, thereby encouraging them to communicate openly, and allowing you to determine job suitability. Close-ended questions that are casual in nature and focus on non-job-related topics will accomplish this goal.

Here are some examples of neutral, rapport-building, close-ended questions:

"Did you have any trouble getting here?"

"Were you able to find parking nearby?"

"How was the traffic getting here?"

"Were the directions we gave you helpful?"

"Isn't it a beautiful day?"

"When do you think it will stop raining?"

"What do you think about this string of 80-degree days we're having in late October?"

As you can see, all these questions are about the same two topics: commuting and the weather. Boring, yes; but they are clearly the safest areas to inquire about without running the risk of saying something controversial or job related. And do not worry about being repetitive in asking the same set of rapport-building, close-ended questions of every applicant. They are not likely to compare notes with one another after their interviews. Chapter 9 will further discuss establishing rapport.

Introductory

This stage represents approximately 3 percent of the interview and is intended to accomplish two key objectives: to help still-nervous applicants feel at ease and to allow the interviewer to start assessing their job suitability. These objectives are best accomplished by posing two to three open-ended questions. This is the most effective type of question to ask at this stage because the applicant will begin talking and relax more, while you actively listen to the responses and start making some preliminary decisions.

Introductory questions should be about topics familiar to the applicant, so as not to create undue pressure, and broad enough to generate additional questions by you. One question that satisfies both of these criteria is, "Would you please describe your activities during a typical day at your current job?" This question actually accomplishes a great deal:

- It helps to relax a still-nervous applicant by allowing him to discuss a familiar subject.
- The open-ended nature of the question encourages the applicant to talk, giving you an opportunity to assess verbal and organizational skills.
- It allows you time to begin observing the applicant's pattern of body language.
- It provides information on which you can build additional questions.

The question is not foolproof, however. An applicant could respond, "Well, that's kind of hard to do. No day is really typical." If this happens, be a little more specific in your wording to help the applicant get started. Try adding, "I can appreciate that. Why don't you just pick a day—say, yesterday—and describe what you did?"

Once the applicant begins to outline specific tasks you can interject, "Do you do that every day?" By breaking the question down and encouraging the applicant to talk, you should be able to get the required information and move on to the next question.

Additional effective open-ended questions to start off with include the following:

> "Can you give me an overview of your experiences with benefits administration?"
>
> "Let's begin with your current job. Would you describe your involvement in the day-to-day operation of your department?"
>
> "In your job as a public relations manager, how do you go about preparing press releases?"
>
> "Working as a legal assistant sounds very challenging. What are your primary responsibilities?"
>
> "If you were asked to write a summary of your primary duties and responsibilities, what would you include?"
>
> "I'm interested in learning more about what being an internal consultant entails. Please tell me what you do in that capacity."

The introductory stage will be referred to again in Chapter 9.

The Core Stage

As the term implies, this is the most substantive segment of the interview. Here, the interviewer gathers all relevant information about the applicant based on the four categories of technical skills, knowledge, behavior, and interpersonal skills, examining them in relation to the requirements and responsibilities of the job. This stage represents 85 percent of the interview, with as much as 65 percent of it devoted to competency-based questions. That leaves about 20 percent of the time to be divided among four other types of questions: close-ended, open-ended, probing, and hypothetical. The last two should receive shared emphasis, say about 5 percent each, with open-ended questions receiving about 8 percent and close-ended carrying the balance. Let us now look at the role of each type of question.

Close-ended questions allow you to zero in on specific issues, usually for purposes of verification or clarification. They are useful when you need a tightly worded response in order to proceed with the interview.

Open-ended questions generally focus on how an applicant approaches tasks. They serve as effective set-ups for subsequent competency-based questions, testing out the validity of preceding answers.

The probing questions asked during the core of the interview will allow you to ascertain additional information from answers to competency-based questions, open-ended questions, and hypotheticals. Their main function, whether rational, clarifier, or verifier probes, is to allow you to delve deeper. Think of them as follow-up questions. Asking too many consecutive probing questions can come across as an interrogation. It also means you are not asking a sufficient number of substantive questions.

Hypotheticals lend balance to the competency-based questions. While the latter focus on specific examples from past job experiences, hypotheticals present realistic job-related problems for solution. Where one is founded on facts, the other is based on supposition. Interviewers can compare what a person has done with how she might act, looking for similarities and further examining situations that stand out. Hypotheticals are also valuable for applicants with limited or no prior work history. Remember that hypotheticals evaluate how the applicant thinks as opposed to what she knows.

Consider this Chapter 7 reference to an opening for the assistant to the director of human resources. The partial list of tasks reads as follows:

1. Recruits and interviews applicants for nonexempt positions; refers qualified candidates to appropriate department managers.

2. Performs reference checks on potential employees.

3. Helps director of human resources plan and conduct each month's organizational orientation program.

4. Assists in the implementation of policies and procedures; may be required to explain or interpret certain policies.

5. Assists in the development and maintenance of up-to-date job descriptions for nonexempt positions throughout the company.

6. Assists in the maintenance and administration of the organization's compensation program; monitors salary increase recommendations as they are received to ensure compliance with merit increase guidelines.

We have already developed more than fifty competency-based questions for these six tasks. Now let's simulate a segment of the core stage, integrating probing, hypothetical and open-ended questions to support the competency-based questions (each question is identified by **CB** for competency-based question, **P** for probing, **H** for hypothetical, **OE** for open-ended, and **CE** for close-ended):

Interviewer: How would you describe your ability to handle a disagreement with a department head over the requirements for an opening? (**OE**)

Applicant: I'd like to think I'm pretty diplomatic.

Interviewer: Why don't you pick a situation that occurred recently. Tell me about it. (**CB**)

Applicant: Well, we had an opening for a security guard at one of our branches two weeks ago. The branch manager wanted me to hire someone who was at least six feet tall and weighed more than 200 pounds.

Interviewer: Why? (**P**)

Applicant: We'd had a string of attempted robberies at that branch. The manager thought someone who looked big and imposing would threaten would-be thieves.

Interviewer: What happened? (**P**)

Applicant: I explained that height and weight requirements had a greater negative impact on women and men of certain ethnic groups and therefore could not be justified.

Interviewer: How did the manager respond? (**P**)

Applicant: Not very well, actually. He insisted that height and weight requirements were job related.

Interviewer: What did you say to that? (**P**)

Applicant: I said that if he could show me that, statistically, security guards who were at least six feet tall and weighed 200 pounds were more successful in thwarting robbery attempts, then I would be able to use these as job requirements. Otherwise, I felt we were opening the company up to possible charges of discrimination.

Interviewer: And? (**P**)

Applicant: He backed off and realized what he was asking for was unrealistic. The job is still open, by the way.

Interviewer: Would you say that your rapport with the manager has been adversely affected by this exchange? (**CE**)

Applicant: No.

Here's another example:

Interviewer: How would you describe your skills in checking references on candidates under serious hiring consideration? (**OE**)

Applicant: Good.

Interviewer: Tell me about a time when you checked a reference on a candidate the department wanted to hire, only to find that the person's former employer had several less than favorable things to say about him. (**CB**)

Applicant: That's never happened.

Interviewer: Imagine that happening, if you will. How would you handle the situation? (**H**)

Applicant: Well, I'm not sure.

Interviewer: Okay. Let me ask you this: Have you ever received information from an applicant that conflicted with what was on the resumé? (**CE**)

Applicant: Yes.

Interviewer: Think about one of the times that occurred and tell me what did you do. (**CB**)

Applicant: Oh, sure. Okay. I see what you're going for. I did a lot of probing and comparing of information until I uncovered the truth. In the situation you described, I guess I would ask a series of questions to determine if the former employer was being factual or had a bias.

Interviewer: What are some of the questions you would ask? (**P**)

Applicant: I'd ask for specific examples to back up his statements. Then I'd compare what he said with what I learned during the interview. I'd also try to contact more than one former employer to see if there was a pattern.

The combination of hypothetical, open-ended, probing, and close-ended questions in support of competency-based questions in these two examples will allow the interviewer to evaluate the candidate's job suitability effectively.

Confirmation Stage

The confirming stage offers the interviewer an opportunity to verify what has been learned thus far about an applicant's job-specific proficiencies; no new topics should be introduced. It represents about 5 percent of the entire interview and should be divided between open- and close-ended questions, with a slightly heavier emphasis on open-ended. A competency-based question occasionally may be appropriate.

Consider these close-ended examples based on the interview for the assistant to the director of human resources interview described in the core stage:

> "Based on what you have told me thus far, may I assume that you view yourself as being diplomatic when it comes to handling disagreements with department heads?"
>
> "Am I correct in understanding that you have not experienced

checking a reference on a candidate the department wanted to hire, only to find that the person's former employer had several less than favorable things to say about him?"

"When we talked earlier about job descriptions, you stated that you assist in their development and maintenance. Is that for exempt and nonexempt job descriptions?"

The single-word answers to these questions will verify whether you have drawn accurate conclusions. The applicant will also have an opportunity to clarify any misunderstood points, if need be.

Sample open-ended questions during the confirmation stage for this same position include the following:

"I'm interested in learning more about your role in your company's monthly organizational orientation program. Would you please clarify for me the extent and nature of your responsibilities?"

"Earlier you stated that you currently assist in the implementation of policies and procedures. What exactly does that mean?"

"I need a clearer picture of when and to whom you explain or interpret these policies and procedures. Would you give me some additional information about this, as well as two specific examples?"

"Tell me more about your responsibilities regarding your organization's compensation program. Specifically, tell me about monitoring salary increase recommendations in relation to compliance with merit increase guidelines."

Not only will these open-ended questions (and occasional competency-based questions) help clarify and confirm preceding information, they inform the candidate that you have been paying attention.

Closing Stage

This is the "last-chance" stage of the interview. The interviewer can ensure coverage of all relevant proficiencies needed to make a screening or hiring decision, and the applicant has one last opportunity to sell himself. It represents 5 percent of the interview, and should be devoted to competency-based questions such as:

"What additional examples of your work with difficult customers would help me make a hiring decision?"

"What else can you tell me about your dealings with the GHK model that will help me understand your level of expertise in this area?"

"What more can you tell me about your work with employee assistance programs to enable me to understand your experience in this area?"

"What additional examples of your knowledge and/or expertise can you offer in support of your candidacy for this position?"

If applicants leave your office believing they have had every opportunity to present a complete and comprehensive picture of their job suitability, then it probably means you have acquired the information needed to determine a job match.

Questioning Techniques to Avoid

I once received a resumé that was later dubbed my "ay/yi/yi" resumé. Three pages were devoted to a string of no fewer than fifty "I" statements: "I am analytical." "I have excellent interpersonal skills." "I am good at solving problems." And so on. At the end of the third page, I still didn't know anything about the applicant's skills, abilities, or knowledge. That's because I had just finished reading a classic "trait" resumé—one that is big on meaningless rhetoric but short on substance.

Applicants may also provide trait responses during the interview as a substitute for specific examples. This is likely to happen in response to an open-ended question when a candidate lacks sufficient expertise and is hoping to impress with fancy words and phrases. For example, if you were to ask, "What is your greatest strength?" the applicant could reply, "I excel at problem solving." Good question; good answer, right? Not really. What have you learned about the candidate? If you want to know about a person's strengths, try the two-pronged approach. Ask, "What is your greatest strength?" and follow up with a competency-based question: "Give me an example of how you have used your greatest strength at your current job." Now if the applicant says, "I excel at problem solving" in response to the first question, she must back it up with a specific example. If she cannot, or rambles on with more rhetoric, you know she is giving you just so much verbiage.

Trait responses are also more likely to take you away from exploring negative areas. Applicants naturally stress strengths and attributes, and interviewers have a tendency to focus on the positive, hoping for the perfect match. Consequently, relevant negative characteristics tend to be overlooked, only to surface after the person has been hired. Interviewers are urged to explore negative information by asking competency-based questions that will provide evidence about past mistakes and problems. Open-ended, hypothetical, probing, and close-ended questions in these areas will also yield a balanced picture of the candidate's strengths and areas requiring improvement.

When a candidate is bombarding you with self-praise, it is hard to remember that he probably cannot do everything equally well. So when you ask about a person's strengths, examine the flip side and ask: "Tell me, what is it about yourself that you would like to improve on? Be specific about a time when that attribute or characteristic surfaced and hindered your ability to achieve desired results."

Another type of question to avoid is the *loaded or multiple-choice* question. Applicants should never feel they must choose between two or more alternatives. That kind of set-up implies that the correct answer is among the options you have offered, negating any additional possibilities. The applicant is likely to feel inhibited, and you are likely to miss out on valuable information.

Sometimes interviewers resort to loaded questions because they have lost control of the interview. If you want to regain control, ask a series of close-ended questions; then return to more meaningful competency-based questions or one of the other types of questions described earlier in this chapter.

Consider the following example of loaded questions—ones *not* to ask. Each one is paired with a rewording of the question that is more meaningful.

Don't Ask:	"How do you go about delegating tasks: according to what a person has proven he can do, demonstrated interest, or random selection?"
Do Ask:	"Describe how you go about delegating assignments. Give me an example of when you did this."
Don't Ask:	"Would you describe your management style as being akin to theory X, Y, or Z?"
Do Ask:	"How would you describe your management style? Give me an example of when you applied this style."
Don't Ask:	"Would you say the greatest motivator for working is money or the pleasure one derives from doing a good job?"

Do Ask: "What would you say is the greatest motivator for working? Why do you think this is so?"

Don't Ask: "Would you describe your previous manager as easy-going, or was he a stern taskmaster?"

Do Ask: "How would you describe your previous manager in terms of his work style and interaction with employees?"

Don't Ask: "Would you like to stay in this field for the rest of your career, or do you think you would like to do something else?"

Do Ask: "What are your short- and long-term goals?"

One other type of question to avoid is the *leading question,* one that implies that there is a single correct answer. The interviewer sets up the question so that the applicant provides the desired response. Here are some examples:

"You do intend to finish college, don't you?"
"Don't you agree that most workers need to be watched very closely?"
"When you were in school, how much time did you waste taking art and music classes?"

It is obvious from the wording of these questions that the interviewer is seeking a particular reply. When leading questions are asked, the interviewer cannot hope to learn anything substantive about the applicant.

Summary

Competency-based questions should be supplemented throughout the interview by a combination of open-ended, hypothetical, probing, and close-ended questions. Open-ended questions, requiring full, multiple-word inquiries, are most meaningful when asked during the introductory, core, and confirmation stages. Most open-ended questions can be made more substantive when followed by competency-based questions. Hypothetical questions are based on anticipated or known job-related tasks, phrased in the form of problems and presented to the applicant for solutions; they evaluate a person's reasoning abilities and thought processes. Hypotheticals are suitable during the core stage of the interview. Probing questions are short and simply worded, allowing interviewers to delve more deeply for additional information. Like hypotheticals, they are reserved for the core stage. Close-ended questions may be answered with a single word, usually yes or no. They should never be substituted for open-ended or competency-based questions. Close-ended questions should constitute the rapport-building stage and contribute to the core and confirmation stages.

There are three types of questions interviewers should avoid asking: trait, leading, and loaded. Trait questions generate answers that are filled with rhetoric but little substance. They also prohibit you from exploring negative information, that is, examining both a candidate's strengths and areas requiring improvement to provide a balanced picture. Loaded or multiple-choice questions offer limited options from which the applicant is forced to choose. And leading questions imply that there is a single correct answer.

Chapter 9

Conducting the Interview

Just as there are various interviewing techniques, so too, there are different employment interviews. The two that we will examine are the exploratory and the job specific. These types differ in content, structure, and overall objectives. Since the end result of an exploratory interview is a decision whether to continue with a job-specific meeting, elements of the job-specific interview—determining a format, establishing rapport, bridging small talk with the first question, practicing active listening, interpreting nonverbal communication, expressing words of encouragement, using silence, providing information, and knowing when and how to end the interview—are only touched upon during an exploratory interview.

Some modification in the application of these components during the job-specific interview may become necessary when meeting less-than-ideal candidates—ones who are excessively shy or nervous, overly talkative, overly aggressive or dominant, or highly emotional or distraught.

Sometimes, too, it is necessary to deviate from the standard one-on-one interview and instead conduct team interviews. Multiple interviewers can help or hinder interview results, depending on your approach and degree of preparation.

Conducting Exploratory Interviews

Exploratory interviews may be conducted under many circumstances, most typically during job fairs, at open houses, with a candidate in response to an ad, with professional applicants traveling a considerable distance at considerable expense (usually yours), during campus recruiting, and with walk-ins. In each instance the objective is the same: to establish continued interest on both sides and determine preliminary job suitability. Assuming these two conditions are satis-fied, the next step is to set up a job-specific interview. Under no cir-cumstances should interviewers substitute exploratory interviews for the in-depth job-specific interview or make a decision to hire based on the exploratory meeting.

Some exploratory interviews are conducted over the telephone (discussed in Chapter 5). These are usually with candidates in re-sponse to an ad or with professionals who will be traveling some distance for an interview. Most others, however, are conducted face to face. What distinguishes an exploratory interview is the amount of time allotted to asking questions. Interviewers must focus on key job-related issues, usually in a period of time ranging from fifteen to twenty minutes for a nonexempt applicant, and about thirty minutes for a professional candidate, and decide if a follow-up interview is warranted.

Under these conditions, interviewers often feel pressured into making a decision based on what they perceive to be limited informa-tion. Consequently, it can be tempting to dismiss a person for giving an inappropriate answer or even because of the way he dresses or shakes your hand. Using such non-job-related reasons as the basis for rejection, even at this early stage in the interview process, can be counterproductive for a number of reasons: you may be passing up a viable candidate, the applicant leaves with negative feelings about your organization (ones that he may well share with others), and it could lead to claims of discrimination based on "intent" (say, the minute you saw that the candidate was black, he was excluded from further consideration).

Time is limited in an exploratory interview, yet you can still make decisions based on solid, job-related information. The process of deciding who "passes" an exploratory interview begins with the job description. First, segregate those tasks that are essential; from that list, try to identify the tasks that require 20 percent or more of the incumbent's time. Many companies write their job descriptions so that each duty is coded as being essential or nonessential. Addi-tionally, they note an approximate percentage of time devoted to each task. These two steps, then, may already be completed. If there are none or just a few tasks that require 20 percent or more of the incum-bent's time, adjust the percentage downward so that you have some-where between four and eight essential tasks isolated. If necessary, isolate all essential tasks, even those requiring 5 percent or less time, in order to come up with half a dozen or so duties.

To illustrate, here is a sample job description for a business office manager. Preceding each task is an **E**, signifying an essential task, or

NE, for nonessential. Following each task is the approximate percentage of time devoted to each task:

    E   1. Plans, organizes, and controls the billing, receiving, and paying functions for the office. (25 percent)

    E   2. Reviews financial resources and collects delinquent accounts by direct contact or referral to collection agency. (20 percent)

    E   3. Prepares and distributes the payroll; establishes and maintains payroll records. (15 percent)

    E   4. Maintains flow of financial information with other departments. (10 percent)

    NE   5. Keeps current on new systems, methods, and equipment. (5 percent)

    NE   6. Performs HR functions in absence of manager; specifically, hiring, training, evaluating performance, and recommending salary increases. (5 percent)

    E   7. Ensures compliance with government regulations and participates in audits, as required. (5 percent)

    E   8. Informs management of current financial position and effect of operations by preparing and analyzing various reports. (10 percent)

    NE   9. Revises policies and procedures relevant to the business office function. (5 percent)

By segregating the essential functions, we end up with this:

1. Plans, organizes, and controls the billing, receiving, and paying functions for the office. (25 percent)
2. Reviews financial resources and collects delinquent accounts by direct contact or referral to collection agency. (20 percent)
3. Prepares and distributes the payroll; establishes and maintains payroll records. (15 percent)
4. Maintains flow of financial information with other departments. (10 percent)
5. Ensures compliance with government regulations and participates in audits, as required. (5 percent)
6. Informs management of current financial position and effect of operations by preparing and analyzing various reports. (10 percent)

Now we can isolate tasks that encompass 20 percent or more of the incumbent's time:

1. Plans, organizes, and controls the billing, receiving, and paying functions for the office. (25 percent)
2. Reviews financial resources and collects delinquent accounts by direct contact or referral to collection agency. (20 percent)

Since only two duties take up 20 percent or more time, other tasks need to be isolated:

3. Prepares and distributes the payroll; establishes and maintains payroll records. (15 percent)
4. Maintains flow of financial information with other departments. (10 percent)
5. Informs management of current financial position and effect of operations by preparing and analyzing various reports. (10 percent)

Now we have five out of the nine primary responsibilities that represent 80 percent of the job. This condensed job description will enable you to focus on the salient aspects of a candidate's experience and qualifications to determine preliminary job suitability.

Also, look at the category of "education, prior work experience, and specialized skills and knowledge." Eliminate excess verbiage and separate key requirements. For the business officer manager's job, you might extract the following:

1. Extensive experience—billing, receiving, payroll, and collection
2. Ability to prepare/analyze/present financial reports
3. Accounting degree desirable

Now, when interviewing candidates in a limited amount of time, you can focus on just five key tasks and three requirements.

The third and final step in preparing for an exploratory interview is to plan your format and the types of questions you will ask. Begin by explaining the purpose of the meeting, verify the available position, and, if your company policy permits, supply the starting salary or salary range. Ask what the applicant currently does (open-ended) and what her current salary is (close-ended). Then, based on the isolated tasks and educational requirements, ask a series of about six competency-based questions to determine the level and nature of her expertise. Wind down with one or two open-ended or close-ended questions, or both types, to confirm what she has told you. Your final question should be, "What else should I know about you in relation to your application for this job?" Probing questions are rarely intro-duced in exploratory interviews, unless the applicants' responses to competency-based questions are incomplete. Hypotheticals are omit-ted, as well, except where the applicant has no prior work experience to draw from.

Here is a sampling of questions from an exploratory interview with a walk-in for the business office manager's position:

> Good morning, Jessie. Thank you for stopping by today. I understand you are interested in our opening for a business office manager. Is that correct? [*answer*] That's fine.
>
> Jessie, this is an exploratory interview. That means we spend a few minutes discussing your interest and qualifi-cations. Then, if it appears that there is a sufficient match between your skills and the position requirements, and you are still interested in continuing, we can arrange a more in-depth interview for another time. How does that sound to you? [*answer*].
>
> Let me also confirm that you understand the salary range for this job is $37,500 to $44,000. Do you want to pro-ceed? [*answer*] Okay, fine. I'm going to ask you a few ques-tions now.
>
> First, why don't you begin by telling me about your activities in a typical day at your current job as an office manager. [*answer*]
>
> What are you currently earning? [*answer*]
>
> I'm interested in learning more about your billing, re-ceiving, and paying responsibilities. Give me one example to illustrate each of these areas. [*answer*]
>
> Tell me about a particularly difficult collection you had to make by direct contact. [*answer*]
>
> Describe a time when the payroll was delayed. What did you do? [*answer*]
>
> Tell me about another department with which you maintain a steady flow of financial information and the na-ture of that information. [*answer*]
>
> Describe the contents of the most recent financial re-port you prepared. [*answer*]
>
> May I safely assume from what you have told me that the bulk of your work is in billing and receiving? [*answer*]
>
> Am I also to understand that you have not had any experience in direct contact collections? [*answer*]

What else should I know about you in relation to your application for this job? [*answer*]

All right. Thank you again, Jessie, for your time and interest. I need to review your answers and will get back to you no later than Friday. Enjoy the rest of the day.

This sample exploratory interview would probably last about twenty minutes. Regardless of the outcome, the applicant should leave feeling that she had an opportunity to present her qualifications and will be judged on her abilities in relation to the job requirements. The interviewer, too, can leave the interview knowing he has asked enough relevant questions to make a preliminary decision whether to reject the candidate or continue with a fuller, job-specific interview.

Establishing the Format

Every job-specific interview requires a structured format. It should be practical and incorporate five concrete components:

1. Asking the applicant questions about his education and prior work history as they relate to the requirements of the job
2. Providing information about the job opening
3. Selling the company, in terms of its salary and benefits packages, growth opportunities, and the like
4. Allowing the applicant to ask questions
5. Telling the applicant what will happen following the interview.

Many interviewers believe that it is best to begin the interview by providing information about the job and the company before asking the applicant any questions. This is done for three primary reasons:

1. By providing this information at the outset, they are less likely to forget something.
2. If they wait to cover these areas until the end of the interview, they may run out of time.
3. With the interviewer doing most of the talking at the beginning of the interview, applicants are likely to feel more at ease.

This technique has one major drawback: providing too much information about the job before the applicant describes his capabilities. In many cases, interviewers inadvertently describe the kind of person they are looking for to such an extent that applicants can simply repeat this information later in the interview when describing their skills. An interviewer who is unaware of what is happening may erroneously assume that she has just found the ideal candidate.

Other approaches might be substituted. One suggestion is to begin by offering general information about the organization. This might include a brief description of its overall function and any historical information considered interesting. (Note that some interviewers prefer to test the applicant's knowledge of the company later in the interview.) You might also begin by briefly describing the job opening, to ensure that the person is applying for the same position that you are prepared to discuss. Or you can dive in with your first question. However, be aware that this can be unnerving if the applicant has not had a chance to get settled.

Some interviewers prefer to begin with a definitive statement as to what will take place. It might go something like this:

> "Good morning, Mr. Turner. My name is Daniel King. I am going to be interviewing you for the position of marketing representative with our company. I will begin by giving you an overview of our organization and then ask you some questions about your background and qualifications. I will then describe the responsibilities of the available position. At that point, I will answer any remaining question you may have about the job or our company. Before we conclude, I will let you know when you may expect to hear from us."

This is a very formal approach. If it is accompanied by the appropriate body language and tone of voice, applicants can be made to feel comfortable. Certainly, with this format there will be no doubt as to the content of the interview.

Other interviewers have a more relaxed style, and therefore their format is less structured. They might begin by saying:

> "Hi, Bob. I'm Dan King. I see you're applying for a marketing rep opening. Why don't I talk a little bit about our company, and then you can tell some things about yourself. If you think of any questions as we're talking, just jump right in and ask me."

Still others are extremely flexible and capable of conducting both formal and informal interviews. These interviewers quickly assess an applicant's general composure and comfort level prior to the interview, and adjust their approach accordingly. Applicants who appear to be nervous will be met with a casual, relaxed approach. Candidates who seem rather formal will benefit from a more structured format.

It is important that the system you decide on reflects your own personality and style. If you are more comfortable outlining the format of the interview at the outset, that is fine. If you prefer to begin with a brief overview of the company and the job, then proceed to answer any questions, filling in as you go along, that will work as well. As long as you feel at ease, the applicant is likely to respond well to whatever format you select.

Establishing Rapport

Regardless of the format you use, take a few moments at the beginning of the interview to establish a rapport with the applicant. As discussed in Chapter 8, this is generally accomplished during the first stage of the interview with icebreakers: comments and questions that have no real bearing on the job. Their sole purpose is to put the applicant at ease before the substantive part of the interview. Some popular icebreakers were identified in that segment.

Just how much time should be spent on icebreakers depends on how comfortable the applicant appears to be. Typically fifteen to thirty seconds is sufficient. Sometimes a little longer will be needed. But under no circumstances should this stage of the interview continue for more than a few minutes. Applicants who are still uneasy after this amount of time will probably not respond to additional small talk. The best thing to do in this instance is to ask your first job-related question.

Asking the First Question

Getting started with the core of the interview is often difficult. Some interviewers get caught up in small talk and do not seem able to move on. Others want to get started but have difficulty making the transition from the icebreakers to the first important question. Still others simply do not know what to ask first.

If you tend to get too involved with icebreakers, consciously limit your time to two minutes. Be certain to select topics that cannot be developed into lengthy discussions. You may also want to limit yourself to two questions. Self-discipline is the key.

For those who need help in making the transition from small talk to the first question, consider integrating the topic of your icebreaker into a transitional statement. For example:

"I'm glad you didn't have any trouble getting here. I'm anxious to begin talking with you about your interest in our opening for a marketing representative."

"I'm sorry you had trouble finding parking. I know that those meters where you finally found a space allow only one hour. Why don't we get started, so that you can be sure to get back to your car before the meter expires?"

"With the weather so beautiful, I'm sure that you're anxious to get back outside, so why don't we get started?"

"Why don't we get started with the interview. It should help take your mind off the fact that you got soaked coming over here."

These statements create a bridge between one stage of the interview and another, thereby eliminating the awkward silence or stammering that can easily occur. Having made this link, you can move on to ask job-related questions, as discussed in Chapter 7 and 8.

Practicing Active Listening

To make sure that you do not miss anything the candidate is saying, learn and practice active listening skills. Listening to what the candidate says in response to the icebreaker questions at the beginning of the interview is very different from listening to the answers during the core of the interview. Icebreaker listening is very casual; active listening requires greater concentration. Following are some guidelines to active listening:

• *Talk less; listen more.* Many interviewers talk entirely too much. No more than 30 percent of your time should be devoted to talking: asking questions about the applicant's qualifications, clarifying points, providing information about the job and the organization, and answering job-related questions. The remaining 70 percent of time should be spent actively listening.

• *Listen for connecting themes and ideas.* By not focusing on every word, interviewers are better able to concentrate on key job-related information.

• *Summarize periodically.* Applicants do not always provide complete answers to questions at one time. Frequently, you must fit the pieces together. To make certain that you are doing this accurately, periodically stop and summarize. To illustrate: "Let me make certain that I understand exactly what you have accomplished in this area. You weren't directly responsible for running the department, but your boss was away about 25 percent of the time, and during that time you ran the department. Is this correct?" The applicant may then say, "Well, I didn't exactly run the department. If there were any problems, it was up to me to get in touch with the boss to find out what we should do." This clarifies the scope and extent of the applicant's responsibility.

• *Filter out distractions.* Distractions can include people coming into your office, the telephone ringing, and having your thoughts focused elsewhere, which can easily occur when applicants are not interesting to listen to. Maybe the work they do strikes you as being dull, or perhaps they speak in a monotone. When this happens, you may find yourself thinking about that last vacation in Mexico and how you would prefer to be there right now. If you find this is happening, consider that not all positions require effective verbal communication skills. The fact that an applicant is not a skilled speaker may be irrelevant to the job. It is unfair to judge people on the basis of how well they are able to hold your interest. By not listening actively, you are likely to miss important information that could influence the final hiring decision.

• *Use free information.* Every time an applicant opens his mouth, you get free information. If you do not listen actively, you are going to miss valuable insights. Free information should be the foundation for many of your interview questions.

• *Screen out personal biases.* Do not allow personal views or opinions to interfere with active listening.

• *Use thought speed.* This is a wonderful tool. Most people think at a rate of approximately 400 words per minute; we speak at a rate of approximately 125 words per minute. Obviously, this means that we think faster than we speak, but there is much more to thought speed than this. While the applicant is talking, you can use thought speed to accomplish the following:

• Prepare your next question.
• Analyze what the applicant is saying.
• Piece together what the applicant is saying now in relation to something said earlier in the interview.

- Glance down at the application and/or resumé to verify information.
- Observe body language.
- Consider how this candidate's background relates to the job requirements.
- Take notes.

Thought speed can also work to your detriment, if you anticipate how applicants are going to complete their responses before they finish, jump to conclusions too soon, compare a candidate's responses with those of a previous applicant, get too involved in note taking, or just tune out the applicant.

Interpreting Nonverbal Communication

As discussed in Chapter 5, perception of nonverbal communication is a vital aspect of the interviewing process. It can clarify conflicting verbal messages and often speaks for itself—or it can easily be misused and erroneously interpreted. In addition to what was already mentioned in Chapter 5, here are some more points to keep in mind with regard to nonverbal communication, or body language.

Body language encompasses more than facial expressions, body movements, and gestures. It also refers to pauses in speech, speech rate, vocal tone, pitch, and enunciation. Together, all of these factors "speak" to an interviewer from the very first moment of contact. Often the message can be confusing. For example, body movements such as finger or foot tapping can contradict facial expressions such as smiling. Similarly, an applicant may maintain direct eye contact while answering a question, an indication that she has a high degree of self-confidence, but the vocal tone conveys just the opposite. The situation may be further complicated when, coupled with this, the interviewer tries to assess the content of what is being said. The conflict between the verbal and nonverbal message can be confusing, leaving the interviewer wondering which message is the more accurate. Since verbal messages are clearly easier to control than nonverbal ones, when there is a conflict between the verbal and the nonverbal, the nonverbal is often more persuasive. This may be accurate, however, only to the extent that the person's nonverbal messages are being interpreted correctly.

Nonverbal communication cannot be universally translated. That is, a gesture that you use to express a certain feeling may mean something entirely different when someone else uses it. For example, in the United States, nodding the head commonly indicates an affirmative answer or understanding. In the Middle East, a single nod means no.

This difference in interpretation occurs not only across diverse cultures. As a result of our individual socialization processes, each of us develops our own pattern of nonverbal messages. We tend to react to a situation in the same nonverbal way each time that it occurs. For example, the applicant who nervously clasps his hands while waiting to be interviewed is likely to do the same thing each time he is nervous. Therefore, although there are no universal interpretations to body language cues, each of us has our own nonverbal pattern that may be consistently translated if observed over a period of time.

Even though there are no universal translations of any one gesture, people tend to interpret certain movements in a given way. The following list illustrates this point:

Nonverbal Message	Typical Interpretation
Making direct eye contact	Friendly, sincere, self-confident, assertive
Avoiding eye contact	Cold, evasive, indifferent, insecure, passive, frightened, nervous
Shaking head	Disagreeing, shocked, disbelieving
Yawning	Bored
Patting on the back	Encouraging, congratulatory, consoling
Scratching the head	Bewildered, disbelieving
Smiling	Contented, understanding, encouraging
Biting the lip	Nervous, fearful, anxious
Tapping feet	Nervous, impatient
Folding arms	Angry, disapproving, disagreeing, defensive, aggressive
Raising eyebrows	Disbelieving, surprised
Narrowing eyes	Disagreeing, resentful, angry, disapproving
Flaring nostrils	Angry, frustrated

Wringing hands	Nervous, anxious, fearful
Leaning forward	Attentive, interested
Slouching in seat	Bored, relaxed
Sitting on edge of seat	Anxious, nervous, apprehensive
Shifting in seat	Restless, bored, nervous, apprehensive
Hunching over	Insecure, passive
Having erect posture	Self-confident, assertive

Paul Ekman, a researcher in nonverbal communication, focuses on facial expressions as a means for interpreting certain emotions. His Facial Affect Scoring Technique (FAST) claims to identify six constants that assess the facial aspect of nonverbal communication. Ekman maintains that disgust is shown in the nose, cheeks, and mouth; fear appears in the eyes; sadness, in the brows, mouth, and eyes; anger, in the forehead and brows; and surprise, in any facial area.

Interviewers are cautioned against assigning a specific meaning to a given movement or facial expression until they have identified certain nonverbal patterns and can be fairly certain that their interpretation is correct. For this reason, applicants should not be sized up within the first few minutes of an interview, and complete interviews should last for at least thirty minutes.

Interviewers should be aware of any sudden changes in nonverbal communication. For example, if an applicant has been sitting quite comfortably for twenty minutes or so, and then suddenly shifts in her seat when you ask why she left her last job, this is a clue that something is amiss. Even if the applicant offers an acceptable response without hesitation, the sudden change in body language should tell you that something is wrong. Additional probing is necessary. The conflict between the verbal and the nonverbal should not be ignored.

Also be careful not to interpret a person's body language erroneously according to his reaction to yours. If you are not aware of your own body language, you may incorrectly assume that an applicant is initiating a nonverbal message instead of reacting to your own. It is critical to be aware of your own body language in terms of how you react to certain emotions or situations.

Your nonverbal responses can be controlled once you are aware of them. It is important to do this during an interview, since your goal is to evaluate the applicant as objectively as possible. It is difficult enough to make a value judgment; adding elements that may not be valid can only serve to make it harder. For example, suppose that you had a fender bender on the way into work and consequently are in a bad mood. If you are not conscious of the body language that you are projecting as a result of this mishap, the applicant may assume that you are reacting negatively to something on his resumé or something that he has said in response to one of your questions. This is perfectly understandable. After all, how many of us are so secure or self-confident that we would think, "Oh, I know it couldn't possibly have anything to do with me"?

Also, remember that when it comes to perception versus how you really may be feeling, it is perception that counts. Try asking a friend or colleague to observe you during a meeting or throughout a typical workday. Periodically ask for feedback. Ask the person what she perceives your mood to be at a given moment based on your nonverbal messages. Remember, the interpretation may differ from what you are actually feeling. This simple exercise can help you understand your patterns and thus help you control your body language during an interview.

By being aware of your own nonverbal communication, you can consciously choose to project certain nonverbal messages to applicants. For instance, by knowing that nodding one's head is generally interpreted as a sign of understanding, you can use this gesture to encourage an applicant to continue talking. If you are aware that leaning forward in one's chair implies interest or attentiveness, you can assume this position when interviewing in order to indicate interest in whatever the applicant is saying.

Encouraging the Applicant to Talk

One of the greatest challenges for an interviewer is encouraging an applicant to talk. Of course, some applicants are well prepared, self-confident, and more than willing to converse with you. Indeed, it is difficult to prevent some of them from talking too much and for too long. With others, however, talking to an interviewer can be intimidating and unnerving; regardless of how much they may want the job, selling themselves may be very difficult. Therefore, you must help them. Here are six ways in which you can encourage an applicant to speak freely:

1. *Use repetition.* This encourages the applicant to continue talking and also helps to clarify certain points. Repeating the last few

words of an applicant's statement and letting your voice trail off as a question mark will encourage the person to elaborate. For example, suppose that the last point an applicant made was, "The most difficult part of being a manager was that I was in charge of twenty-five people." You could follow up by saying, "You supervised twenty-five people . . . ?" The applicant might then reply, "Well, not directly. I was in charge of three supervisors, each of whom monitored the work of about seven workers." To clarify, you might say: "So you were directly responsible for supervising three people. Is this correct?" The applicant would then state, "Yes, that is correct, although my supervisors always came to me when they were having trouble with their workers."

This dialogue presents a far more accurate picture of the applicant's supervisory responsibilities than did the original statements. Using repetition encouraged the applicant to provide valuable additional information.

2. *Summarize.* Like repetition, this allows the candidate to clarify the points made thus far in the interview and to elaborate as necessary. It further ensures an accurate understanding on your part. Summarization may be used at specific time intervals in the interview, say, every ten minutes or so after a certain topic has been discussed. For instance, you and the candidate may have just devoted approximately ten minutes to reviewing his prior work experience as it relates to the available position. At that point, you might say: "Let me make certain that I understand what you have said thus far. All of your employment since graduating high school has been as a mechanic. This includes the time that you spent in the Marine Corps. You enjoy this line of work and want to continue doing it. However, you feel that you were underpaid at your last job and that's why you left. Is all of this correct?"

The applicant can now confirm all or part of what you have just summarized. Be careful not to include more than four or five statements in your summary. If part of it is inaccurate or requires clarification, it will not be difficult to isolate. Also, in order to ensure accuracy, make certain to employ the active listening guidelines outlined earlier in this chapter.

3. *Try close-ended questions.* Asking competency-based questions will yield the most information, but some applicants have difficulty talking and may initially respond better to a series of *direct, close-ended questions.* These are effective when used for the limited purpose of allowing the applicant to achieve a certain comfort level before moving on to the more information-producing forms of inquiry.

4. *Employ certain phrases to encourage an applicant to continue talking.* These phrases include "I see." "How interesting." "Is that right?" "Really?" and "I didn't know that." None of these phrases expresses an opinion or shows agreement or disagreement; they merely show interest and understanding.

5. *Use encouraging body language.* In order for these phrases of understanding to be effective, they must be accompanied by *encouraging body language*—for example, nodding, smiling, direct eye contact, and leaning forward. Conveying these nonverbal messages consistently throughout the interview will establish your interest in what the applicant is saying, thereby encouraging the person to provide additional information.

6. *Silence.* Most people find silence to be awkward and uncomfortable. Consequently, interviewers often feel compelled to talk whenever the applicant stops. However, unless you are prepared to ask another question, talking when you need additional information from the applicant will not help with your hiring decision. When the applicant stops talking and you want him to continue, try silently and slowly counting to five before speaking. This pause often compels a candidate to go on. Of course, you must be careful not to carry silence too far. The interview can easily become a stressful situation if you simply continue to stare at an applicant who has nothing more to say or needs your encouragement to continue. However, if you combine silence with positive body language, the applicant should continue talking within a few seconds. Silence clearly conveys the message that more information is wanted.

Providing Information

Ascertaining information about the applicant is only part of the interview; providing information to the applicant is also important. Just as interviewers must decide if candidates are appropriate for a job, candidates must decide whether the job and company are right for them. This is particularly true when unemployment is low and applicants can afford to be selective about job opportunities.

Many interviewers erroneously assume that applicants come to the interview armed with information about both the company and the job opening. Perhaps there was a detailed description in the newspaper advertisement to which the applicant responded. Maybe the applicant has been referred by a long-term employee who has extensive knowledge of the company and the available job. Or perhaps, while waiting in the reception area, the applicant was seen perusing the company's annual report or newsletter. It is also possible that the candidate is a former employee or has been away on a leave of absence. Regardless of how much the applicant may presumably or actually know, interviewers are responsible for informing all job candidates about certain aspects of the company and the available position. In this way, applicants will be certain to understand key elements of their prospective employment.

Information about the job and company may be provided at the beginning of the interview or may be sprinkled throughout, between asking and answering questions. However, care must be given not to give away too much regarding the characteristics of an ideal candidate in the early stages of the interview.

Generally interviewers should inform applicants about the organization in terms of what it does and how long it has been in business, as well as providing brief statements about its origins, growth to date, and projected growth. They should also provide a brief summary of company benefits. Then they can offer more specific information concerning the department that has the opening: its function, the different tasks performed, how it interrelates with other departments, a description of who is in charge, the chain of command, and the work environment.

This naturally leads to a description of the specific job opening, details of which may be offered by providing the applicant with a copy of the job description. Allow her a few moments to read it and then encourage questions based on its contents. If the job description is comprehensive and well written, this process will ensure a clear understanding of what the job entails and requires. Be certain to cover growth opportunities available through job posting, career planning, training programs, tuition reimbursement, or other in-house or outside means for career development. Also review any negative features as they pertain to, say, working conditions or the work schedule. Let the applicant react now, during the interview, rather than later, as a disgruntled employee.

Whether salary is discussed depends on your company's policy. It is advisable for interviewers to provide at least general information about the range for an given job. Tell the applicant if the salary is fixed and nonnegotiable.

Also offer a brief description of the neighborhood surrounding the workplace: transportation options, restaurants, stores, and, since we have become increasingly health conscious, any local health or exercise facilities.

Finally, be certain to inform the applicant what will occur after the interview is over: approximately when she may expect to hear from you, whether it is likely that there will be additional interviews, and what to do if she has additional questions. Be certain you have the applicant's current telephone number and address so there will be no problem with future communication.

Interviewing Less-Than-Ideal Candidates

Most applicants are eager to make a good impression on the interviewer. They try to answer all questions as fully as possible, project positive body language, and ask appropriate questions. Occasionally, however, you will find yourself face-to-face with a less-than-ideal or difficult candidate, someone who falls into one of the following categories: excessively shy or nervous, overly talkative, overly aggressive or dominant, or highly emotional or distraught.

At the first indication that you are dealing with a difficult candidate, make certain adjustments in how you conduct the interview.

Excessively Shy or Nervous Applicants

Within the first few seconds of the icebreaker portion of the interview, it will become apparent if an applicant is especially shy or nervous. This type of person needs to be drawn out slowly; a broad, open-ended question might be too intimidating if used right off the bat. Instead, try a few close-ended inquiries to put the candidate at ease. Make them simple, relating to areas likely to make the applicant feel comfortable. Also make certain that your first competency-based or open-ended question pertains to a topic within the individual's experience, thereby ensuring a certain degree of ease. In addition, try using a softer tone of voice than you may typically, exaggerated positive body language, and words of encouragement. Let the applicant know that you are interested in what she has to say.

Overly Talkative Applicants

Some candidates seem capable of talking nonstop. They not only answer your questions, but volunteer a great deal more information, much of which is irrelevant, unnecessary, and sometimes inappropriate for you to know. Such people are often very personable and really quite delightful to talk with. However, remind yourself that you are not there to engage in a social conversation. Your goal is to acquire sufficient information on which to base a hiring decision.

The key to dealing effectively with applicants who talk too much is control. Remember that you are in charge of the interview, and control the amount of time devoted to questions and answers. When you have gathered enough data, say to the applicant: "Everything you have told me is very interesting. I now have enough information upon which to base my decision. Thank you very much for your time. You will be hearing from us by the end of this week."

Sometimes applicants do not respond to a cue to leave. They remain seated and resume talking. If this occurs, escalate your efforts somewhat. Tell the applicant, "I am afraid that is all the time we have. I do have other applicants waiting." At this point, stand up and extend your hand. As you shake hands, gently guide the applicant to the door.

Overly Aggressive Applicants

Some applicants present themselves in an overly aggressive or hostile manner. Perhaps they have been out of work for a long time, or maybe they have applied for a job with your company before and were rejected. When confronted with an angry applicant, stay calm and maintain your objectivity. Try to find out why the applicant is so upset. Explain that you cannot continue the interview as long as he remains agitated. Try to complete the interview and judge the applicant as fairly as possible, taking into account extenuating circumstances.

Dominant Applicants

At times an applicant will try to gain control of the interview, usually to cover up for a lack of sufficient job experience. The attempted takeover may manifest itself in a variety of ways, for instance, by steering the conversation to a discussion of the interviewer's career or interests, or discussing books or photos in the office. If this takes place during the interview, all is not lost. Remind yourself that you are in charge and say to the applicant: "Excuse, me, but we seem to have strayed. Let's get back to. . . ."

Highly Emotional or Distraught Applicants

An applicant who begins to weep in your office can be quite unnerving. If this happens, extending empathy rather than sympathy will enable you to remain objective, in charge, and better able to help the individual regain composure. Offering the person a few moments of privacy usually enables most applicants to continue with the interview. In some instances, however, it may be preferable to reschedule the interview.

Occasionally, applicants become emotional or distraught when you challenge an answer to a particular question. If this occurs, stop and return to the question later, perhaps after a better rapport has been established. Emphasize to the applicant that the information is vital for continued consideration. This message is usually sufficient encouragement for even the most reluctant applicant.

Sometimes it is helpful to pose a series of very specific, close-ended questions. Another way to encourage applicants to answer is to indicate that a reference check will be made.

Team Interviewing

Most interviews involve two people: the interviewer and the applicant. Occasionally, however, the team approach is used. This involves up to three interviewers: usually an HR representative, the department supervisor or manager, and possibly a division head. Team interviews are commonly done for one of two reasons: (1) to save the time it would take to schedule three separate interviews and (2) to compare impressions of the applicant.

If carefully planned, team interviews can be highly effective. The role of each participant should be agreed upon ahead of time. Perhaps the HR representative will begin by introducing everyone, making small talk to establish rapport, and asking some broad questions to determine overall job suitability. Then the supervisor or manager will ask more detailed, technical questions. Finally the division head will pursue the candidate's potential and other intangible factors.

Applicants should always be advised in advance that the team approach will be used. Otherwise, it can be unnerving to see more than one interviewer in the room.

Seating should be carefully arranged. Unlike a one-on-one interview, where the proximity of the interviewer's chair to the applicant's is inconsequential, improper seating in a team interview situation can create an uncomfortable environment. Do not, for example, surround the candidate's chair. As Figure 9-1 illustrates, this places one seat on either side and one directly in front, resulting in a "tennis match" sort of interview, with the candidate continually turning his head from one side to the other, trying to address all members of the team.

Figure 9-1. Surrounding the candidate.

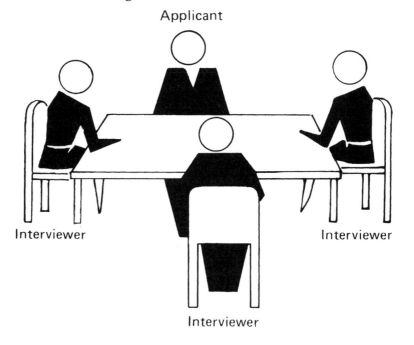

Applicant

Interviewer   Interviewer

Interviewer

Instead, offer the applicant a seat and form a soft arc in front of him. As Figure 9-2 illustrates, this setting is less structured and more conducive to a productive exchange.

Avoiding Stress Interviews

In a stress interview the applicant is deliberately put on guard, made to feel ill at ease, or "tested" for some purpose known only to the interviewer. *This technique is not recommended under any circumstance.* Proponents of stress interviewing claim that they ferret out some significant job-related traits: how applicants will handle uncomfortable situations that cannot be discovered through questioning, assessing nonverbal communication skills, weighing intangible factors, and so forth. In truth, stress interviews are often nothing more than a smokescreen for ineffective interviewing skills.

Since stress interviews are occasionally used, however, examples are cited here *Readers are urged to view these* as *illustrations of what to avoid!*

Stress Interviews in the Office

Stress interviews in the office usually involve various "props," such as chairs, exaggerated body language on the part of the inter-

Figure 9-2. Suggested arrangement for a team interview.

Applicant

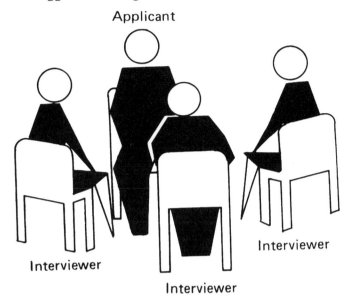

Interviewer

Interviewer

Interviewer

viewer, or unnecessary, sometimes inappropriate, comments. Here are some examples:

• The interviewer slowly eyes the applicant from head to toe, staring for some time at the candidate's feet. Finally he says, "I never would have worn those socks with those shoes."

• The interviewer makes certain that her chair is considerably higher than that of the applicant.

• The interviewer invites the applicant to sit in an oversized chair, making it difficult for the applicant to rise up out of it.

• The interviewer invites the applicant to sit in a chair with one leg slightly shorter than the others, causing it to wobble.

• The applicant is offered a chair more suitable for a five-year-old.

• The applicant is offered a chair that faces the window. On a sunny day, with the drapes open, the interviewer repositions the chair according to the time of day so that the sun will shine directly in the applicant's eyes.

• The interviewer positions himself in front of a window on a sunny day with the drapes open, thereby causing a "halo" effect around his head.

• The interviewer begins firing questions at the applicant as soon as she enters the room.

• The interviewer does not ask the applicant any questions. Rather, he simply stares at the applicant, waiting to see what the person will say or do.

• The interviewer asks questions while looking down at her desk or while doing other work.

• The interviewer answers the telephone during the course of the interview, puts the person on hold, turns to the applicant, and says, "Go ahead. I can keep him on hold for a minute."

• The interviewer makes a series of telephone calls during the interview.

• The interviewer leaves the room for several minutes.

• The interviewer begins by saying, "Go ahead. Impress me."

• The interviewer begins by saying, "Is there anything you'd like to tell me?"

• The interviewer asks the applicant, "Do you always wear your hair that way?"

• The interviewer takes her watch off, places it on the desk, and says, "We have exactly forty-five minutes."

• After responding to a question, the applicant is asked, "Are you sure that's the answer you want to give?"

• The interviewer stares at the applicant for some time and finally says, "You're rather young, aren't you?"

• The interview is conducted in an open area, where other interviews are taking place simultaneously. The interviewer begins listening to a conversation between another interviewer and applicant and soon begins asking questions of the other applicant.

Mealtime Stress Interviews

Mealtime interviews are generally reserved for professional-level applicants. They can be appropriate and, indeed, quite comfortable for both the interviewer and the applicant if the same guidelines that govern office interviews are adhered to. Unfortunately, meals also provide an ideal arena for proponents of stress interviews, based on the justification that eating and drinking habits may be a valid reflection of decision making on the job. Consider these examples:

• The interviewer waits until the applicant has a mouthful of soup before asking a question.

• The applicant is rejected because he orders food that requires direct handling with his hands (say, a cheeseburger). The premise here is that an applicant should assume that he will be asked to review papers during the course of a mealtime interview. This cannot be done with greasy fingers.

• The applicant is rejected because she orders shrimp scampi when the interviewer orders a chef's salad. The point here is that the scampi takes approximately eight bites to complete, while the salad requires more like one hundred bites to consume. Therefore, the applicant will be finished eating long before the interviewer, leaving the latter feeling rushed.

• The applicant accepts the offer of a alcoholic beverage and is rejected on the basis that he might have a tendency to drink too much.

• The applicant refuses an offer of an alcoholic drink and is rejected on the basis that she might formerly have had a drinking problem.

• The applicant is rejected for refusing to check his coat upon entering the restaurant, the assumption being that this person is insecure about parting with possessions.

• The applicant is evaluated on her knowledge of the correct utensils to use during various points in the meal.

• The applicant is found acceptable because he orders something from the menu that costs the same as or less than what the interviewer orders.

• The interviewer fires a steady stream of open-ended questions at the applicant as soon as her food arrives, to see whether she can eat and talk at the same time.

• The interviewer tries to slip in some non-job-related questions during the meal.

• The interviewer assesses the applicant's level of assertiveness in dealing with a disagreeable waiter.

• The interviewer identifies several other diners who work at the same organization. Later in the meal, the applicant is asked about them to determine how closely he was paying attention.

Knowing When and How to Close the Interview

Just as some interviewers have trouble knowing how to begin interviews, others are uncertain how to terminate them. To help you decide if it is time to end an interview, ask yourself the following questions:

- Have I asked the applicant enough questions about her education and previous experience to determine job suitability?
- Have I adequately described the available position and provided sufficient information about this organization?
- Have I discussed salary, benefits, growth opportunities, and other related topics to the extent the policy of this company permits?
- Have I allowed the applicant to ask questions?

If your answer to all four questions is yes, then you are ready to make your closing remarks. These should entail telling the applicant what will happen next—for example:

> "Well, Ms. Ryan, I believe that I have all the information I need. If I have answered all your questions, I would like to close by telling you what will happen now. We still have a dozen or so candidates to interview throughout the remainder of this week. After that, we will check references and make our final selection. Everyone will be notified by mail regarding our decision. In the interim, if you have any additional questions, please do not hesitate to call me. I want to thank you for coming in. I have enjoyed talking with you."

Interviewing Guidelines and Pitfalls

With all that has been said thus far about the face-to-face interview, it is a good idea to review these important guidelines:

1. Conduct exploratory interviews to determine continued interest and preliminary job suitability.

2. Establish a format that encompasses all of the important ingredients of an interview. Be sure that it reflects your own style and personality.

3. Establish rapport by taking a few moments out at the beginning of an interview to put the applicant at ease.

4. Carefully select your first question so that the answer will yield additional categories to explore.

5. Practice active listening skills, concentrating closely on what the applicant says and talking no more than 30 percent of the time.

6. Practice positive nonverbal communication skills. Employ gestures and movements that are likely to be interpreted in an encouraging way. Also, strive for consistency between your verbal statements and nonverbal expressions.

7. Encourage the applicant to talk via repetition, summarization, direct close-ended questions, encouraging phrases, positive body language, and silence.

8. Provide information, making certain that the applicant has a clear and complete understanding of both the organization and the job.

9. Consider different types of interview questions and the most appropriate stages for asking them. Choose from among competency-based, open-ended, hypothetical, probing, and close-ended questions. Make certain all questions produce information about relevant education and prior work experience.

10. Adjust your approach when dealing with less-than-ideal applicants, such as those who are excessively shy or nervous, overly talkative, overly aggressive or dominant, or highly emotional or distraught.

11. Plan team interviews carefully, including the seating arrangement as well as the role played by each team member.

12. End a job-specific interview when you have acquired sufficient information upon which to base a hiring decision, have allowed the applicant to ask questions, and have explained what happens next.

In addition to these guidelines, there are some pitfalls that interviewers should try to avoid:

- Avoid interrupting the applicant, as long as he is saying something relevant.
- Avoid agreement or disagreement. Instead, express interest and understanding.
- Avoid using terminology that the applicant is unlikely to be familiar with.
- Avoid reading the application or resumé back to the applicant.
- Avoid comparisons with the incumbent, previous employees, yourself, or other candidates.
- Avoid asking unrelated questions.
- Avoid talking down to an applicant.
- Avoid talking about yourself.

- Avoid hiring an unqualified applicant simply because you are desperate to fill an opening.
- Avoid trying to duplicate someone else's interviewing style.
- Avoid allowing applicants to interview you or to control the interview.
- Avoid hasty decisions based solely on first impressions, information from others, a single response, nonverbal communication, or your biases.
- Avoid asking questions, even in a roundabout way, that might be considered violations of equal employment opportunity laws.
- Avoid judging applicants on the basis of cultural or educational differences.
- Avoid conducting stress interviews of any sort.

Summary

Conducting a face-to-face meeting involves more than just asking a series of questions. Exploratory interviews require the isolation of key job skills and requirements, focusing on whether there is sufficient interest and ability to continue with a job-specific interview. The latter encompasses the integration of numerous components, including establishing a format, building rapport, bridging small talk with the first question, practicing active listening, accurately interpreting nonverbal communication, encouraging the applicant to talk, providing information about the job and company, and knowing when and how to end the interview.

Interviewing becomes especially challenging when meeting with less-than-ideal candidates—those who are excessively shy, overly talkative, overly aggressive or dominant, or highly emotional.

Sometimes it is preferable to deviate from the standard one-on-one interview set-up, and conduct team interviews. This can be effective as long as the applicant is advised in advance and all the interviewers prepare for the role they will play.

All interviewers, even seasoned ones, will find it helpful to review periodically the enumerated summary of interviewing guidelines and pitfalls.

Chapter 10
Writing Up the Interview

One benefit of active listening is that interviewers can take notes while the applicant is talking without losing track of what is being said. Thanks to thought speed, you can write down key words and ideas during the interview and then, immediately after, develop your notes more fully. Doing this right away will ensure that you retain important facts.

Why Take Notes

Some interviewers believe that note taking will offend applicants or make them uneasy. If you feel this way, tell the applicant at the beginning of the interview that you will be taking some notes to make certain that you have sufficient information with which to base an effective evaluation. Many applicants will not mind, even preferring that you do take notes. After all, most jobs have many candidates competing for them. With so many people being considered for each position, how can the interviewer differentiate among candidates without notes? In fact, *not* taking any notes could convey a lack of interest; consequently, the applicant may lose interest in the job.

The notes taken are a permanent record of your interview and should be written with care. Whether you use a separate preprinted form (as illustrated with Appendix G) or a blank piece of paper, the same guidelines relating to your notes or documentation apply. (Interviewers are advised against writing directly on the employment application or resumé.)

In addition to serving as a permanent record of an interview, documentation enables the interviewer to assess a particular applicant's job suitability. After the interview process is completed and all candidates have been seen, the interview notes for each should be placed side by side with the job description. The interviewer may then compare the applicant's relevant experience, skills, and accomplishments, as documented, with the requirements, duties, and responsibilities of the available opening, as outlined in the job description.

Postinterview documentation may also be used to compare the notes on those applicants in the final running. All relevant factors should be identified with the backgrounds and qualifications of each candidate measured against the others.

Moreover, these notes will prove useful to the original interviewer as well as others considering rejected applicants for future job openings. Finally, postinterview documentation is frequently scrutinized as potential evidence in employment discrimination suits.

Avoiding Subjective Language

Avoiding subjective language, even if complimentary, is an important requirement for effective postinterview documentation. Stated another way, all comments that are written down should be objective. For example, saying that an applicant is attractive is a subjective statement. On the other hand, writing that "the applicant's appearance is consistent with the employee image desired by the organization for this position" is objective.

As you can see from this example, objective language generally takes longer to write and requires greater effort. It is clearly much easier to say that someone is attractive than it is to write the objective version of the same thought. However, the term *attractive* may not mean the same thing to everyone as it does to you; hence, it would not be useful to future interviewers reviewing your notes, or even to you if your opinion as to what constitutes attractiveness changes over time. In addition, it could create an issue in an equal employment opportunity investigation.

Following are some additional examples of subjective language to avoid:

Abrasive	Boring
Acted high	Calculating
Acted like a real know-it-all	Careless
Appears to be rich	Chip on his shoulder
A real sales job	Cocky
A real workaholic	Cultured
Arrogant	Curt
Bad dresser	Diligent

Easily distracted	Personable
Eccentric	Polished
Energetic	Pompous
Erratic	Pontificates
Fake smile	Pretentious
Fidgety	Refined
Full of hot air	Reserved
Good sense of humor	Restless
Greedy	Rude
Has a bad attitude	Sarcastic
Ideal candidate	Sharp
Ingenious	Shrewd
Interesting	Sloppy
Jovial	Sluggish
Lacks luster	Smart
Looks like a model	Snappy dresser
Looks too old	Somber
Makes lots of mistakes	Tactful
Manipulative	Too hyper
Money hungry	Too much makeup
Narrow-minded	Too pushy
Needs polish	Tried too hard
No roots	Uptight
No sense of humor	Vain
Not serious about working	Very nervous
Perfect	

To contrast, here are some examples of objective language:

"This job requires prior customer service experience; applicant has two years' experience as a customer service representative."

"This job calls for excellent verbal skills; applicant exhibited job specific verbal skills during our sixty-minute interview."

"This job includes working with highly confidential matters; applicant has never worked with confidential matters before."

"This job requires employees to be on-call; applicant said one of the reasons he was leaving his current job was because he was on-call and found it 'disruptive' to his personal life."

Avoiding Recording Unsubstantiated Opinions

Interviewers are cautioned as well against recording their opinions without sufficient job-related backup. Opinions that stand alone without concrete support imply that the interviewer has drawn some conclusions, but fail to identify what information these conclusions were based on. These statements generally begin with phrases such as the following:

"I feel . . ."
"In my opinion . . ."
"I believe . . ."
"It is apparent to me that . . ."
"In my judgment . . ."
"I am of the opinion that . . ."
"I think . . ."
"It is my view that . . ."
"To my way of thinking . . ."
"It is obvious to me that . . ."
"To me it is clear that . . ."
"Without a doubt, this applicant . . ."

Such broad, summarizing statements do not refer to specific requirements and matching qualifications. Interview notes containing statements such as these would not be useful in determining the applicant's job suitability.

Following are some expressions that illustrate the ineffectiveness of recording opinions. None of the original statements tells us anything about the candidate's qualifications for a given job, and all should, therefore, be avoided. However, these statements become effective when they are enhanced by job related information:

Don't Say: "I feel Ms. Jenkins would make an excellent manager of product planning."

Say: "I feel Ms. Jenkins would make an excellent manager of product planning based on her experience in her present capacity as manager of product planning at Avedon Industries."

Don't Say: "In my opinion, Mr. Martin does not have what it takes to be a sales representative."

Say: "In my opinion, based on his lack of sales experience and failure to answer key questions, Mr. Martin does not have what it takes to be a sales representative."

Don't Say: "I believe Ms. Castro is just what we're looking for!"

Say:	"Based on her test scores and accounting expertise, I believe Ms. Castro is just what we're looking for!"
Don't Say:	"It is apparent to me that Mr. Brock can't do this job."
Say:	"It is apparent that Mr. Brock can't do this job due to his lack of experience in a high-volume working environment."
Don't Say:	"In my judgment, Ms. Princeton will make an excellent project manager."
Say:	"In my judgment, after assessing her two years' experience as a project coordinator, Ms. Princeton will make an excellent project manager."
Don't Say:	"I am of the opinion that Mr. Valentine will make a good addition to our staff."
Say:	"I am of the opinion that Mr. Valentine will make a good addition to our staff based on his experience in dealing with crises and working under pressure."
Don't Say:	"I think Mr. Turner will make a good mechanic."
Say:	"I think Mr. Turner will make a good mechanic based on his previous mechanic's experience."
Don't Say:	"It is my view that we would be making a mistake if we hired this applicant."
Say:	"It is my view that we would be making a mistake if we hired this applicant due to her lack of public relations experience."
Don't Say:	"To my way of thinking, Ms. Davis appears to be perfect for the office assistant position."
Say:	"To my way of thinking, because of her demonstrated interpersonal skills, Ms. Davis appears to be perfect for the office assistant position."
Don't Say:	"I consider Ms. Hastings to be excellent secretarial material."
Say:	"I consider Ms. Hastings to be excellent secretarial material based on three outstanding references and high test scores."
Don't Say:	"It is my view that Ms. Heller will do quite well as a data processing operator."

Say:	"It is my view that Ms. Heller will do quite well as a data processing operator after having worked in this capacity for the past two years."
Don't Say:	"As I see it, Mr. Green is just right for this job."
Say:	"As I see it, Mr. Green is just right for this job due to his accounts receivable background."
Don't Say:	"To my way of thinking, Ms. Mendoza will make a great programmer-analyst."
Say:	"To my way of thinking, Ms. Mendoza will make a great programmer-analyst because of her experience with multiprocessing systems."
Don't Say:	"If you ask me, we've found our next assistant vice president of marketing."
Say:	"If you ask me, after assessing his background in marketing for the past five years, we've found our next assistant vice president of marketing."
Don't Say:	"I believe, with a little training, this candidate will work out fine."
Say:	"I believe, with a little training to supplement her limited sales experience, this candidate will work out fine."

Referring to Job-Related Facts

There are two documentation techniques that best enable the interviewer to assess job suitability, compare the qualifications of several candidates, measure the applicant for future job matches, and preclude the possibility of referencing any information that might violate EEO laws.

The more effective of these two techniques requires that only job-related facts be referred to. This is a rather simple process, if the job descriptions are well written and if active listening techniques were practiced during the interview. As soon after the interview as possible, refer directly to each duty and requirement of the position and then indicate whether the applicant has the necessary skills and experience. In addition, you may want to record direct quotes made by the applicant.

The latter is of particular significance when a candidate possesses all of the concrete requirements of the job but is lacking in some intangible, nonrecordable quality. For example, you are about three-quarters of the way through an interview; even though the candidate can clearly handle the duties of the job, you have an uneasy feeling about her attitude toward a number of factors. Since recording that the applicant has a "bad attitude" would be subjective, continue to probe until you come across some job-related reason for rejecting her. Among other things, you explore with her the fact that this job requires extensive overtime with little advance notice. Your question to her in this regard might be, "Describe a time in your last job when you were asked to work overtime at the last minute; how did you react?" She replies, "I told my boss I didn't like the idea of being asked at the last minute! I mean, obviously I stayed, but I didn't like it." You might then say, "Are you saying that you have a problem with working overtime, especially on short notice?" She might then reply, "Don't get me wrong; I'll do it—but I would appreciate receiving sufficient advanced notice. After all, there is life after work!"

When it is time to write up this interview, you might state: "This job requires extensive overtime with little advance notice. When asked how she felt about this, the applicant replied, 'I'll do it—but I would appreciate receiving sufficient advanced notice.' "

By writing up your notes in this manner, you have clearly indicated that the applicant has effectively eliminated herself because she finds objectionable one of the requirements of the job: working overtime with little advance notice.

Recording direct quotes can also be helpful when comparing several candidates with similar backgrounds and qualifications.

Following is another, more comprehensive illustration of the usefulness of referring directly to the position's duties and requirements and recording direct quotes from the applicant.

You are trying to fill the position of secretary to the president of your company. Here is a partial list of essential duties and responsibilities, encompassing approximately 85 percent of the job:

• Takes, transcribes, and edits dictation. Dictation may be taken directly, over the telephone, or from a machine. Editing of dictation includes research for the completion of correspondence and/or reports involved.

• Schedules all appointments and meetings for the president. Arranges the president's travel itinerary, including commutation, reservations, and accommodations.

• Screens all calls and visitors to the president's office.

• Opens, reroutes, and disposes of all correspondence directed to the president.

- Replies to routine inquiries.
- Supervises record keeping and filing system of all correspondence and reports in the president's office, including confidential information.
- Supervises the work of the president's clerical staff.
- Prepares and writes formal minutes of all board of directors meetings, as well as shareholders and executive committee meetings.
- Prepares various reports required for meetings of the board of directors, shareholders, and executive committee.

As you interview each candidate applying for this position, refer to the specific job requirements. A partial interview might go something like this:

Interviewer: Please describe the extent of your experience taking dictation over the past three years in your present position as senior secretary.

Applicant: Well, my boss, who is the vice president of public relations, dictates into a dictaphone about three times a week. Sometimes she dictates directly to me, and I take down everything in shorthand and then transcribe it.

Interviewer: How much research is involved in order to complete any correspondence or reports?

Applicant: None. I just type exactly what she says.

Interviewer: What word processing program do you use?

Applicant: WordPerfect.

Interviewer: What kind of things do you type on a regular basis?

Applicant: The usual: letters, memos, that kind of thing.

Interviewer: What kind of things do you type periodically?

Applicant: I type a monthly project status report and then a quarterly report that covers our division's accomplishments over the past three months and the goals for the next quarter. I also type our department's budget twice a year.

Interviewer: What are your responsibilities with regard to meetings, such as board of directors meetings?

Applicant: I type up reports for distribution.

Interviewer: Do you take the minutes?

Applicant: No. The president's secretary does that.

Interviewer: What are your responsibilities with regard to scheduling appointments, meetings, and trips?

Applicant: Oh, I do all of that. I even arrange international trips, because my boss travels to Europe about a half-dozen times a year.

It's up to me to book her hotel reservations, develop her travel plans, and everything like that.

Interviewer: What do you do when someone calls or stops by your office and wants to speak with or see your boss?

Applicant: By now, I pretty much know who she wants to see and who I should turn away. I use my judgment and may tell someone she's in a meeting and cannot be disturbed. I will also offer my help. Sometimes the person has a question that I can answer.

Interviewer: Tell me about a time when someone insisted, saying it was urgent that they see her?

Applicant: That actually happened last Friday morning. I remember because she was in a meeting—her weekly staff meeting. The VP of human resources said it was an important matter concerning one of her employees. I buzzed her, and she came right out.

Interviewer: What are your responsibilities with regard to the mail?

Applicant: I open all the mail, including envelopes marked "confidential." Then I stamp everything and put the pile on my boss's desk. She likes to go through everything herself. She's kind of a control freak, if you know what I mean. Anyway, after she's gone through everything, she attaches notes to everything telling me what to do.

Interviewer: What do you mean when you say she's a "control freak"?

Applicant: Well, she likes to add her personal touch to most things.

Interviewer: Like what?

Applicant: In addition to sorting through her own mail, she likes to place her own phone calls. She also likes to greet people rather than having me take them in to her. I guess that's about it.

Interviewer: How do you feel about that?

Applicant: I don't mind. It's that much less for me to do!

Interviewer: Let's turn our attention to another aspect of this job. What is the extent of any supervisory responsibility you may have?

Applicant: I don't have any.

Interviewer: Am I correct in understanding, then, that you do not delegate any work to anyone else?

Applicant: Right. I do it all myself.

This partial interview illustrates the importance of writing down facts as they relate to the duties and requirements of a job. The interviewer correlated each question to a particular responsibility listed in the job description. As the applicant responded, the interviewer might have jotted down the following key words and phrases:

> Sr. sec'y.—VP
> Dictates (mostly dictaphone; some direct)—3x's/wk.
> No research
> WordPerfect
> Regular typing: letters; memos
> Period. typing: monthly proj. status report; quarterly report re: division's accomplishments and goals; department's budget twice a year
> Also types reports for meetings; no minutes
> Schedules appointments, meetings and trips
> Screens visitors; offers help; puts through if urgent
> Opens/stamps mail, including "confidential"; responds according to directions
> Refers to boss as "control freak" re: mail, calls, greeting peo. O.K. with app.—". . . less for me to do!"
> No super/delegation

After the applicant has left, the interviewer can review these thoughts and elaborate on her notes. By once again referring to the position's requirements, she can determine overall job suitability. The final set of notes, based on this portion of the interview, might read like this:

> Applicant has worked as secretary to VP, PR for three years.
> Job requires taking, transcribing and editing/researching dictation (phone, direct, machine): app. regularly takes and transcribes dictation by dictaphone plus some direct; no research.
> Lots of typing: letters; memos; monthly proj. status reports; quarterly reports re: division's accomplishments and goals; department's budget twice a year. WordPerfect.
> Job requires preparing reports for meetings: app. types reports for meetings.
> Job requires preparing and writing minutes of meetings: no exper. with minutes.
> Job requires scheduling appointments and meetings plus making travel arrangements: app. schedules appointments, meetings and trips.
> Job requires screening calls and visitors: app. screens visitors; offers help; puts through if urgent.
> Job requires opening, rerouting and disposing of correspon-

dence: app. opens/stamps mail, including "confidential"; responds according to directions only.

Refers to boss as "control freak" re: mail, calls, greeting peo. O.K. with app.—". . . less for me to do!"

Job requires supervising and delegating work to clerical staff: app. has no super/delegation exper.

Everything written is a job-related fact, including the quote that reflects an intangible quality important to this position.

Being Descriptive

The second technique that is effective in postinterview documentation entails recording a description of the applicant's behavior, speech, attire, or appearance. This technique may be utilized by interviewers conducting interviews for entry-level jobs as well as volume interviews—that is, they schedule perhaps forty or more interviews a week. After seeing so many people, the interviewer has difficulty referring back to each person's application or resume and differentiating one from another. Even notes that are objective, factual, and job related may not succeed in jogging your recollection of a specific candidate. To help you with this, consider the occasional use of descriptive phrases. Their purpose is limited to identifying the person and aiding you in recalling the specific interview.

Care must be taken in the use of such phrases for two primary reasons: first, descriptive phrases can easily become subjective; and second, even though factual, they are not job related. To illustrate, "Applicant was dressed entirely in yellow" is an objective descriptive phrase. The addition of just one word, however, makes it subjective: "Applicant was garishly dressed entirely in yellow."

Here are additional examples of objective descriptions:

- Smiled during the entire thirty minutes of the interview
- Hair extended below waist
- Wore black nail polish
- Wore pearl cufflinks
- Twirled hair through entire ninety minutes of the interview
- Played with paper clips
- Tapped fingers
- Taller than 6'6" (doorway to office is 6'6")
- Laughed frequently
- Chewed gum
- Rocked in chair

Interviewers are cautioned against using any of these descriptive terms in the selection process. They are intended *only* to help you remember the applicant, not to determine job suitability.

Tape-Recording Interviews

Some interviewers feel that there are too many problems related to note taking, including the amount of time it takes and the possibility of writing something down that violates EEO regulations. Instead of following the simple rules just cited, they reason that it is easier to tape-record the entire interview. It certainly is easier to record than to write. However, there are two very good reasons for avoiding this practice:

1. If the applicant knows that you are recording the interview, this is almost guaranteed to make him feel nervous and reluctant to speak freely. It also causes some candidates to become angry and defensive.

2. If the applicant does not know that you are recording the interview, you are violating his right to privacy.

The only time that a tape recorder can reasonably be used as part of the employment process is after an interview is completed. The interviewer may then choose to record her observations before the next scheduled candidate arrives. Even in this case, however, the interviewer should transfer the dictated thoughts to paper; written notes should accompany every application or resumé.

Assigning Numerical Values

Some organizations incorporate a point system in the note-taking stage of the interview: The interviewer assigns a numerical value to each factor evaluated. Factors appear on a preprinted form with a key that briefly explains the point value of each rating. For example, the overall rating for a five-point value system might look like this:

1   Superior overall skills and qualifications
2   Above-average skills and qualifications
3   Meets the requirements of the job
4   Fails to meet all of the requirements of the job
5   Not qualified

Then each individual factor might be evaluated according to the following scale:

1	Outstanding
2	Very good
3	Good
4	Fair
5	Poor

There are a number of problems with this kind of system:

• The accompanying point value form may contain factors that are subjective and are not job related—for instance, appearance, personality, awareness, maturity, tact, and self-confidence.

• Using subjective terms such as *outstanding* or *poor* to judge someone is meaningless.

• Busy interviewers who are relying on forms with several preprinted categories tend to check off boxes quickly, without giving enough thought to each person's actual skill level.

• Without written details concerning each applicant, it will be extremely difficult to distinguish one person from another at a later date.

If forms are used, they should include only job-related categories, such as various aspects of education and experience. In addition, ample space should be allotted for the interviewer's notes. Overall evaluation categories of "meets job requirements" and "fails to meet job requirements" may be included as well. A sample interview evaluation form appears in Appendix H.

Of course, a form need not be used at all; a blank piece of paper attached to the application or resumé will suffice. Just remember to restrict your comments to objective, factual, and job-related information, with occasional distinguishing notes as needed.

Interviewing for Jobs With No Requirements

You may find yourself recruiting for jobs that do not carry any experiential or educational requirements. These are usually entry-level positions requiring very simple, repetitive tasks. Naturally, when this occurs, you cannot evaluate someone's demonstrated skill level. In these instances, consider posing hypothetical questions relative to the specific tasks of the job and recording the applicant's reply. For instance, suppose that the opening for a messenger calls for picking up presorted mail from the mailroom and distributing it to each employee. During the course of the interview, you might ask an applicant, "What would you do if an employee told you that she was expecting a very important letter, but it wasn't included in the mail you had just brought to her?" The applicant might reply, "I would give her the name and extension of my supervisor to check on it." Your notes for this interview might then include the following reference to the job-related activity: "When asked how would handle missing mail, said, 'Tell employee to check with supervisor.' "

Hence, even with applicants who lack prior work experience, postinterview documentation can be objective, factual, and job related.

Taking Effective Notes

At this point it is helpful to illustrate both effective and ineffective note taking. In Chapters 7 and 8 we saw an abridged job description for the position of assistant to the director of human resources. Here, related tasks have been expanded upon and added to; excerpts from an interview for this position are also presented. Note that the interview excerpts include only questions asked by the interviewer and responses by the applicant. They do not include detailed information provided about the job and the company or questions asked by the applicant. Following the interview excerpts are examples of effective and ineffective note taking.

Job Description for the Assistant to
the Director of Human Resources

1. Recruits applicants for nonexempt-level positions via various recruitment sources.

2. Interviews and screens all applicants for nonexempt positions; refers qualified candidates to appropriate department manager/supervisor.

3. Assists department manager/supervisor with hiring decisions.

4. Performs reference checks on potential employees, by telephone and in writing.

5. Processes new employees in terms of payroll and benefits; informs new employees of all pertinent information.

6. Is responsible for conveying all necessary insurance information to employees and assisting them with questions, processing of claims, etc.

7. Assists in the implementation of policies and procedures; may explain or interpret certain policies as required.

8. Assists in the maintenance and administration of the organization's compensation program; monitors salary increase recommendations as they are received to ensure compliance with merit increase guidelines.

9. Advises managers/supervisors of employee performance review schedule; follows up on delinquent or inconsistent reviews.

10. Is responsible for the orderly and systematic maintenance of all employee records and files.

11. Assists EEO officer with advising managers/supervisors on matters of equal employment opportunity and affirmative action as they pertain to the interviewing and hiring process and employer-employee relations.

12. Assists in the maintenance of up-to-date job descriptions of positions throughout the company.

13. Maintains all necessary HR records and reports; this includes unemployment insurance reports, flow-log recording, EEO reports, change notices, and identification card records.

14. Conducts exit interviews for terminating nonexempt employees.

15. Assists HR manager and HR director with the planning and conducting of each month's organizational orientation program.

16. Performs other related duties and assignments as required.

Prior Experience and/or Education

1. Thorough general knowledge and understanding of the HR function.
2. Prior experience as a nonexempt interviewer, preferably in a manufacturing environment.
3. Ability to work effectively with all levels of management and large numbers of employees.
4. Ability to deal effectively with applicants and referral sources.

Partial Interview for Human Resources Assistant

Interviewer: Good morning, Ms. Oliver. Thank you for coming in. Please be seated.

Applicant: Thank you. I'm glad to be here, and, by the way, it's Mrs. Oliver, but you can call me Sandra.

Interviewer: Did you have any difficult getting here, Sandra?

Applicant: No, my daughter attends school about two miles from here, so I'm very familiar with the area.

Interviewer: Well, I'm glad that you didn't have any trouble. I'm anxious to begin talking with you about your interest in our opening for the assistant to the director of human resources.

Applicant: Oh, I'm ready! I've been looking forward to this all week. I really want this job!

Interviewer: Fine. Then why don't we begin discussing your qualifications as they relate to the responsibilities of this job.

Applicant: Sure; no problem.

Interviewer: To begin with, this job requires recruiting, interviewing, and screening applicants for all of our nonexempt positions. Please describe your experience in this regard.

Applicant: Well, that's exactly what I've been doing for the past year at Circuits, Inc.

Interviewer: Please explain what you mean.

Applicant: Well, whenever I receive an approved job requisition, it's up to me to start recruiting. The first thing I do is talk with department heads to make sure that I understand the requirements and duties of the job. I also try to visit the department in order to get a feel for the work environment and to see firsthand what the person will be doing. It also helps beef up my rapport with the department head. Let's see; where was I? Oh, yes; then I start to explore different recruitment sources.

Interviewer: Such as?

Applicant: The usual: agencies, want ads, walk-ins, employee referrals.

Interviewer: Any others?

Applicant: That's usually all it takes. We don't have any trouble attracting applicants. We have a fine reputation in the manufacturing industry, as I'm sure you know.

Interviewer: Please, continue.

Applicant: Well, I interview and screen all the applicants and then refer those qualified to the department head.

Interviewer: Where did you learn to interview?

Applicant: I have a degree in HR administration, as you can see from my resumé, and then I received on-the-job training when I first joined Circuits, Inc.

Interviewer: How much time was devoted to on-the-job training?

Applicant: About three months. Then I was left on my own.

Interviewer: I see. Please go on.

Applicant: Okay. As I said, I refer qualified candidates to the department head. Then we get together and decide on who to hire.

Interviewer: Who finally makes the actual hiring decision?

Applicant: The department heads and I usually agree, but if we disagree, then they decide. After all, they're the ones who have to work with the person.

Interviewer: What are your responsibilities with regard to reference checks?

Applicant: I run both written and telephone references on only those applicants we're interested in.

Interviewer: Tell me about a reference check that didn't confirm the information you had on a candidate. What happened?

Applicant: That's happened several times actually. Each time I tried to get at least two additional references to confirm either the employer's information or the applicant's. Then I turned all the information over to the department manager for a final decision.

Interviewer: Tell me about a time when you felt it appropriate to discuss the conflicting information with the applicant. What happened?

Applicant: There was this applicant who warned me in advance that I might get some negative information from his old boss. He was right. I called the applicant and told him what his former employer had said. He called the guy, who ended up calling me to explain why he said what he did. It was pretty amazing. We ended up hiring the applicant. He worked out fine.

Interviewer: Once an applicant is selected, what do you do?

Applicant: I arrange the starting date and schedule the person for orientation. It's also my job to put the new employee on payroll and take care of the benefits.

Interviewer: So is it your responsibility to explain all of the company benefits?

Applicant: No, not exactly. I just process the paperwork. Someone from the benefits department explains all of that during orientation.

Interviewer: I understand. Tell me. Sandra, does Circuits, Inc. have a policies and procedures manual?

Applicant: Yes, it does.

Interviewer: What are your responsibilities with regard to this manual?

Applicant: Sometimes if my boss, the human resources manager, is not around, I try to answer questions from department heads.

Interviewer: Give me a specific example.

Applicant: Well, last week one of the managers from accounting called for clarification on our vacation policy for part-timers.

Interviewer: Were you able to help?

Applicant: Yes.

Interviewer: Good. Tell me, in addition to recruiting, interviewing, screening and processing payroll, and benefits paperwork, what other areas of human resources are you involved with?

Applicant: Well, let's see. Let me think for a minute. Oh yes, I'm in charge of performance reviews.

Interviewer: In what way are you in charge of performance reviews?

Applicant: I keep a log of when each nonexempt employee's review is due and notify the department head if they don't get them in on time.

Interviewer: Tell me about a time when a department head did not submit a past-due review despite repeated requests.

Applicant: We have this one department head—I won't name names—who never gets anything in on time. So what I did was start bugging him about two months before the review was really due. By the time he finally got around to sending it in, it was only a little late!

Interviewer: I see. That's certainly an interesting approach. Tell me about your responsibilities with regard to salary administration.

Applicant: I don't have any. We have a wage and salary manager who takes care of that.

Interviewer: What about EEO and affirmative action?

Applicant: Nope. Our EEO officer handles that. I know a lot about those areas though.

Interviewer: You know a lot about EEO and affirmative action?

Applicant: Yes. I studied it in school and attended a three-day seminar on it about six months ago. I'd like to specialize in EEO some day.

Interviewer: That's very interesting. What other human resources responsibilities do you have at Circuits, Inc.?

Applicant: Well, I help with job descriptions.

Interviewer: In what way?

Applicant: Whenever there's a nonexempt job opening, I check with the department head to make sure that the job has not changed significantly and that the existing job description is still valid. If it needs revamping, I tell my boss and she takes over from there.

Interviewer: What are your responsibilities with regard to HR files?

Applicant: I keep an applicant flow log and process employment change notices.

Interviewer: Do you process any other forms?

Applicant: None that I can think of.

Interviewer: What about your involvement with exit interviews?

Applicant: Oh, yes, I forgot about that! I do all exit interviews for nonexempt employees. I enjoy that!

Interviewer: What is it that you enjoy about it?

Applicant: I like finding out why a person is leaving and what the company might do in the future to prevent good people from leaving.

Interviewer: I see. That's very interesting. Describe for me a specific exit interview and what you learned as a result.

Applicant: We recently lost a great programmer-analyst because we ignored his request for a transfer to a less technical department. He didn't care about making less money; he just wanted to change fields. I felt badly about that. We should pay attention to what people want to do as much as what they can do.

Interviewer: What other aspects of your work do you enjoy?

Applicant: I like the interviewing—you know, talking to so many different people.

Interviewer: Tell me about one of the most interesting people you ever interviewed.

Applicant: There was an applicant who came in with a snake draped around her neck—honest! She said it was her pet and that she took it wherever she went!

Interviewer: That's certainly unusual. What don't you like about your job, Sandra?

Applicant: If I had to pick one thing, I guess it would be the paperwork—mostly the employment change notices.

Interviewer: What aspect of your job do you find to be the most difficult?

Applicant: I guess that would be my part in the monthly orientation program.

Interviewer: You participate in the orientation program?

Applicant: Yes, didn't I mention that? I have to give an opening talk of about twenty minutes about the history of Circuits, Inc., why it's such a great place to work—that sort of thing.

Interviewer: What is it about doing this that you find difficult?

Applicant: I get nervous talking in front of people.

Interviewer: I see. Sandra, I'd like to get back for a moment to your educational training in HR administration. What made you interested in this field?

Applicant: It seemed challenging and varied. It also seemed to offer a lot in the way of growth opportunities.

Interviewer: What level do you ultimately want to achieve?

Applicant: I think I'd like to be an EEO officer.

Interviewer: If we contacted your college, what would they tell us about your grades, in both HR courses and other courses?

Applicant: I graduated with a 3.0 average. I did pretty well in everything except math. I got a D in statistics.

Interviewer: What did your HR courses consist of?

Applicant: Everything. The degree prepared us to be generalists.

Interviewer: I know you said that you particularly like EEO. What aspects of human resources do you enjoy the least?

Applicant: That would have to be benefits. I really find it kind of dry and boring.

Interviewer: I understand. Sandra, I have just a few more questions to ask you. Can you tell me about a time when an applicant acted up? By that I mean, became aggressive or cried.

Applicant: I did have a guy start screaming at me when I told him the job he was applying for was already filled. I tried to calm him down by telling him we could still talk; then if something suitable opened up in the future I could call him. It worked. I knew I had to remain objective if I was going to evaluate him fairly.

Interviewer: It sounds as if you got a good handle on the situation. Sandra, what does the prospect of this job offer you that your present job does not?

Applicant: It's time for a change.

Interviewer: A change?

Applicant: Yes. One year in Circuits, Inc. is long enough. It's not the most exciting place in the world to work.

Interviewer: What's your idea of an ideal work environment?

Applicant: One where employees who prove themselves can grow; also, where managers don't look over your shoulder all the time. Of course, I would like to be paid more too!

Interviewer: What type of employee are you?

Applicant: I like to work independently. I don't need close supervision.

Interviewer: What do you feel you could offer our company, Sandra? Please be specific about three of your attributes, and examples of when you have applied them in your current job.

Applicant: Let's see. Well, I'm objective; I gave you an example of that before with the applicant who was screaming at me. I'm also a hard worker. In the last month alone I've worked overtime at least a dozen times without getting paid for it. And I care about keeping good people once we hire them. That's why I get so much out of exit interviews. I also want to say that I love the field of human resources.

Interviewer: Is there anything else I should know about your qualifications that would help me to make a hiring decision in your favor?

Applicant: I can't think of anything else.

Interviewer: Fine, Sandra. I'd like to thank you again for coming in. We will be interviewing for the next five days or so, and will make our decision at the end of that time. All applicants will be notified by mail. If you have any questions in the interim, please do not hesitate to call me. I've enjoyed talking with you.

Applicant: Thank you. I've enjoyed talking with you, too. I really want this job!

Interviewer: I understand. Good-bye, Sandra.

Applicant: Bye.

Example of Ineffective Notes

Here are the ineffective notes taken during the course of the interview:

Married; young daughter
Too anxious
Tends to ramble
Only nine months' real experience; degree okay
Likes P&P involvement
Had trouble remembering what else she does
Interested in EEO; I smell trouble
No real JD experience
Light record keeping
Sounds like a troublemaker; loves to find out why people leave
Dislikes doing orientation
Dislikes benefits
Light experience with problem applicants
Bored with present job; didn't give it much of a chance
Wants more money and to move up in a hurry
Doesn't like supervision

Summarizing Statement

I don't feel Sandra would make a very good HR assistant. She just doesn't seem reliable. Also, she hasn't demonstrated a thorough knowledge of HR.

As you can see, these statements are highly subjective. In addition, many of the comments are not job related and some violate EEO regulations.

Example of Effective Notes

Now, let's review effective notes (to be subsequently elaborated upon in relation to job-specific requirements and responsibilities) based on the same interview:

Circuits, Inc., manufacturing
Nonexempt interviewing experience: 9 mos; 3 mos. OJT
Degree in HR admin.
Recruiting, interviews (enjoys), screens, and recommends for hire
Telephone and written references
Processes payroll and benefits paperwork
P&P manual; most questions handled by HR mgr. (boss)
No. Sal. admin. respon.
Expressed interest in pursuing field of EEO
Checks on accuracy of existing JDs
Flow log and employee change notices (enjoys least)
Exit interviews for all nonexempt employees (enjoys)
Participates in monthly orientation prog.: "nervous talking in front of people"
Least favorite: benefits
Reason for leaving: "time for a change"
Has dealt with applicants who have acted up; knew it was important to remain objective
"Like to work independently"
"I'm a hard worker; I love the field of human resources."

Summarizing Statement

This job calls for a thorough general knowledge and understanding of human resources, as well as prior experience as a nonexempt interviewer. Ms. Oliver has had three months' on-the-job training and nine months' actual experience in the following areas of HR at Circuits, Inc.: nonexempt recruitment, interviewing, screening, references, processing payroll and benefits paperwork, checking accuracy of job descriptions, flow-logs and employee change notices, exit interviews, monthly orientation. Also has a degree in HR administration. Recommends hiring; interested in EEO; enjoys exit interviews; least favorite—benefits. "Wants a change"; "Likes to work independently"; "hard worker"; "loves HR."

These statements are all objective factual, and job related. Anyone reading them would have an immediate understanding of the applicant's skill level as it relates to the requirements of the job.

Summary

Notes serve as a permanent record of an interview. They also help interviewers assess an applicant's job suitability in relation to the job description and as compared with other candidates, are useful to the original interviewer and subsequent interviews considering rejected applicants for future openings, and can be used as evidence in employment discrimination suits.

Effective documentation relies on objective language. Additionally, any personal opinions should be supported by job-related information.

There are two effective documentation techniques that enable interviewers to assess job suitability. The first requires that only job-related facts be referred to. The second technique relies on a description of the applicant's behavior, speech, attire, or appearance to help interviewers differentiate among applicants.

Interviewers are discouraged from tape-recording interviews. They are also urged to avoid using point value systems tied in to forms that cite subjective categories.

Directly quoting applicants' responses can prove useful for jobs that do not carry any experiential or educational requirements. These quotations are also helpful when a candidate meets the concrete aspects of a job but falls short with regard to one or more intangible requirements.

Chapter 11

Preemployment and Employment Testing

We live in a society that relies on testing. Children and young adults may be subjected to twenty or more years of testing, beginning in preschool and continuing through graduate school and beyond. The process continues at work, as tests are given to screen out, evaluate, classify, predict, and promote. We may be asked to take tests to determine if we are strong enough, smart enough, or healthy enough. Then there are honesty tests, drug tests, and personality tests. It is doubtful that many of us have ever stopped to think about how many tests we have taken so far in our lives, but if we did, the resulting number would undoubtedly be startling.

What is this fixation we have with tests? More significantly, why do so many people believe in a test's reliability to predict suitability, say, for employment? Are tests, in fact, valid indicators of job success?

Employers may believe so strongly in tests as virtually infallible and reliable predictors of job suitability that they will not even conduct the face-to-face interview without first administering a series of tests and assessing the results. Others feel that tests are basically worthless, perhaps even dangerous, in that they may result in inaccurate, inappropriate, or incomplete conclusions. These companies usually place a great deal of emphasis on the employment interview to determine job suitability. And, not surprisingly, there are still others who view test scores as one part of the selection process.

In addition to the controversy over the benefits of preemployment and employment testing, there are legal issues of test validation and the relationship between tests and discrimination. In this regard, many questions need to be addressed, including what constitutes a valid test, when tests should be given, who is qualified to administer various types of tests, and how to interpret test results.

If tests are to be considered as part of your recruitment and selection process, carefully and objectively analyze testing in terms of its characteristics, guidelines for validation, scoring, and relationship to discrimination. Then review various types of tests for applicability to specific jobs. Numerous classifications exist, including intelligence, personality, physical ability, honesty, and drug use. Knowing which tests are most suitable for a particular job can be a challenge in and of itself.

Testing Characteristics

In simplest terms, preemployment and employment tests are defined as procedures for determining job suitability. This is accomplished by examining the skills, knowledge, or physical capabilities of employees or employment candidates according to a predetermined set of objective guidelines. The results are assessed in relation to the requirements and responsibilities of a given position, and conclusions are drawn as to the appropriateness of the applicant's qualifications.

Many tests evaluate a job candidate's achievements and, hence, measure current skill level; others focus on aptitude, or a person's potential ability. Tests may also indicate how motivated a person will be in a certain type of job or work environment. In addition, they may be used to screen out individuals with certain undesirable traits, such as drug use.

Based on this description, tests certainly seem to be useful recruitment and selection tools. They can aid employers in selecting candidates who are capable, motivated, and less likely to bring unacceptable qualities to the job. Also, they can help distinguish between otherwise similarly qualified candidates. In addition, the objective nature of testing can help employers make unbiased, job-related employment decisions. This lends itself to another benefit of testing; that is, when tests are fair representations of the skills and knowledge needed to perform a given job, employers are likely to be portrayed as impartial. This, in turn, may serve to enhance the overall image of the organization.

Not surprisingly, there are some disadvantages to testing. A tendency to overrely on tests for screening or hiring purposes is one of the greatest concerns expressed by opponents. Even if a test is well designed and properly used, the results can, at best, indicate which individuals are most *likely* to do well. No test can point with certainty to those people who *will* do well. Hence, employers are cautioned against using test scores exclusively to make employment decisions;

tests should instead be viewed as one of many factors contributing to selection.

Although there are several multipurpose tests, many tests are designed to emphasize—and, therefore, spotlight individuals who possess—specific skills or knowledge. This can screen out candidates who might otherwise make good employees. In some instances, the qualities being sought through testing may be acquired through a minimal amount of on-the-job training or education.

Opponents of testing also point out that many people react negatively to the mere idea of a test; others, who may in fact be qualified, simply do not do well on tests. The result may be a distorted or incomplete picture of a candidate if too much emphasis is placed on test scores.

Weighing the pros and cons of testing can render difficult a decision as to when testing is appropriate, how much weight to place on test results, and whether to use tests at all. To resolve these issues, begin by ascertaining the specific skills, knowledge, and abilities needed to perform the duties and responsibilities of a job. This usually calls for a written job description. Ask yourself whether an applicant could acquire the required skills on the job relatively quickly or should come to the job already possessing certain abilities. Also, anticipate any possible consequences of hiring (or promoting or transferring) someone into the available position without the required knowledge. Next, determine the degree of excellence in relation to the requirements of the job. If the job opening can readily be filled by any number of candidates with comparable abilities, then testing to distinguish superiority may not be necessary. Also, decide if there might be other, equally effective means of determining job suitability. Certain verifiable credentials and certifications might adequately indicate an acceptable skill or knowledge level. Information acquired through the face-to-face interview and through employment or educational reference checks may also provide sufficient data, precluding any need for formal testing.

Uniform Guidelines on Employee Selection

Even proponents of testing admit that there are a myriad of stipulations and conditions that must be met before legitimate preemployment and employment tests can be administered. Fortunately, the Equal Employment Opportunity Commission (EEOC), the Department of Labor's Office of Federal Contract Compliance Programs (OFCCP), the Civil Service Commission (renamed the Office of Personnel Management), the Department of Justice, and the Department of the Treasury together set forth, in 1978, a comprehensive set of *Uniform Guidelines on Employee Selection Procedures* that can steer employers through the testing process. The primary purpose of these guidelines is to provide a framework for determining the proper use of preemployment tests relative to referral or hiring decisions and employment tests pertaining to promotions, demotions, transfers, training, retention, and other employment decisions. Selection procedures other than tests, including interviews, application forms, references, and performance evaluations, are also covered by the guidelines. Therefore, the more encompassing expression *selection procedure* is preferred over the term *test*.

These guidelines apply to private employers with fifteen or more employees, state and local governments, many employment agencies, labor organizations, and contractors and subcontractors of the federal government.

The guidelines are designed to ensure that tests and other selection procedures do not adversely affect the employment opportunities of individuals of a particular race, sex, religion, or national origin. Consequently, employers are required to conduct validity studies of tests where adverse impact has occurred and generally are advised to use only valid tests, even if adverse impact has not been shown. *Validation* refers to a demonstration of the job relatedness of any test or other selection procedure. *Adverse impact* is defined by the guidelines as "a substantially different rate of selection in hiring, promotion or other employment decision which works to the disadvantage of members of a race, sex, or ethnic group."

Validation begins with a thorough analysis to define the requirements of the job. The next step identifies selection devices and standards that characterize those applicants or employees meeting the job requirements. Testing current employees and applicants, without using the test scores to influence any employment-related decisions, can measure the effectiveness of the selection device being tested. This process should take place over a long period of time and be applied to a large sample population in order to yield credible results. The last phase is to prepare a detailed validation report that outlines and documents the steps taken.

The *Uniform Guidelines* recognize three methods of determining validity:

1. *Criterion-related validity*—a statistical demonstration of a relationship between scores on a selection procedure and the job performance of sample workers

2. *Content validity*—a demonstration that the content of a selection procedure is representative of important aspects of performance on the job

3. *Construct validity*—a demonstration that a selection procedure measures something believed to be an underlying human trait or characteristic (e.g., honesty) and that this trait or characteristic is essential for successful job performance

Although the *Uniform Guidelines* do not indicate a preference of one validity method over the others, it is generally agreed that the criterion-related process, while effective, can be a long and expensive procedure to administer. Construct validity has been the source of much debate, in that the soundness of any trait claimed to demonstrate successful job performance is difficult to establish. Consequently, most employers rely on content validation, believing that it most accurately predicts job success.

Employers using a test with adverse impact may be engaged in discriminatory practices and held liable for various penalties, including back pay, attorney fees, and the loss of government contracts. However, if an employer has substantial evidence of validity or has a study under way that is designed to document within a reasonable time the evidence required by the guidelines, the employer may continue to use a test that is not yet fully validated. In such instances, however, employers should refrain from making hiring decisions based on invalidated test results. Rather, alternative selection procedures should be explored.

To validate their selection procedures, many employers turn to industrial and HR psychologists with expertise in validation research techniques. These trained psychologists may be faculty members in colleges and universities, independent consultants, or members of a consulting firm. Additional information regarding individuals qualified to conduct validation studies may be obtained from:

American Psychological Association
1200 17th Street, Northwest
Washington, D.C. 20036

In addition to test validation, employers are advised to consult with trained professionals when creating employment tests or tailoring existing tests to meet their needs better. "Homemade" tests developed by nonprofessionals place employers at greater risk of liability since such tests are more difficult to validate than are professionally developed and researched tests. Tests developed by professionals are also more likely to be more accurate predictors of job success than the homemade variety.

Employers should exercise caution when purchasing prepackaged tests from any vendor, including expert psychologists. Check the credentials and reputation of any vendor carefully. Bypass those who use terms like *valid, reliable,* and *court defensible* without substantial documentation. In addition, review the vendor's publication record. Most important, determine the test's relevance to your objectives.

Purchasing or using a test that does not have a sound base can only increase your potential liability; furthermore, it will do little to ensure that you have hired candidates with the best chance for success on the job.

Testing and Discrimination

Title VII of the Civil Rights Act of 1964 made illegal discrimination against any individual with respect to any term or condition of employment on the basis of race, color, religion, sex, or national origin. Two years later, one of the first cases to focus on specific employment testing discrimination was litigated in Illinois, *Myart v. Motorola.* Myart, an African-American applicant for a job at a Motorola factory, alleged that the hiring practices at Motorola were racially discriminatory in that he had been asked to take a qualifying test containing questions requiring familiarity with a predominantly white, middle-class culture. A hearing examiner for the Illinois Fair Employment Practices Commission agreed that this was discriminatory, but the Illinois Supreme Court overturned the examiner's ruling. Nevertheless, news of this case alerted the public to the issue of testing and discrimination.

Griggs v. Duke Power Co. drew even greater attention to the issue of testing and discrimination with its landmark ruling in 1971. Until the passage of Title VII, Duke Power Co. openly practiced racial discrimination by employing African-American workers only in the labor department, where they were paid less than workers in other, all-white departments. Once Title VII rendered such practice illegal, the company opened up job opportunities to minorities in all departments, but established a new set of hiring requirements, including a high school diploma and satisfactory scores on two aptitude tests: the Wonderlic Personnel Test and the Bennett Mechanical Aptitude Test. African-Americans argued that the tests and diploma requirements had an adverse effect, were arbitrary, and were not job related.

The trial court ruled that the tests did not violate Title VII, because Duke Power did not have a discriminatory intent. The U.S. Supreme Court disagreed. It stated that Title VII was concerned with the consequences of employment practices, not motivation, drawing an important distinction between intent and effect. The Court further criticized employment testing in general. Although *Griggs v. Duke Power Co.* left companies free to use tests, it limited the use of tests having an adverse impact on minorities. The Court held that "Congress has forbidden giving [testing or measuring procedures] controlling force unless they are demonstrably a reasonable measure of job performance."

Employment tests are governed not only by federal laws, but also by state laws covering fair employment practices. This is significant; many state laws allow discrimination claims to be tried by juries, which may award punitive damages in addition to back pay. On the other hand, it takes much longer—often years—to go to trial in state court.

Testing Policies

Companies administering tests should have a written policy clearly stating that the primary objective of preemployment and employment testing programs is to select qualified candidates, regardless of race, color, religion, national origin, gender, age, or disability. The policy should then describe how various tests are administered, evaluated, and interpreted. Details of this policy should be made available to those directly involved in the testing process. In addition, a testing policy statement should be distributed to all managers who participate in employee hiring decisions.

Those involved in the testing process should be trained in proper administration procedures. Following are some general guidelines for test administration:

• Tests should be given only when job-related criteria indicate a direct correlation between test results and job performance.

• Tests should never be given exclusively to members of selected groups: women, minorities, or people with disabilities.

• The testing environment should be the same each time a test is given. This includes factors such as lighting, ventilation, seating, space, and noise.

• The same tools or materials should be distributed in exactly the same order and manner each time a test is given.

• The purpose of the test should be explained to test takers at the outset. The language used to describe the purpose of the test should be identical each time the test is administered.

• Oral instructions should be recited at the same rate of speech, using the same tone of voice and at the same pitch and volume. In addition, identical words should be used. Since even the same person's voice can vary from time to time, many employers use prerecorded instructions.

• Take care not to project expectations about the test results.

• Make every effort to eliminate known anxiety-producing factors, such as an excessively long waiting period before the test, uncomfortable seating, noise, faulty equipment, flickering lights, or inadequate heating or air-conditioning.

• Limit the number of people who have access to copies of the test, as well as any answer or scoring sheets.

• Exercise care when scoring objective tests—those in a multiple-choice format or those resulting in numerical scores—to use the correct answer key. Computers may be used to score these types of tests. Subjective tests, such as personality and intelligence tests, should be scored only by experts with the appropriate training.

• Afford across-the-board opportunities for retesting and reconsideration.

Computer-Administered Tests

To help ensure the uniformity of test administration, many test publishers now offer computer-administered versions of standard employment tests. These tests allow test takers to read the instructions and questions from a computer monitor and then respond by using either a light pen, which allows "writing" directly on the screen; a "mouse," to click on items on the screen; or a keyboard, for typing out answers. Regardless of the method used, the answers to test questions are then keyed directly into the computer.

Proponents of computer-administered tests maintain that these procedures eliminate any possibility of administrator bias, thereby ensuring standardized testing procedures. On the other hand, test scores may be adversely affected if users are not comfortable or familiar with computers. In addition, supplying a sufficient number of computer terminals for all test takers can be costly.

Gaining in popularity is a modified version of the computer-administered test: adaptive testing or tailored testing. With this method, the computer selects questions of appropriate difficulty for the test taker, based on that person's demonstrated ability to answer questions earlier during a preliminary evaluative test. This technique is favored by those concerned with test security, since different candidates are asked different questions. It also saves time and reduces frustration for test takers who are asked questions that are either too easy or too hard.

Opponents argue that uniformity, one of the principal requirements of testing, is adversely affected when different questions are asked of different applicants for the same job. They are also concerned about premature decisions based on the preliminary test results.

All variations of computer-based testing are subject to the standards and requirements for selection procedures as outlined in the *Uniform Guidelines on Employee Selection Procedures.*

Test Takers With Disabilities

The uniformity rule of testing is generally put aside for test takers with disabilities necessitating special accommodations. For example, visually impaired applicants may require tests offered on cassette tapes, with the assistance of a reader, or written in large print or braille. They may also need additional time to complete a test. Local agencies providing vocational rehabilitation for the visually impaired can suggest sources that will prepare adapted tests for applicants with special needs.

Hearing-impaired test takers also require special accommodation. Spoken instructions must be replaced with written information and possibly sign language. Allowances must also be made for the fact that people born with hearing impairments may suffer significant language deprivation and, consequently, score poorly on word-oriented tests.

Test takers with motor disabilities may require a variety of accommodations to compensate for their inability to walk, write, or work with specific tools. Special access to test sites should be provided for applicants in wheelchairs. Computer-administered tests may assist motor-disabled test takers who find it easier to work a keyboard than to hold a pencil or turn pages. In addition, specially adapted equipment or personal help may be required. In certain instances, it may be appropriate to waive the test altogether and permit an alternative demonstration of job ability.

Disclosing Test Results

Test scores and results should be disclosed only to test administrators, HR representatives, and any managers directly involved in the testing and hiring process. Disclosing test results to the test takers themselves may be dictated by state law. Some states allow employees and former employees, but not applicants, access to the HR files and all the information they contain that was used to make an employment decision. Unless specific exceptions are cited, test information is also accessible. State and local civil service laws generally require government employers to notify test takers of their total scores and of the cutoff for qualification.

Many employers disclose test results to test takers as a matter of fairness. Those reluctant to reveal the results would argue that disclosure without explanation may result in a misinterpretation of the scores. In addition, there is concern over compromising test security.

Types of Tests

In an attempt to diminish any confusion over the vast array of tests available, we will look at two primary classifications with several subclasses: (1) achievement and aptitude tests and (2) physical and security-related tests.

Achievement and Aptitude Tests

Achievement tests are designed to measure current skills and indicate a person's existing abilities. *Aptitude tests* are intended to measure a person's potential ability to perform a given task. Professional testers recognize the distinction in terms, but prefer to categorize achievement and ability tests together, maintaining that both measure developed ability and therefore yield related results. Examples of achievement and aptitude tests are tests of job knowledge, work samples, intelligence tests, and personality tests.

Job Knowledge Tests

Tests of job knowledge, also known as trade tests, require applicants to demonstrate the degree of existing knowledge they have concerning how a job is performed. Hence, these tests screen prospective employees to ensure they possess the experience they claim. Such challenges are based on the premise that the tests closely resembling a job and closely measuring performance against sample tasks are better indicators of actual job performance. The majority of companies that conduct job knowledge tests require them for clerical as well as other office positions, production and service jobs, and technical work. Tests may include office math, office procedures, general clerical ability, stenographic skills, secretarial procedures, mechanical familiarity and knowledge, accounting procedures, and word processing.

Job knowledge tests may be oral or written. Oral tests may consist of a series of questions asked by a test administrator or may be more structured, with a panel asking applicants a preselected set of questions. A structured scoring system determines the results. Oral tests generally take less time to administer than do written tests but are not easily standardized, making a legal challenge more probable. Written tests of job knowledge are more common and are usually scored on a pass-fail basis. They are more easily administered and standardized, and more comprehensive than are most oral exams. Such tests may, however, be costly to develop and, by virtue of the fact that they are written, tend to emphasize literacy. This last point could pose problems if literacy skills are not relevant to the job.

Most job knowledge tests are developed according to the content-validation approach and are considered to possess high validity overall. Many companies develop and validate their own tests internally; others purchase commercially developed tests. Anyone intending to purchase a test should first conduct a thorough job analysis to determine its appropriateness. Additional information regarding commercially developed job knowledge tests may be obtained from Employers' Tests and Services Associates in Chambersburg, Pennsylvania (717/264-9509), the Psychological Corporation in San Antonio, Texas (512/299-1060), or Purdue University in West Lafayette, Indiana (317/743-9618).

Work Samples

Work samples differ from job knowledge tests in that they require applicants to demonstrate a level of skill as opposed to a degree of knowledge. Work samples may be used with job-related equipment, such as a keyboard, or performed on simulated equipment, as with a repair test. Since work samples test an existing level of achievement, they are used to select experienced workers having a degree of proficiency in a particular area. For this reason, they are often useful in making promotion decisions.

There are two basic types of work samples: motor and verbal. An example of a motor work sample is a programming test. Common verbal work samples include in-basket tests for managers and tests of ability to write business letters. Both motor and verbal work samples are considered to be highly valid predictors of job proficiency. Because of this, and the fact that they are generally well accepted by job applicants and employees, work sample tests are growing in popularity. They are, however, time-consuming to administer.

In developing work samples, the most critical factor is a complete and thorough job analysis. Furthermore, in order to protect themselves adequately from challenges to a work sample's validity, employers should fully document all the steps in its development.

Large companies generally contact outside professionals for assistance in preparing work samples. The Educational Testing Service in Princeton, New Jersey (609/921-9000); National Computer Systems Professional Assessment Services in Minneapolis, Minnesota (800/328-6759); and QUIZ, Inc. in Atlanta, Georgia (404/843-1124) are but a few of the suppliers that can help an organization custom-develop work samples or provide prepared samples for selected fields and skills.

Intelligence Tests

Experts cannot agree as to just what intelligence is. Some experts maintain that there is an intelligence quotient (IQ) measuring a person's ability to perform all cognitive or thinking tasks. Others believe that intelligence is multidimensional, consisting of separate mental abilities that cannot be "averaged out" to equal one level. Others define intelligence in terms of many cognitive abilities that together result in an overall mental ability.

The controversy over a definition of intelligence leads, not surprisingly, to disagreement over its measurement. Some use general intelligence tests that concentrate on abstract functions involving the use of verbal or numerical reasoning. The effectiveness of such tests for specific jobs is questionable, however, so many employers instead choose to use aptitude tests that evaluate more practical abilities. A number of such aptitude tests are available for measuring clerical, mechanical, and computer-related abilities. There are also several multiple-aptitude tests that measure a variety of job-related skills.

Employers intending to purchase intelligence tests should ask for evidence that the test is valid relative to the type of job for which it will be administered. In general, multiple-aptitude tests have a higher validity rate than do single tests. Additional information regarding an intelligence test's validity may be found in such test directories as the *Mental Measurements Yearbook*.

Personality Tests

Personality tests may focus on a variety of psychological characteristics. For example, there are tests for measuring a person's emotional stability, ability to work under pressure, and susceptibility to depression, paranoia, hysteria, or schizophrenia. Even eating disorders may be identified.

Test publishers generally sell personality tests only to those trained in psychological testing. Information regarding the services of industrial psychologists to assist your organization with the development or implementation of validated psychological tests may be obtained from the American Psychological Association (202/955-7600).

There is a great deal of controversy surrounding personality tests. Proponents of this assessment tool maintain that an objective personality test, coupled with other traditional selection devices, can provide a clear picture of a person's abilities, interests, and potential. This, it is argued, can result in lower turnover rates and greater productivity. Proponents also maintain that personality tests disclose information in such a way that those taking such tests are unaware of exactly what they are revealing. Hence, the probability of charges of discrimination and resulting lawsuits is greatly diminished.

Opponents of personality tests argue, however, that personality is extremely difficult to measure. Even if tests could perfectly measure an individual's personality, there is no reason to assume that this would result in greater productivity. There is also concern over the inherent assumption that personalities do not change, implying that matches deemed appropriate or inappropriate through testing will remain so. Furthermore, there is doubt as to the validity of personality tests that fail to take into account the role of motivation: an unmotivated employee is not likely to perform well on the job, even with the desired personality traits.

Physical and Security-Related Tests

Physical and security-related tests are intended to ensure a workforce that is physically capable of performing the essential functions of each job, does not threaten the health or safety of others, has been honest in the presentation of its respective skills and background, and may be trusted with the daily dealings of the job. Physical and security-related tests include preemployment physical exams, physical ability and psychomotor tests, drug tests, genetic testing, polygraph tests, and written honesty tests.

Preemployment Physical Exams

Preemployment physical examinations can identify individuals who are not physically able to perform the essential functions of a job in a safe and effective manner. More specifically, such exams may disclose a person's past and current state of health, prior exposure to harmful substances or an injurious environment, family health history, and genetic composition. (Additional information regarding genetic testing follows.) Predictive screening can also assess an applicant's susceptibility to future injury.

Employers are subject to the preemployment physical restrictions and guidelines of their respective states. These generally include requiring the employer to pay for the entire cost of the exam, providing the employee with a copy of the results, and maintaining the confidentiality of the results. State regulations may also control the timing of tests and who may not be tested. Some states restrict preemployment physicals to applicants receiving an offer of employment. In these cases, employment is generally conditioned on the successful completion of the medical exam. Other jurisdictions stipulate that preemployment medical exams must be given to all applicants, including those with prevailing disabilities. Depending on the test results, accommodation for those with physical or other impairments may be required, barring undue hardship to the employer. Note also the provision in the Americans with Disabilities Act (see Chapter 6) that people with disabilities cannot be singled out for physical exams.

Employers are advised to ascertain relevant state requirements before beginning, or continuing with, preemployment physical tests. This can be accomplished by examining state fair employment acts or civil rights acts, or by consulting with an attorney knowledgeable in this area.

In these litigious times, ever-increasing numbers of employers are requiring applicants and employees to sign a waiver acknowledging that the company does not guarantee the accuracy of its physician's conclusions. This sort of waiver is an attempt to limit the employer's liability for negligence, if the employee later suffers an on-the-job injury as a result of a condition that was not detected during the preemployment physical.

Preemployment physical exams can be significant detective and evaluative tools, assuming the administering physician is familiar with the tasks that are essential to the performance of each applicable job and evaluation is limited to the candidate's ability to perform those tasks. Test results are not always accurate, however, and they offer limited predictive qualities. Consequently, they are effective, but only as one of several selection devices.

Physical Ability and Psychomotor Tests

Many on-the-job injuries occur because the tasks require more strength and endurance than the employee can exert without excessive stress. These injuries can lead to increased absenteeism and turnover, not to mention claims for workers' compensation and health insurance. Since it is extremely difficult, if not impossible, to judge a person's strength and level of endurance on the basis of body size and appearance, physical ability tests, also known as strength and endurance tests, can be helpful preemployment selection devices for positions requiring physical performance.

Several strength and endurance factors may be relevant to employee selection:

- Dynamic strength, involving the power of arm and leg muscles to support or move the body's own weight
- Trunk strength, which is dynamic strength specific to trunk muscles
- Explosive strength, which involves a burst of muscular effort
- Static strength, the muscular force needed to lift, push, or pull heavy objects
- Dynamic flexibility, the ability to make repeated trunk or limb flexing movements
- Gross body equilibrium, which measures the body's ability to maintain or regain balance
- Stamina, the ability to sustain physical activity over long periods of time

The preferred validation method for physical ability tests is content validity. Simply stated, a thorough job analysis has determined that a given test accurately reflects the primary duties and responsibilities of a job. Many employers contact private agencies or clinics for assistance with physical ability testing.

Psychomotor tests measure such abilities as manual dexterity, motor ability, and hand-eye coordination. They are used primarily for semiskilled, repetitive work, such as packing and certain forms of inspection. Most psychomotor tests are simulation tests, although relevant written exams may be useful. The most valid psychomotor test should call for the use of the same muscle groups as required on the job. Custom-made tests that reproduce the combination of motor abilities needed have been shown to have fair validity.

Drug and Alcohol Tests

Drug testing is one of the most anxiety-producing issues confronting HR specialists and managers today. Chances are that 10 percent of your workforce uses illegal drugs, and even more abuse alcohol. The impact on businesses is disturbing and costly. Lost productivity accidents and medical claims due to drug and alcohol use cost businesses more than $140 billion a year: $60 billion is attributable to drug use, with the balance due to alcohol. Seventy-five percent used drugs on the job, 64 percent admitted drugs affected their work, 44 percent sold drugs to other employees, and 18 percent stole from coworkers to support their habit.

Compared with the average employee, a typical drug-using employee is 2.5 times more likely to be absent eight days or more per year, 3 times more likely to be late for work, 3.6 times more likely to be involved in workplace accidents, 5 times more likely to file a workers' compensation claim, and incur 300 percent higher medical claims (*Drugs in the Workplace*; Vol. XI, No. 8 (August, 1997)).

In spite of these statistics, objections have been raised to drug and alcohol testing in the workplace. For instance, across-the-board testing as part of a "zero tolerance" policy, designed to deter drug and alcohol use off the job as well as on the job, has been criticized by some courts as an unwarranted invasion of privacy. In addition, opponents object to drug and alcohol testing because of potential legal liability, the excessive costs for properly conducted testing programs, an adverse effect on employee morale, and the possibility of erroneous results.

Still, an increasing number of employers favor some form of drug and alcohol testing. Typically employers use urine testing to screen for drugs. Screening tests are the tests of choice for many employers. Viewed by most experts as an initial drug screen, it will reveal the presence of drugs, but it does not indicate what or how much. Screening tests alone are not legally defensible, so when positive results occur, employers generally conduct a second, confirmatory test. If the second test reveals illegal drug use, employers may deny an applicant employment or may terminate an employee after ample opportunity is provided for treatment or cessation of drug abuse.

This process can have legal ramifications in the form of suits filed by applicants or employees claiming to have been falsely accused of drug use. One common basis for such lawsuits is the allegation that positive test results do not necessarily prove any act of wrongdoing. Urine can retain traces of drugs for anywhere from a few days, as in the case of cocaine, to a month, as with the drug classification cannabinoids. Consequently, although a urine test may indicate use of an illegal drug, it cannot establish with certainty that the drug was used during working hours, impaired the employee's ability to perform work, interfered with the work of others, or endangered the safety of others.

Because of the possibility of false positives (and missed drug use), an increasing number of employers are using medical review officers (MROs). These are doctors who examine lab results and interview applicants and workers to determine whether the test should be labeled positive. The MRO can also prevent the firing of an employee for illegal drug use when there is a legitimate medical explanation.

Many employers use the federal drug testing program, which is administered by the Substance Abuse and Mental Health Services Administration and is widely respected in terms of accuracy, worker protection, and legal defensibility It is required for all employers with Department of Transportation licenses and affects nearly 4 million workers whose jobs have safety or security implications. However, although it is a model, the federal program is conservative and does not provide sufficient testing to suit some employers. Because prescription drug abuse can prove dangerous, employers may want to test for legal as well as illegal drugs. In fact, some of these drugs, like sedative-hypnotics or benzodiazepines, can have devastating consequences when used by workers in positions that are safety-sensitive.

Testing for methamphetamines is increasingly popular. The potent, cheap, illegal street version of methamphetamine—"crystal meth"—is a synthetic stimulant and the form that laboratories look for. This is the D-isomer variant. The L-isomer variant, which means it has no abuse potential and is not illegal, is of no concern. The Vick's inhaler is an L-isomer variant. Labs must distinguish between the D- and the L-isomers of methamphetamine; otherwise they might report the user of a Vicks inhaler as testing positive.

Physical effects of methamphetamine on human behavior include rapid heart rate, elevated blood pressure, increased body temperature and respiratory rate, pupillary dilation, reduced food intake and decreased sleep time. Psychological effects include feelings of euphoria, increased vigor, and increased sociability. Abusers have been known to mask their addiction behind apparent diligence in the workplace.

Users quickly develop a tolerance for specific doses of methamphetamines and must increase their intake to achieve the same effect. Many methamphetamine users simultaneously drink alcohol to increase the impact of the drug.

Employers concerned about alcohol abuse can test by means of the conventional breath method used by regulated employers or through urine testing. The problem with the latter is diabetes. Alcohol will show up in urine either because the person was drinking or because there is glucose, a sign of uncontrolled diabetes. If there is also some bacteria or yeast in the body, the glucose can ferment and turn into ethanol, resulting in a positive urine test result, even if the person had not consumed a drop of alcohol. Additionally testing alcohol-positive urine for glucose is not effective since the glucose may have already fermented.

Confronted with drug and alcohol testing, some applicants and employees will try to "beat" the system. These attempts at adulteration are often detected by savvy lab technicians. For example, if Urinaid (glutaraldehyde) is used as an adulterant to mask marijuana, labs can determine that tampering had occurred.

Employers planning to use any form of drug or alcohol testing should develop and implement a set of well-defined, written guidelines, made available to all employees. These guidelines should include the purpose of the testing, who is to be tested, what method of testing will be used, where and when testing will take place, who will administer the test, and how the test will be administered. If urine tests are to be conducted, the guidelines should include a description of the manner in which specimens will be collected (privacy and dignity should be preserved without compromising test security or hampering test results). In addition, all applicants and employees being tested should be asked to sign a consent form, agreeing to the test and to the release of the results to the employer.

State laws on drug testing vary and should be checked carefully by employers and their legal counsel. In addition, employers should consult with an attorney before implementing drug and alcohol testing programs of any kind.

AIDS Testing

Acquired immune deficiency syndrome (AIDS) is an area of increasing concern for all employers. Many companies have developed AIDS policy statements affirming that their terms of employment, benefits, training, and termination relating to employees with AIDS do not discriminate. Since such special statements imply that basing employment decisions on AIDS-related factors would be discriminatory, there is little justification for employers to implement an AIDS testing program. In addition, there is no direct test for AIDS itself. Current tests can show only whether a person has developed antibodies in response to the AIDS virus. The presence of antibodies, or of the AIDS virus itself, does not guarantee that the person will develop AIDS or, perhaps more significant, is infectious. According to the surgeon general's report on AIDS, "Everyday living does not present any risk of infection. You cannot get AIDS from casual social contact. . . . Nor has AIDS been contracted from . . . eating in restaurants (even if a restaurant worker has AIDS or carries the AIDS virus). You cannot get AIDS from toilets, doorknobs, telephones . . . [or] office machinery."

The surgeon general's conclusions regarding AIDS have led many courts to declare that there is no risk to coworkers from AIDS virus carriers or AIDS-infected individuals.

In addition to statements by the surgeon general and the courts, the Centers for Disease Control (CDC) has taken a stand with regard to this disease. It has issued recommendations for preventing the transmission of AIDS in the workplace. These recommendations pertain, in particular, to health care workers, persons providing personal services, and those preparing and serving food and beverages. According to the CDC, AIDS is not proved to be spread by casual contact, nor is it known to be transmitted through the preparation or serving of food. Hence, routine AIDS antibody screening for these and other groups is not recommended. The CDC does recommend that testing be made available to health care workers and others who wish to know their AIDS status.

Copies of the CDC guidelines on AIDS may be obtained from:

Office of Public Affairs, Centers for Disease Control
1600 Clifton Road, Northeast
Atlanta, Georgia 30333

In the few instances where you may determine that there is a legitimate basis for testing an applicant or employee for AIDS or, more accurately, for AIDS antibodies, obtain prior consent from the individual. Use a reliable indicator, such as the enzyme-linked immunosorbent assay (ELISA) test. If the results are positive, give a confirmation test, such as the HIVAGEN Test. Inform the applicant or employee of test results, which must be kept in the utmost confidence.

Additional information regarding AIDS and AIDS testing may be obtained by calling the AIDS hot line (1-800/342-AIDS) or by writing to:

U.S. Public Health Service
Public Affairs Office
Hubert H. Humphrey Building
200 Independence Avenue, Southwest
Washington, D.C. 20201

Genetic Testing

Genetic testing is among the most controversial forms of employment testing. It includes diagnostic and carrier testing, as well as prenatal diagnosis, and can identify individuals at increased risk to contract various conditions, including Alzheimer's disease, heart disease, cystic fibrosis, Huntington's disease, and breast cancer. The federal government is currently about midway through a fifteen-year project designed to map the entire human genetic system. Although only an estimated 5 percent of U.S. companies conduct any type of genetic testing (mostly chemical, petroleum, and electronics companies), this Human Genome Project will undoubtedly generate increased interest as the study nears completion. Employers must then consider the pros and cons of yet another type of test.

Proponents contend that employers have a strong incentive to subject applicants and employees to genetic testing. Approximately 390,000 workers contract a disabling occupational disease each year. Occupational diseases are ones that arise out of, and in the course of, employment for which a person is entitled to benefits under workers' compensation or similar laws. Nearly 100,000 of these workers die. Screening and testing for genetic abnormalities could prevent many illnesses and deaths.

Also, between 85 and 90 percent of all individuals with health insurance in the United States are covered under employer group health plans. Businesses struggling to keep their health care costs down can do so by identifying individuals at risk for serious genetic conditions. Decisions can then be made concerning the placement of workers in high-risk jobs, or even hiring them at all, on the basis of test results.

But what if a person does not want to know about her genetic disposition? And what right does an employer have to determine that an individual has a predisposition to a disease? Can businesses legitimately determine whether people work based on their genes?

Even proponents will acknowledge that genetic tests are not terribly reliable. For example, in 1996, doctors at Johns Hopkins Medical Institution found that 56 out of 177 patients undergoing genetic testing for colon cancer would have received false-negative results without additional laboratory tests. Additionally, the tests do not necessarily provide conclusive evidence. A person with a predisposition to breast or colon cancer might experience the onset of disease anywhere from age twenty-five to eighty-five—or never display a single symptom.

Proponents also acknowledge that the cost of genetic testing is prohibitive. Although the price is dropping (a single test currently costing $800 cost $2,000 six years ago), it is still a disincentive. Projections are that the cost will continue to drop, to less than $100.

Opponents also fear that genetic information will be used to discriminate against people rather than help them. Diseases and illnesses peculiar to certain ethnic groups could screen out a disproportionate number of group members. Also, people refusing to take genetic tests could find themselves passed over for promotions and rejected for group insurance.

There is concern as well about maintaining the confidentiality of private medical data. As records are passed back and forth between computer systems, information can and does seep out, despite federal laws requiring a company to maintain HR records separate from medical records. Keeping genetic information private simply cannot be guaranteed.

These last three issues—insurance benefits, discrimination, and invasion of privacy—are intertwined. Since the EEOC expanded the ADA to protect individuals subjected to discrimination on the "basis of genetic information related to illness, disease, or other disorders," any applicant or employee can take legal action on the basis of genetic discrimination. They would, however, be forced to disclose the very information they wanted to keep private in the first place.

Currently, only a handful of states have laws addressing aspects of workplace genetic discrimination and privacy. Some require probable cause for all testing; others require reasonable cause for employees but make no provision for applicants. Many of the laws apply only to specific gene mutations for specific disorders; others prevent discrimination as a result of genetic testing, but not if an employer or insurer obtains the information from an outside source, such as a medical record.

Companies considering the implementation of genetic testing

should ensure that all testing is voluntary. Individuals should have the right to learn test results and, if desired, receive counseling regarding the implications of genetic testing. In addition, test results should remain private. Communication of test results with any third parties without consent of the individual should be prohibited.

Genetic testing statistics are from *Workforce* (July 1997) and *Workforce Tools* (July 1997).

Polygraph Tests

In 1988, the Employee Polygraph Protection Act all but banned from use, by private sector employers, mechanical lie detector tests as screening devices for job applicants. There are certain exceptions where polygraph testing is still permitted, among them when employers hire workers for security-sensitive jobs and pharmaceutical work. Employers that manufacture, distribute, or dispense controlled substances are also exempt. In addition, the Employee Polygraph Protection Act does not apply to the federal government, state or local governments, or industries with national defense or national security contracts. Moreover, businesses with access to highly classified information may continue to use polygraph tests. However, although these employers are exempt, they may not use the results of the polygraphs as the sole basis for making an employment-related decision.

Use of polygraph tests to investigate employees reasonably suspected of stealing or committing other infractions is also permitted. Access to stolen property alone, however, is not considered a reasonable basis for suspicion. An employee believed to have committed an infraction must first receive a written notice that identifies the loss being investigated and the employer's basis for suspicion, and explains the employee's statutory rights under the act. Employees must also be advised of their right to consult with counsel before and during the examination.

Employees and applicants may refuse to take the polygraph test or may terminate it at any time. No test is allowed to last longer than ninety minutes. In addition, upon learning of the test results, they may request a second test or hire an independent examiner for a second opinion. Test takers must not be asked degrading or intrusive questions or questions about sexual behavior, union activities, or religious, racial, or political beliefs. They must be given advance notice relative to testing conditions and, before the test begins, must be permitted to review all questions. Afterward, they must receive a written copy of the test questions, their responses, and any opinions based on the test results.

Employers may test according to these exceptions and guidelines only if they use the services of licensed, bonded examiners.

Violators of the Employee Polygraph Protection Act may be fined; required to hire, reinstate, or promote the employee or applicant; and possibly be required to pay lost wages and benefits, as well as attorneys' fees. Employers must post a notice of this law conspicuously where all applicants and employees may see it.

Some states have polygraph laws that are even more restrictive than the federal statute. Such state laws will not be preempted by federal law unless the state provisions conflict with the federal act. Employers that use polygraph tests unlawfully risk not only violation of federal and state statutes, but also legal liability on the basis of defamation and invasion of privacy.

Written Honesty Tests

Not surprisingly, since the Employee Polygraph Protection Act virtually banned the use of the most popular form of lie detector test, there has been an increase in the use of written honesty or integrity tests. Most of these tests pose a series of direct and indirect questions related to thievery and deceit; others also seek out the potential for unsafe work habits, drug abuse, and counterproductivity. These tests generally take about twenty minutes to complete and are scored by computer in approximately six seconds.

Although most would agree that written honesty tests are less intimidating than polygraphs, there is a great deal of concern expressed over their validity. Indeed, there are reports of companies' simply transferring polygraph questions onto paper.

Test publishers argue that their written honesty exams are highly accurate and based on extensive research. However, many experts express concern over reliance on such test results to determine job suitability.

Alternative Selection Procedures

Even proponents agree that test results should not be the sole determining factor in making an employment decision. Other selection procedures, such as the face-to-face interview, the employment application form, and references, should also be used for making hiring decisions. These procedures are covered by the EEOC's *Uniform Guidelines on Employee Selection Procedures* and are treated in detail in other chapters of this book.

Finally, employers should consider performance appraisals as an alternative selection procedure in matters of promotion, transfer, demotion, changes in salary, job posting, and career pathing. An evaluation program should consist of criteria that are directly related to the primary duties and responsibilities of a particular job. The standards should be specific, observable, and measurable. Factors to be considered might include the amount of time spent performing various duties, their level of difficulty, their frequency of performance, and the consequences of error. The nature of each position, as well as its level of responsibility, should determine the amount of weight assigned to each of these factors. In addition, to be considered valid, an appraisal system should yield consistent data and show a direct correlation between the factors being measured and those that are critical elements of a particular job. Also, a performance appraisal system should be standardized in its design and consistent in its administration. Any employer using the system should be given written guidelines and trained in their implementation.

Summary

The interpretive and evaluative potential of employment testing is controversial, and many specific test categories, like drug testing, AIDS testing, and genetic testing, are the subject of much debate.

Employers interested in exploring the use of tests today must contend with numerous questions—for example:

- What constitutes a test?
- What are the benefits and disadvantages of testing?
- What is validation, and how are certain tests validated?
- Is it advisable to buy a prepackaged validated test?
- What kind of testing policy is most effective?
- What are the differences among certain types of tests?
- How costly is testing?
- How reliable are the results in terms of making sound employment decisions?

It is best to err on the side of caution and use tests as part of the selection process, balanced by alternative selection procedures such as the application form, interview, references, and performance appraisals.

Chapter 12
Making the Selection

Finally, after all your prerecruitment preparation, exploration of various recruitment sources, familiarization with equal employment opportunity (EEO) laws, interviewing, documentation, and testing, it is time to make your selection. For many interviewers, this step is easy: One applicant stands out, and there is no question but that she should be hired. For others, however, this is the most difficult step in the employment process. Often several candidates possess the required qualifications, making the choice difficult; or the interviewer may feel uneasy when there is only one viable candidate, wondering if the recruitment effort has been thorough enough or the screening process too critical. Doubts may also arise because of the heavy responsibility in making a hiring decision, including the potential consequences of a poor selection.

Conducting Reference Checks

Most interviewers do not make a hiring decision without first checking a candidate's references. In spite of well-honed recruiting, screening, and interviewing skills, interviewers do not feel comfortable in extending a job offer, for any level of employment, without more closely examining the background of the candidate of choice. This usually means talking with or acquiring written information from former employers and verifying educational credentials. Most professionals agree that personal references rarely have any merit, since the candidate will obviously list only those people likely to provide rave reviews. Occasionally, however, these may be useful to supplement other character or professional references. In addition, receiving feedback from those who know the candidate on a personal level may serve to ferret out potential negligent hiring and retention situations (see Chapter 6). All of these efforts will help in the selection process by confirming the interviewer's own impressions of the candidate.

Invasion of Privacy and Defamation of Character

Although most employers agree that references can be a valuable employment selection tool, few readily provide information to other employers. In fact companies commonly refuse to give references for former workers. This lack of cooperation is founded on fear of being sued by a former employee for giving a less than flattering reference. Accordingly, many employers verify only dates of employment in an effort to mitigate any legal exposure on the basis of invasion of privacy or defamation of character. Indeed, even if the applicant was off by a month when recording his dates of employment, a former employer may simply state that these dates are incorrect, without giving the right dates. This leaves you to wonder how far off the applicant was and if he was trying to conceal something.

Although it is difficult to blame employers for being careful in this regard, they may be overly cautious, failing to realize that a great deal of information can be legitimately and legally imparted without fear of retaliation from the former employee. Although apprehension of being sued for defamation motivates many employers, understanding the meaning of the term should alleviate this concern somewhat. Defamation occurs when one person makes a statement, orally or written, about another that is false or harms the person's reputation. In employment situations, allegations of defamation frequently arise when a former employer tells a prospective employer why an individual was terminated. The key to whether defamation has actually occurred is the truth or falsity of the information. To be actionable, a statement must be a personal attack, lacking in veracity. Thus, if a former employer gives a prospective employer a false and damaging reason for an employee's termination or gives the discharged person a false basis for the discharge and the applicant repeats this to a prospective employer, then the candidate may have been defamed.

Employers fearing charges of defamation should also be aware that, based on case law, truth is an absolute defense, even if the statements made about a former employee are negative. However, the truth, too, may be actionable if it is volunteered with malicious intent to do harm. Disputable opinions or statements are also protected by a limited privilege; that is, such communications must be malicious to be actionable.

Common Law Doctrine of Qualified Privilege

Employers are further protected by the common law principle of qualified privilege. This doctrine is premised on the public policy that an exchange of information relative to the job suitability of employees is in the best interest of both employers and the general public. Consequently, if the information is defamatory but without malice, it is deemed privileged.

This privilege is not without certain limitations. The information must be provided in good faith and in accordance with the questions asked. For example, if a prospective employer asks about a former employee's ability to work unsupervised, the voluntary statement that she had a problem getting in on time is not protected. Also, information about an individual's private life should not be offered unless it is relevant to work performance. Moreover, former employers should ensure that the information is being provided to the appropriate party and is relevant to the requirements of the job. Failure to comply with any of these conditions could eliminate the protection provided by the qualified privilege.

Good-Faith References

The number of states with reference-checking laws is increasing. These laws protect employers that provide good-faith job references of former and current employees. This added protection enables employers to give and receive references, going beyond the typical "play it safe" policy of verifying only dates of employment for former employees. Even with such legal protection, however, the trend is to proceed cautiously, providing only documented information that can be easily defended in court. In addition to dates of employment, this includes salary ranges, promotions, transfers and demotions, performance evaluations, and attendance records.

References and Negligent Hiring

In spite of the degree of protection afforded former employers by case law, the common law doctrine of qualified privilege, and individual state laws, many still fear liability and hesitate to provide references. The result has been a proliferation of lawsuits based on negligent hiring and retention (see Chapter 6). The only effective defense against charges of negligent hiring is based on a complete investigation of all job-related facets of a candidate's background prior to employment. This may include reference checks of previous convictions and driving record violations, where deemed appropriate. Workers' compensation records for positions requiring physical labor may also be checked to alert future employers to potential problems. Educational records, to be discussed shortly, should also be reviewed, if relevant.

This situation presents quite a dilemma for employers: Former employers can be sued for defamation or invasion of privacy for providing improper references; prospective employers can also be sued for negligent hiring and retention if references are not properly checked. Employment experts have suggested a solution: that job applicants be required to sign waivers relieving former employers of liability if they are not hired because of unflattering references. However, such waivers would be of questionable legal enforceability.

Guidelines for Releasing Information

A more workable solution would establish guidelines governing both the release and ascertainment of reference information. With regard to releasing such information, consider the following guidelines:

• One person, or a limited number of persons, should be in charge of releasing information about former employees. These individuals should be trained in matters relating to laws of defamation and qualified privilege.

• Supervisors and managers should be discouraged from releasing information over the telephone, even though telephone references are the preferred method for acquiring information. Releasing information by telephone may result in loss of the protection afforded by principles of qualified privilege.

• During exit interviews, tell terminating employees what information will be provided during a reference check. If the employee is being asked to leave, make sure she knows the reason.

• If possible, obtain a signed consent form from a terminating employee, authorizing you to provide relevant reference information to prospective employers.

• Always tell the truth, and make certain you have documentation to back it up. Provide examples to support your statements.

• Make certain that the person to whom you are providing reference information has a legitimate and legal right to it.

• Be certain all information provided is job related.

• Do not volunteer unsolicited information.

• Try to say something positive about a former employee to demonstrate that you are acting in good faith.

Guidelines for Obtaining Information

In a 1995 Society for Human Resource Management reference checking survey, employers were asked what they want to learn about candidates from references and, if obtained, how helpful they found the information. Here are the results (numbers may not add to 100):

Category of Information	Received Adequate Information	Received Inadequate Information	Not Applicable
Dates of employment	96%	1%	3%
Salary history	45%	30%	24%
Reason candidate left previous employer	47%	44%	7%
Work habits	41%	48%	8%
Personality traits	24%	52%	22%
Violent/bizarre behavior	11%	54%	34%
Human relations skills	37%	43%	19%
Qualifications for a particular job	56%	30%	12%
Extent of special knowledge or skills	46%	34%	10%
Eligibility for rehire	65%	25%	7%

Source: HR Magazine (December 1995).

As you can see, the more tangible categories—that is, those more readily verifiable—yielded the most satisfactory information. Intangible categories, such as personality traits or behavior, left prospective employers guessing.

To increase your chances of obtaining meaningful information about potential employees, consider these guidelines:

• Conduct all reference checks in a uniform manner. Never single out only women or minorities for reference checks or follow up on only those candidates who strike you as "suspect." Inconsistency may be viewed as discriminatory.

- If an applicant is ultimately rejected because of a negative recommendation, be prepared to document the job-related reason.

- If, while conducting a reference check, you discover that an applicant has filed an EEO charge against her former employer, keep in mind that it is illegal to refuse to employ someone for this reason.

- Obtain permission from applicants, on the application form, to contact former employers.

- Carefully question the validity of comments made by former employers. In spite of possible legal ramifications, it is not uncommon for employers to express negative feelings toward a good employee who resigned for a better position. And employees terminated for poor performance sometimes work out a deal with their former employers that ensures them of positive reference checks. Therefore, probe for objective statements regarding job performance.

- Exercise caution when interpreting a respondent's tone of voice, use of silence, or implication. Be aware, too, of phrases that may be interpreted in more than one way. For example, if a former employer were to say, "She gave every impression of being a conscientious worker," ask for examples.

- Since reference checks are generally reserved for applicants making it to the final stage of consideration, give these individuals the opportunity to refute any information resulting from the reference check that contradicts impressions or information obtained during the interview.

- If possible, check with a minimum of two previous employers to rule out the possibility of either positive or negative bias. This may also disclose patterns in an individual's work habits.

- Reference checks should be conducted by the person who interviewed the applicant. If the interview was conducted by representatives from both HR and the department in which the opening exists, the HR specialist usually does the checking.

- Do not automatically assume that a reported personality clash is the applicant's fault.

- Having been fired does not necessarily mean that an applicant is a bad risk. Employees are terminated for many reasons; get an explanation before jumping to conclusions.

- Since it is unlikely that an applicant will give permission to contact his current employer, it is wise to tell the applicant that any job offer will be contingent upon a satisfactory reference from his current employer.

Telephone References

The most effective means for gathering information on an applicant under consideration for hire is by telephone. Although many employers hesitate to verify much more than dates of employment, it is worth a try. Telephone reference checks will enable you to evaluate the former employer's tone of voice and voice inflections. It also allows for clarification of comments that may have a double meaning, such as, "You'll be lucky to get him to work for you." Not only is a telephone reference likely to produce more valuable information, it takes less time to conduct.

Conducting telephone reference checks is much like conducting an interview. Virtually all the same skills (e.g., active listening and encouraging the other person to talk) are employed. In fact, about the only facet of an employment interview that cannot be incorporated into a telephone reference check is nonverbal communication. Because of this similarity to an interview, preparation for a telephone reference check plays a key role. Begin by deciding who to call. Ask the applicant for the names of her former supervisors and anyone else qualified to comment on the quality of her work. Also get the name of someone to contact in the HR department. It may be necessary to speak with more than one person. The supervisor and others with whom the applicant directly worked will be able to discuss work performance; HR will provide information regarding such matters as job title, dates of employment, absenteeism, tardiness, and salary history.

It is also important to prepare a telephone reference form in advance. As with a written reference form, you may want to have one for exempt positions and one for nonexempt positions. The same form can be used for both written and telephone references. However, in designing the forms, keep in mind that telephone references yield more information and therefore require more space for your notes. It is also likely that you will ask questions other than those on the form. Therefore, allow ample room between questions to take notes. A sample reference form for exempt positions is provided in Appendix I, and a sample for nonexempt positions is found in Appendix J.

When conducting a telephone reference check, first identify yourself, your organization, and the reason for your call. To illustrate:

"Good morning, Mr. Salerno. My name is Peter Fisher. I am the human resources representative for Valdart, Ltd., and I am conducting a reference check on your former employee, Ms. Susan Downey."

If there is any reluctance on the part of the previous employer, offer your telephone number and suggest that he call to verify your identity. If it is a long-distance call, offer to receive the call collect.

Always begin by verifying the information provided by the applicant. This will assist the former employer to recall specific information about the individual—for example:

> "Ms. Downey has informed me that she worked for your organization as an industrial engineer from June 1996 through December 1997. She indicated that she regularly fulfilled four key responsibilities during that time: analyzing current operating procedures; developing flowcharts and linear responsibility charts to improve operating procedures; implementing systems by programming personal computers and by training staff; and advising management of project feasibility after conducting studies. Would you agree with this summary of her primary responsibilities?"

While listening to your opening statement, the respondent's thought speed will enable him to think about other aspects of the candidate's work. At this point, you will be able to proceed with the other categories on the reference form. As soon as you anticipate that the former employer is willing to volunteer information, shift from close-ended questions to competency-based and open-ended questions. Be prepared to ask probing questions when more in-depth information is needed.

Written References

Written references usually consist of form letters designed to verify facts provided by the applicant. Unless directed to the attention of a specific supervisor or department head, these forms are usually routed to, and completed by, HR staff relying on the former employee's file for information. Even when addressed to the applicant's former manager, these inquiries may routinely be turned over to the company's HR department for response because of the increased number of lawsuits resulting from reference-related matters. Indeed, many employers hesitate to provide any unfavorable information and hence will only confirm the person's job title, dates of employment, and the company's policy regarding eligibility for rehire. Therefore, perspective employers are unable to ascertain a true picture of the candidate's skill level.

Another drawback to a written reference is the amount of time it takes to obtain a response. Even if the request is marked "Rush," it generally takes a minimum of one to two weeks for a reply. This is valuable time lost if you are waiting for the reference to be returned before making a hiring decision. In fact, the person you finally select may have accepted another job offer in the interim. The issue of lost time can be avoided by requesting references by e-mail. However, most former employers are uneasy about providing information on employees by e-mail since it may potentially be "read" by many people.

Make certain that your written request is comprehensive but not time-consuming. Each question should be straightforward, easy to understand, and work related. It is also advisable to have two separate form letters: one for exempt employees and another for nonexempt employees. In addition, try to direct your request to the applicant's former supervisor. You may also want to call this person prior to sending the letter, to make certain that she is still employed with the company. In addition, you can stress the importance of a speedy reply. Follow up with a telephone call three to four days after mailing your request to help expedite a reply.

Faxing is faster than the mail, but it is not recommended for references. References contain confidential information that should not be disclosed to everyone retrieving faxes.

Educational References

Applicants must provide written consent before a school can release educational records to a prospective employer. The Family Education Rights and Privacy Act (Buckley Amendment) allows students to inspect their scholastic records and to deny schools permission to release certain information. In an employment setting, a space for this permission should appear on the application form or a separate release form. Once the proper release has been obtained, academic information may be ascertained by the prospective employer, usually for a small fee.

Be certain to include the following questions when you check educational credentials: dates attended, major and minor courses of study, specific courses relevant to the position applied for, degree and honors received, attendance record, work-study program participation, and grade averages.

In considering this last point, remember that the value of scholastic achievement varies from school to school An overall index of 3.5 in one college might be equivalent to an index of 2.8 in another. Therefore, it is important to know something about the standing and reputation of a particular school.

Also, be careful about drawing conclusions based on grades. Not everyone does well on tests or in a classroom setting. This does not mean, however, that the applicant has not gained the knowledge needed to perform a particular job. Moreover, outstanding grades do not, in and of themselves, mean that someone will excel in a position.

Educational references are generally most useful in confirming the validity of information provided by an applicant. This can be important, since applicants have been known to claim degrees that they do not possess. Educational references may also prove to be valuable when an applicant has had little or no previous work experience. Remember, however, that these references should be conducted only when a job description clearly calls for specific educational achievements.

Personal References

Some application forms ask candidates to provide names of personal references. Usually, three names are called for, along with their relationship to the applicant, titles, telephone numbers, and addresses. Although asking someone to provide references guaranteed to offer only praise seems like a waste of time, many interviewers check personal references and maintain that the information gleaned is valid and useful. Specifically, personal references may reveal significant data relevant to the issue of negligent hiring and retention. Some go so far as to ask the references to refer still others who can discuss certain qualities and behavior characteristics. By talking with people not directly referred by the applicant, they are more likely to get a complete and accurate picture. Still others believe that the type of person used as a reference—that is, whether the person is, say a doctor, lawyer, or teacher—is significant. This premise has no relevance.

As with employment references, personal reference checks may result in charges of discrimination if potential employers do not abide by the guidelines already described in this chapter. Incorrectly, some employers believe that these guidelines do not apply when talking with a reference not connected with the applicant's former employment, prompting non-job-related and even illegal questions, in the belief that an acquaintance is more likely to reveal information relevant to the intangible qualities being sought.

Generally personal references should be avoided unless interviewers have absolutely no other source of employment or educational information and when the issue of negligent hiring is a factor. When personal references are checked, the information ascertained should be sifted carefully, and any data that appear biased and not factual should be filtered out.

Evaluating References

Obtaining reference information is important, but there is no real value to it if it is not properly evaluated. By and large, reference checks should be viewed as an interview; that is, the person conducting the check must listen to or read the information carefully in relation to the requirements and responsibilities of the job. In some ways, references are more difficult to assess than are interviews because they tend to be more subjective. Regardless of how well your questions are worded, references will offer biased responses, both positive and negative, that may cloud the picture of a candidate and justify more than one reference check. Also, loss of one job does not necessarily mean failure in another, nor does it indicate employee deficiencies. Conceivably termination could have been avoided if there had been a more appropriate job match or if the employee's personality had been more compatible with that of her supervisor.

The safest way to approach and evaluate reference checks is to view them as just one of the factors to consider in making a final selection. This does not deemphasize their value; it merely puts them in proper perspective. In addition, although each individual's impression is subjective, an overall consensus may be more readily treated as an objective fact.

Considering Other Factors

In addition to checking references, there are additional factors to consider before making the final selection:

1. *Review your objectives.* Remind yourself of the company purpose to be served in filling the job and how it fits in with other positions in the department, division, and organization. Consider its projected impact on both departmental and organizational goals.

2. *Review the job description to ensure thorough familiarity with the concrete requirements, duties, and responsibilities of the position.* Identify

the critical and secondary aspects of the job. In addition, review the approximate amount of time to be devoted to each task.

3. *Review the work history and relevant educational credentials of each candidate.* Identify all experiences and training that would prepare the candidate for the job.

4. *Consider the intangible requirements of the job.* Remember that certain intangible qualities, although subjective by definition, can still be job related. Therefore, identify and evaluate only intangibles that have a bearing on job performance.

5. *Evaluate applicants' reactions to various questions and statements.* For example, if the job requires extensive overtime and standing for long periods of time, cite each applicant's reaction to this information.

6. *Document and correlate each applicant's nonverbal communication patterns with his verbal communication.* Recollect patterns of body language and carefully interpret what was being "said" with certain gestures or movements.

7. *Take each applicant's salary requirements into consideration and compare them to the salary range for the available position.* The salary offered should be comfortable for both the prospective employee and the company.

8. *Assess the reasons offered for leaving previous employers.* If you see a pattern emerging every two years or so (e.g., "no room for growth"), it is possible that within a short time your company's name will be on this candidate's resumé.

9. *Consider the applicant's potential, especially if the opening is a stepping-stone to other positions.* Look for a future employee whose strengths are most likely to further the company's goals.

10. *Determine whether your organization and the available job are appropriate for the applicant.* Since it takes more than words to motivate another person, you can assess what your company offers in the way of career growth and other opportunities. Then correlate this information to your understanding of what the candidate is looking for in the way of a position and a work environment.

Review the position's primary duties, responsibilities, and requirements side by side with a chart describing how each promising candidate measures up against the determining factors. This will enable you to compare the qualifications of each applicant. A sample chart appears in Appendix K.

These steps will often reveal qualities that tip the scales in favor of one final candidate over the others. Also, keep in mind the role of your organization's affirmative action goals in the selection process, as described in Chapters 2 and 6.

Determining Who Should Choose

Reviewing the results of reference checks, going through the steps just outlined, and factoring in your affirmative action goals ideally should be done by all who participated in the interviewing process. This usually means a member of the HR department and representatives from the unit where the opening exists. These individuals should meet to exchange their views regarding the candidates under consideration. As a final step, they should review the selection checklist, identifying the concrete and intangible requirements of the job. In most instances, an assessment of all data collected will point in the direction of one candidate, and all concerned will agree. Occasionally, however, the department representative will favor one person and the HR specialist will prefer another. If after listening to each other's reasons, both parties still disagree, then the departmental representative should make the final selection. After all, she is the one who will be working directly with the employee on a day-to-day basis. HR representatives should go on record with their objections for future reference.

Notifying Selected and Rejected Candidates

After making a hiring decision, many interviewers immediately send letters to those candidates not chosen. It is wiser to wait until the selected applicant has been offered and accepts the job. If an offer is extended to your top choice and he has already accepted another position or lost interest, you may be forced to select someone else. It is most awkward to approach your second choice, having just sent out a letter of rejection.

Offers for each job should be made in writing. This can be done after a verbal offer has been made and accepted. Letters are usually sent by the HR specialist, with copies to the department. The contents of these letters should be concise and accurate, with no room for misunderstanding. Include the following elements:

- Official job title
- Department and division

- Hours of work
- Starting salary in weekly terms
- Time to report to work
- Location
- Person to see
- Arrangements regarding a preemployment physical, if relevant
- Arrangements regarding preemployment orientation, if relevant
- Agreement regarding a reference check with the present employer
- Identification and instructions for the completion of any literature enclosed (e.g., benefits forms)
- Who to contact with questions

The sample letter shown in Figure 12-1 incorporates these elements. Note that the language in this job offer avoids any commitment for a specific term of employment. Since this letter could be interpreted as representing an employment contract, it would be imprudent to give any indication that the position offered is permanent. In this regard, it may be desirable to go a step further by inserting an employment-at-will clause, similar to the one in the application. This step is not essential, however, and many employers believe it detracts from the welcome being extended to new employees. Accordingly, reference to the employment-at-will doctrine on the application form, as well as in the employee handbook distributed and explained to every new employee, preferably during orientation, is considered sufficient by most experts.

Once a candidate has been selected and your job offer has been accepted, it is time to notify the other applicants. Rejection letters should refer to the specific position for which an individual applied. In other words, do not reject the person overall; you may want to consider him for another position in the future.

The tone of your letter should be professional and sincere. Avoid including detailed information about the successful candidate. Doing so without permission of the new hire could be an invasion of privacy. In addition, a rejected applicant could use the disclosures as the basis for a claim of discrimination.

Rejection letters should be brief, beginning and ending on a positive note. They are usually sent by the HR representative who interviewed the candidate. The sample letter shown in Figure 12-2 encompasses these points.

Figure 12-1. Sample letter confirming a job offer.

September 28, 199X

Ms. Elizabeth Downey
55 Poplar Street
Plainfield, New Jersey 07060

Dear Ms. Downey:

We are pleased to confirm our offer for the position of industrial engineer in the operations department of Valdart, Ltd., at a starting salary of $1,400 per week. As discussed, your regularly scheduled core hours of work will be 10:00 a.m. to 4:00 p.m., Monday through Friday, with an additional two hours of work preceding and/or following these hours each day. Please see Ms. Taylor, the operations vice president, when you report for work on Monday, November 9, 199X, at 10:00 a.m. She is in room 219 on the second floor of our building, located at the address noted above.

The nursing office has been apprised of your starting date and will be expecting you for your preemployment physical exam anytime before that date, Monday through Thursday, between 8:00 a.m. and 12:00 noon.

As agreed, you will resign from your present position upon receipt of this job offer. Upon doing so, please notify this office in writing so that we may conduct a reference check. It is understood that this job offer is contingent upon receiving a satisfactory reference from your present employer.

Enclosed is a benefits package describing your health and life insurance options, as well as other company benefits. Also enclosed is our employee handbook for your review. Please bring both items when you begin work on November 9. There will be an orientation program scheduled for later that morning, during which time these and other matters will be discussed.

If you have any questions, please call me at 212/555-2200, extension 442.

We look forward to having you join our organization.

Sincerely,

Peter Fisher
Human Resources Representative

Encl. (2)

Figure 12-2. Sample rejection letter.

```
October 8, 199X




Ms. Mary Parker
128 Field Avenue
Union, New Jersey 07083

Dear Ms. Parker:

    Thank you for taking the time to meet with me to
discuss Valdart's opening for an industrial engineer. I
learned a great deal about your accomplishments and
aspirations, and appreciate the interest you expressed
in our company.

    When filling an opening, Valdart looks at a number of
factors, such as experience, demonstrated skills,
knowledge, and the ability to handle key job-related
situations. This can make the selection process difficult
when we are fortunate enough to attract many qualified
candidates like you. With only one opening, however, we
are forced to turn away many fine applicants. Accordingly,
we regret that we are unable to extend an offer of
employment to you at this time.

    Your credentials are impressive, Ms. Parker. We hope
you again consider us for employment in the future.

Sincerely,




Peter Fisher
Human Resources Representative
```

Summary

Reference checks can assist an interviewer in deciding whether to hire one candidate over another. Unfortunately, fears of invasion of privacy and defamation of character charges prevent many employers from divulging useful job-related information, in spite of protection by the common law doctrine of qualified privilege and, in some states, reference-checking laws. Not only does this lack of information render a hiring decision difficult for prospective employers to make, but making the wrong decision can result in negligent hiring and retention lawsuits.

In addition to checking references, employers should compare the qualifications of each candidate in relation to the position's primary responsibilities and requirements, and consider the organization's affirmative action goals.

Once the selected candidate has been notified and has accepted the offer of employment, contact those who were rejected, making certain your letter is brief, and beginning and ending on a positive note.

Chapter 13

The Fundamentals of Employee Orientation

Well, you have finally done it! After all your preparation, planning, analyses, and comparisons, the job opening has been filled. If you have followed the guidelines mapped out in previous chapters, the new employee should have a clear idea as to what his job will entail, in addition to what it will be like to work for the company. Regardless of how much may be anticipated, however, starting any new job can be unnerving. Even former employees returning after a lengthy leave of absence report an uneasiness during the first few days or weeks back on the job. Until the new employee becomes familiar with the surroundings, feels comfortable with the details and routine of a typical day, and develops an understanding of company and departmental expectations, it will be difficult for him to focus on job performance.

For these reasons, all organizations, regardless of size, should conduct orientation programs. To many employers, the term *orientation* means sending new employees to a brief meeting, usually no more than two hours in duration, during which the company's history, rules, and benefits are described. Often there is no opportunity for interaction among attendees and little time, if any, for questions. Literature is distributed, placing the onus on the employees to read, understand, and apply the contents, and then immediately start work in their departments, only to discover that department heads or managers are often unavailable or unable to answer any questions that may come up.

Although this is an accurate description of how orientation is handled by many organizations, it does not represent an effective program. The company's history, rules, and benefits are certainly important elements of an individual's introduction to the new work environment; however, this cannot be accomplished effectively in a couple of hours. It is also impractical to assume that a new employee will come away knowing all that is required. Each employee's supervisor, manager, or department head, or a knowledgeable designee, should be available to provide the guidance needed for proper acclimation during the start of any new job.

In this connection, a comprehensive orientation program for new employees consists of three main components: the first day of work, a multitiered formal organizational orientation program, and a less formal, but still structured, departmental orientation. Careful preparation for these segments will ensure better employer-employee relations. In addition, employers who customize their orientation programs to reflect the needs of their employees and follow up by evaluating the program's effectiveness are most likely to create a good first impression and put new employees in synch with the company's culture, goals, and work environment.

The First Day of Work

As soon as a prospective employee's starting date is confirmed, his supervisor or manager should make a notation to keep that day as free of appointments as possible. In this way, full attention may be given to meeting the needs of the new worker. If a clear calendar cannot be arranged, then at least some time during the day—preferably first thing in the morning and then again at the end of the day—should be set aside to spend with the new employee. Arrangements should also be made for someone else, say, another supervisor, manager, or colleague from within the department, to assist the new employee in getting settled.

Introductory Remarks

When the new employee reports to work for the first time, devote several minutes to putting her at ease and establishing rapport. To accomplish this, employ the same techniques used during the interview process, including icebreaker questions and statements. Consider the following examples:

> "I'm sorry we couldn't arrange better weather for your first day of work. The weather report predicts that the rain should stop early this afternoon, however—just in time for rush hour!"

"We at Valdart try to think of everything. We even arranged a beautiful sunny day for your first day of work!"

"I'll bet the construction on the expressway cost you about twenty minutes this morning. Before you leave today, I'll have someone give you directions for an alternate route."

"You're lucky you didn't start here two weeks ago when the transit workers were on strike. Commuting then was a nightmare."

"Were you able to locate your assigned parking space without much difficulty?"

Be careful that your initial icebreaker statements do not make the new employee feel unduly pressured. For instance, a greeting such as, "Thank goodness you're finally here! The work on your desk is already a mile high!" could make the employee wonder if she made a mistake in accepting your job offer. All you want to do at this stage is to calm first-day jitters and make the individual feel comfortable.

Following your icebreaker remarks, take a few moments to describe the scheduled activities of the day. If a great deal has been planned, then hand the new person a prepared agenda. Otherwise, briefly describe what is lined up. To illustrate:

"Janet, after we finish talking, I'll take you around the department to meet everyone. Then I'm going to turn you over to Bruce Jenkins, our production manager. He'll show you your office, tell you where everything is, and essentially explain how to get around. I'll meet you back here at 11:45 so we can go to lunch. I've made reservations for us at the officers' dining room. The food there is quite good. Then at 1:30, Bruce will take you over to the Human Resources Department for the first part of the organizational orientation program. When that ends at 4:30, come back to my office so we can talk. I'll answer any questions you may have formed throughout the day, and we can discuss what's been scheduled for tomorrow."

Before moving on from this step in the employee's first day of work, be sure to tell the person how you wish to be addressed. This may not seem terribly important to you, but to a nervous employee who wants to make a good impression, it can avoid some awkward moments. Simply say:

> "By the way, we're very casual around here, so please call me Phyllis. Everyone is on a first-name basis except when you get to the executive vice presidents' level and above. They like things a bit more formal. In fact, they'll address *you* as Ms. Bower. The only time they relax on this is at the annual picnic. I guess when they're playing softball and eating hot dogs, they feel it's okay to use first names!"

These introductory remarks take only a few minutes, yet they contribute a great deal to a new employee's perception about the company. These perceptions will affect the employee's attitude toward her job, which will affect her productivity. Therefore, care should be taken to be as encouraging, supportive, sincere, and upbeat as possible.

Introductions

Now it is time to introduce the new worker to others with whom she will be working. Generally these individuals are in the same department. Sometimes, however, introductions extend to employees in other units. This may occur when the new person will be working on a regular basis with other departments. If there are to be more than a half-dozen introductions, it is a good idea to prepare a sheet in advance with everyone's name, title, office location, and telephone, e-mail, and fax extensions. This can make the experience less overwhelming, since the new employee can refer to it after the introductions.

As you take the new employee around, be careful not to express your opinions about others—for example, "Janet, the next person you're going to meet is Bob Johnson. Watch out for him during staff meetings. He's notorious for stealing ideas and submitting them as his own!" Or, "When I introduce you to Fred Waters, don't take it personally if he acts as if he doesn't like you. He applied for your position through job posting, but was rejected. He thinks you cheated him out of a promotion."

Positive statements should be avoided as well—for example, "Janet, I'd like you to meet Rod Perret. Rod can always be counted on to help you meet impossible deadlines."

New employees should be permitted to form their own opinions about coworkers. Therefore, avoid any statement that is subjective or judgmental. Instead, focus on being descriptive. As you approach the office or work station of each worker, briefly describe his overall function. Limit yourself to one or two sentences per person so that the new employee will be able to remember what you said. Think in terms of action words, as described in Chapter 5. For instance, you might want to say, "The next person you will be meeting is Terry Carson. Terry is our office manager. She receives all the work to be prepared from the department's assistant vice presidents, distributes it among the secretaries, reviews the final product, and then returns it to the appropriate AVP." Therefore, if the new employee were making notes, she could quickly write, "Terry Carson: office manager: receives, distributes, and returns work to AVPs."

Familiarization With the Office

Once the introductions have been completed, it is time to show the employee exactly where she will be working and to explain where things are located. Generally a sponsor will be assigned to the new person for this purpose. Be certain that the person selected is thoroughly familiar with the office layout and can devote the amount of time necessary to offer sufficient explanations.

Preparation for this stage of the new employee's first day should include a checklist of items to ensure that no details are omitted. This list might include the following:

1. *Show the employee her office or work station.* It is likely that this is the first time the individual will be seeing exactly where she will be working. If she is to be situated at a desk in close proximity to other workers, explain what the others do in relation to her responsibilities. If the employee has a private office, describe any company policies pertaining to pictures on the walls, plants, or other personal touches. Some organizations are rather inflexible about such matters, and the employee should be so informed at the outset.

The desks of all employees should be filled with the necessary supplies: pencils, pens, markers, pads, staplers, rulers, letter openers, paper clips, rubber bands, tape, scissors, and so on. Additional equipment, such as calculators, computers, and dictaphone machines, should also be provided, as appropriate. Relevant reference materials, such as a dictionary and a thesaurus, should be available.

2. *Show the employee where supplies are located, and explain how to order supplies.* Describe departmental procedures regarding additional supplies. It may be that there is a central supply room and

employees merely go there and take whatever they need. If this is the case, take the employee to the room, and briefly show where everything is located. If your organization requires employees to fill out requisition forms for additional supplies, explain where to get the forms, who to give them to when completed, and approximately how long it takes to receive the requested items. Also explain any exceptions to the regular policies. For instance, ordering a new chair or desk will undoubtedly require more paperwork, and probably more signatures, than will requesting a hand-held calculator.

3. *Provide the employee with a telephone directory.* All employees should know how to reach others within the company. A directory of departments, key employees with corresponding titles, and telephone exchanges should be provided. They will also need a directory of primary contacts outside the organization, such as customers, clients, vendors, consultants, agencies, or suppliers.

4. *Explain how the telephone system works.* Many organizations have rather complex telephone systems. It is rare that one can simply pick up a telephone and punch the desired number. Therefore, be certain to explain thoroughly the use of such factors as prefixes, special codes, intercom systems, outside lines, transferring calls, holding calls, voicemail, and conference calls.

5. *Show the employee the location of rest rooms and water fountains.* It is amazing how many employees hesitate to ask about the location of these two indispensable items. It only takes a moment to point out where the rest rooms and water fountains are located. If there are several throughout the department, point all of them out.

6. *Explain the time and location of the coffee wagon.* Everyone wants to know how and when they can get coffee, pastries, and the like. If your organization has a food wagon that comes to each department, tell approximately what time it comes each day and exactly where it stops. You might also include information as to what is offered and a sampling of prices.

7. *Show the location of photocopy and fax machines and explain how they are used.* Explain any required procedures for their use. In some companies all the duplicating and fax transmissions are done by a clerk. If this is the case, specify who is in charge of these tasks and where he is located. In other offices, everyone does his own photocopying and fax work. In this event, demonstrate how the machines are operated and provide the name of a contact should the machines malfunction.

8. *Show the location of paper files and backup disks.* Show where the department's files and disks are located and explain how they are arranged. Also, describe any sign-out procedures.

9. *Show the cafeteria and/or executive dining room.* Take the new employee on a brief tour of the cafeteria. Describe the kind of food offered and the price range. Also provide the hours of operation. If by virtue of her title, the employee is entitled to eat in the executive dining room, include this in your tour as well. Be sure to provide information regarding its hours, reservations if required, method of payment, and policy pertaining to guests.

10. *Show the location of the employee lounge.* If your organization has an employee lounge, take the employee on a brief tour. Describe the hours it is open, which activities are permitted there, and which are prohibited (e.g., smoking, watching television, listening to the radio, or playing games).

11. *Explain the use of company cars.* An employee required to travel from one organizational location to another is often provided with a company car. If this is the case, explain who the employee should contact for details.

12. *Explain the use of expense accounts and reimbursable expenses.* If an employee's position entitles her to an expense account, explain how the process works, including what expenses may be charged back to the company and any limits. Also, explain what constitutes reimbursable expenses, the paperwork, as well as how often and to whom expense reports should be submitted.

13. *Show any exercise facilities, and share information about your health program.* More companies are reflecting the times by providing their workers with an exercise facility or health program. These may include a running track, gymnastic equipment, and even group exercise classes scheduled before and after working hours, as well as during lunch hours. If your organization has such a program, be certain to describe eligibility for and frequency of use, required gear (e.g., sneakers), and hours. Some companies also sponsor workshops to help employees quit smoking, eat more sensibly, or learn about stress reduction. Tell the new employee where she can obtain a schedule of these workshops.

14. *Show any child and elder care facilities.* If your organization has an on-site child or elder care facility, take the new employee on a brief tour, and explain how it operates. Be sure to include eligibility requirements, a description of who watches the children or cares for the elderly relatives, the ratio of child or elderly person per caretaker,

a sampling of activities, and the cost. If your company has off-site facilities, arrange for the new employee to visit them within a few days. Describe any satellite programs your business participates in as well. Provide the employee with the name of who to contact for additional information.

15. *Explain procedures for medical care.* Explain the procedure in the event that an employee requires nonemergency medical care, including any forms to be filled out and where to go.

It is a good idea to provide to the new employee a list highlighting these fifteen categories so that she can jot down notes as you talk. A sample checklist for new employees appears in Appendix K. If available, also provide the employee with a floor plan.

Some of the tours mentioned, such as visiting the cafeteria, employee lounge, exercise facility, and child and elder care facility, may be conducted as part of the organizational orientation. At this stage, repetition can only serve to reinforce what the employee is being told and shown.

Taking the New Employee to Lunch

By the time lunch hour rolls around on a new employee's first day of work, she is probably feeling somewhat overwhelmed. Therefore, arrangements should be made for someone to take this person to lunch—usually the employee's immediate boss or the sponsor in charge of showing the person around. In any event, it should be someone who in all likelihood will be eating with this person again on a somewhat regular basis.

If your company has a cafeteria, it is a good idea to eat there, so that the individual can become familiar with its offerings. In addition, informal introductions to other employees in the cafeteria at that time can be made. If the person is an exempt employee, plan on eating in the executive dining room.

Remember that your purpose in taking a new employee to lunch is to provide a welcoming and comfortable atmosphere. Be careful not to get carried away, as did the executive who insisted on taking a new clerk in his department to the executive dining room for lunch. His intentions were good, but the gesture was inappropriate, The clerk enjoyed the experience immensely and fully expected a repetition. It was his first job, and he did not realize that a meal in the executive dining room was an exception to the normal procedure for this position. He waited for the vice president to invite him again, and when the invitation was not forthcoming, assumed that there was a problem with his job performance. Eventually his work was affected, and his six-month performance review reflected less than satisfactory work.

The End of the Day

It is strongly recommended that new employees attend orientation for at least part of the first day. If this cannot be arranged, then the balance of the day should be devoted to introducing the employee to departmental policies and procedures in some other fashion. A full discussion of departmental orientation appears later in this chapter.

Regardless of how the day is spent, it should conclude the way it began: with a meeting between the new employee and her manager. Set aside approximately thirty minutes to discuss what took place during the day and to answer any questions the employee may have. In addition, review the next day's agenda.

An Overview of Organizational Orientations

Virtually all organizations have an orientation program for new employees. Unfortunately, many employers hesitate to invest more than a minimal amount of energy, money, or staff time in this critical stage of a new employee's career. Indeed, some consider it a waste of valuable time that could be better spent working. This kind of thinking can have a detrimental effect on both employee performance and attitude and, in turn, result in disciplinary problems as well as increased turnover. Taking the time to acclimate the new worker to the company can have the opposite effect. The employee is more likely to form positive impressions and consequently care more about the quality of his work.

The Purpose of Orientation

A well-planned organizational orientation is designed to make new employees feel welcome and knowledgeable about their new organization. More specifically, it will:

- Give new employees an overview of the organization's history and current status
- Describe the company's overall functions
- Explain the organizational structure
- Describe the organization's philosophy, goals, and objectives

- Explain how vital each employee is in helping to achieve company goals
- Describe the benefits and employee services offered
- Outline the company's standards of performance, rules, regulations, policies, and procedures
- Outline safety and security practices

The exact information provided and the amount of time required for an orientation program vary with each organization. In small companies, for example, a one-day session will probably be adequate. In very large corporations, a full week devoted to orientation may be appropriate. Follow-up sessions several weeks or months later are also recommended. Regardless of the duration of your program, it is critical that the ingredients already outlined be included and that representatives from HR and other key departments present the information. Detailed information regarding the contents of sample organizational orientation programs follow in Chapter 14.

Participants

All new employees should be required to attend the organizational orientation program. In some companies, new employees in all job classifications participate in the same program. In other companies, one presentation is offered to exempt employees and another to nonexempt employees. This is frequently done for two reasons: First, there are too many new employees for a single program; and second, there is a substantial difference in the specific information offered (e.g., managerial benefits and policies pertaining to executives may differ). Still other companies separate employees new to the workforce from those with prior experience. The former group usually consists of new graduates needing help to make the transition from the academic to the business world. They are also more receptive to corporate philosophies since they have no prior experiences for comparison. The experienced group, on the other hand, brings with them established habits and attitudes that may conflict with the new work environment. For example, employees accustomed to working independently in an unstructured setting may need time to adapt their work style so that it fits within a more structured environment. They will also need to be sold on the company's philosophy.

It is not prudent to conduct a separate orientation program for new employees with disabilities. These individuals may indeed need special accommodations: for example, someone with a hearing impairment may necessitate a sign language interpreter, close-captioned video presentations, or written information, or a sight-impaired employee may require audio presentations, live readers, or materials written in braille. Isolating them from other new employees sends the message, albeit well intentioned, that they are different. Make every effort instead to provide suitable accommodations for the organizational orientation. Employees with disabilities should not have a separate orientation unless they determine that attending the one scheduled for other new employees would create a hardship.

Although orientation programs are designed with the new employee in mind, consider inviting existing staff to attend as well. A refresher on such matters as corporate goals and standards of performance can prove useful to all employees. It can also motivate existing employees, making them feel of continuing importance to the company. Having such individuals attend the same session as new employees also allows for an exchange between the newcomers and the existing workers. Usually, however, a separate session is scheduled in order to avoid unnecessary repetition of certain points.

Because discussion is an important element of an effective orientation program, the number of participants should be limited to a maximum of twenty; the ideal group size is from twelve to fifteen. This encourages an exchange between the new employees, while allowing for questions to be asked and responded to. Having fewer than six employees can make the participants feel conspicuous and self-conscious.

Location and Setting

The site selected for the organizational orientation program should be centrally located and convenient for most employees. It should easily accommodate the number of people scheduled to attend, but not be too large. Tables should be provided, since literature is likely to be distributed, and employees will probably want to jot down notes during the course of the presentation. Tables and chairs should be arranged in a casual manner; round tables are preferred over a classroom-style arrangement. For these reasons, auditoriums should be avoided.

Content

There are eight main areas to be covered in an organizational orientation program. These may be expanded to encompass additional components. Depending on the size and complexity of your organization, the following topics may be considered for inclusion:

EEO and affirmative action policies	Personal days
Employees' club	Philosophy, goals, and objectives
Employment and termination-at-will	Present status of the organization
General expectations of all employees	Promotions
General industry information and special terminology	Rules and regulations
Grading system	Safety and security practices
Growth opportunities	Salary increase guidelines
History	Savings incentive plans
Holidays	Sick days
Insurance	Standards of performance
Job posting	Structure
Leaves of absence	Training and development
Overall function	Transfers
Payday	Tuition reimbursement
Pension plan	Unique organizational features
Performance review process	Vacation

Generally an orientation program should emphasize what employees can expect from the organization and what the organization expects to receive from them. In addition, the orientation should expose employees to the larger picture of the overall function, status, structure, philosophy, and goals of the organization. This holistic view can benefit individuals in their jobs, assist them developing a sense of commitment to the organization, and help them plan a future with the company.

Employee Handbooks

Orientation is an ideal time to distribute and explain the one document that can encompass all of these categories: a well-prepared employee handbook. Like an HR policies and procedures manual, an employee handbook serves several objectives, among them:

• It provides a written declaration of a company's commitment to fair employment practices and equal employment opportunity with regard to all employees in all work-related instances.

• It expresses the basic philosophies of senior management, through both content and tone.

• It serves as a basic communication tool pertaining to various areas of work.

• It outlines company rules and requirements and clarifies an organization's expectations of its employees.

• It provides a brief history of the organization, including a description of its primary products and services.

• It outlines the benefits and privileges of working for an organization.

• It may boost employee morale.

• It states the employer's commitment or lack thereof to employees with regard to continued employment.

Although employee handbooks should be self-explanatory, users must be afforded an opportunity to ask questions and seek clarification. In addition, because of legal ramifications, companies must ensure that recipients understand its contents. Although there is no guarantee that an employee will comprehend the contents of any document despite all reasonable efforts, employees can be asked to sign a statement that they have received a copy of the company handbook, have read its contents, and understand them. Consider the sample shown in Figure 13-1.

Departmental Representation

The next area to consider in orientation planning is departmental representation, that is, who should conduct or be actively involved with the program. Three different groups should be considered: HR representatives, experts in each topic, and officers from major departments.

In general, someone from HR should be in charge of the overall program. This entails:

• Planning the content
• Scheduling the speakers
• Preparing the presentation media and supplemental material
• Reserving space
• Scheduling employees
• Making opening and closing remarks
• Introducing each speaker
• Conducting tours

Because of this wide range of responsibilities, the HR representatives selected should be knowledgeable about the organization and

Figure 13-1. Handbook acknowledgment.

> This is to acknowledge that I have received and read Valdart's employee handbook in its entirety. Any statements, rules, policies, or procedures I did not understand were explained to me.
>
> I understand that the contents of this handbook do not constitute a binding contract, but comprise a set of guidelines concerning my employment with Valdart, Ltd.
>
> I understand that these guidelines are not intended to confer any special rights or privileges upon specific individuals or to entitle any person to any fixed term or condition of employment.
>
> I understand that no Valdart, Ltd. employee has the authority to enter into a contract with me, binding upon Valdart, unless such contract is in writing and signed by the President or the President's delegate.
>
> I understand that Valdart may modify any of the provisions in this handbook at any time. I further understand that I am to, and will, observe and abide by all rules and regulations contained herein, as well as any and all amended rules and regulations that may be given to me in writing and made a part of this handbook.
>
> I acknowledge receipt and retention of a copy of this signed statement and Valdart's employee handbook. A copy of this signed statement will be placed in my HR file.
>
> Name _____
>
> Signature _____
>
> Department _____
>
> Date _____

should have good presentation skills. The latter is important if enthusiasm and interest are to be generated among the participants. Also, to preclude orientation leaders from going stale, a rotational system is recommended, so that no one person conducts orientation every time it is offered.

Experts in various topics should also be involved—for example:

- A benefits expert to discuss insurance, the pension plan, and the savings incentive plan
- A salary administrator to discuss the grading system, the performance review process, and salary increase guidelines
- A member of the training and development department to discuss growth opportunities and tuition reimbursement

As with the HR representative, these topical experts should be knowledgeable and possess group dynamic skills. Particularly with dry subjects, such as insurance, it is critical that the presenters are able to generate interest and facilitate retention.

Finally, all employees, regardless of classification, should be familiar with key organizational officers. Having representatives from senior management participate in the orientation program should accomplish this end. In addition to welcoming new people into the organization, officers might briefly describe the primary functions of their respective departments and discuss how each unit relates to the organization as a whole. This information will add to the employee's holistic view of the company. Furthermore, minority and women representatives from senior management may serve to promote an organization's equal employment opportunity and diversity-driven work environment to inspire future growth.

Format

Orientation information can be imparted in a variety of ways. In fact, variety is essential to the success of a program where a great deal of new information is to be presented.

There are several formats from which to choose:

- Lecture by one or more speakers
- Transparencies or charts
- Handout materials
- Films, slides, or videotapes
- Question-and-answer periods
- Tours

Having representatives from various departments participate in orientation is highly desirable. However, regardless of how interesting departmental presentations may be, a straight lecture format is discouraged. Supplemental transparencies and charts highlighting key points will further employee understanding and retention of what is being presented. Providing handout materials illustrating what has been said is also recommended. Use of professionally prepared films or slides can be very effective. The primary objection to using a film, rather than slides, is that updating a film is far more difficult and expensive than replacing slides. In addition, questions raised during the course of a film must be delayed until the end.

Growing in popularity is the use of videotape in a modular format. This offers the advantage of an entire orientation program that is portable, allowing for a range of viewing possibilities. For example, before a new employee's first day of work, he might be sent a videotape providing a broad overview of the company, its history, philosophies, goals, and products. Having this information when reporting to work on the first day can render the environment less intimidating and consequently put an employee more at ease. It is also a good public relations technique, since the new employee may invite family members and friends to view the tape too. Of course, this presumes that all new employees own or have access to a videotape machine. It also presumes that the new employee will actually view and comprehend the presentation. To ensure this, some organizations show these segments again at orientation; others offer a special session to address any questions home viewers may have. Videotapes also allow employers greater flexibility as to where segments of the orientation may take place. For instance, if a large number of employees is hired for a new satellite location, the videotape portion of the orientation may be conducted there rather than at headquarters.

Answering questions as soon as they arise is far more preferable than having a formal question-and-answer period. Encouraging a free exchange between speakers and participants promotes a more relaxed, less intimidating atmosphere.

A tour of major company departments is also recommended. This will enable employees to appreciate how their jobs relate to the work performed in other units of the organization.

Timing

Employees should be encouraged to attend orientation as soon as possible after employment has begun. Indeed, some organizations require new employees to attend before their first day on the job. This is not generally recommended. Since most people continue to work for another employer until beginning a new position, taking time off to attend an orientation program is usually quite impractical.

The first day of work is the best time to begin orientation. Employees are not yet caught up in the details of their jobs, and there is little chance of their receiving inaccurate information from other sources. More specifically, the afternoon of the first day is considered ideal. The first morning should be devoted to departmental introductions and office familiarization. Once new employees have had the opportunity to become somewhat acclimated to their new environment, they are prepared for more detailed information about the organization.

Duration

The duration of an orientation program depends largely on the size and complexity of the organization. In relatively small companies, a minimum of one day is recommended; in very large corporations, a full week or more is usually needed to cover the key points.

One alternative growing in popularity is the flexible mode orientation program, whereby a general session during the first few days of employment is followed by detailed modules of varying duration in subsequent weeks and months. This method provides employees with basic information at the very beginning of their employment and then provides more specific information after they have had an opportunity to become familiar with their work and surroundings. This progression from general to detailed information also ensures greater retention. The only real drawback is the potential scheduling conflict with departmental deadlines. However, advance notification of session scheduling and cooperation on the part of department heads should preclude any problems of this nature.

An Overview of Departmental Orientations

In addition to the topics covered on the employee's first day and during the organizational orientation, there are other areas with which a new employee should become familiar. These are topics unique to each employee's job and workplace that are most effectively covered during an orientation session conducted within the employee's own department. The person conducting this orientation should be the same person who helped the new employee become acclimated on the first day of work. A rapport with this person will have already been established, making the employee feel more comfortable.

Content

Managers are responsible for more than just introducing new employees to coworkers and others with whom the employee will have frequent on-the-job contact, touring the department and surrounding facilities, and introducing them to their work assignments. They should also focus on covering and answering questions about job-related areas.

Following are some topics considered relevant for inclusion in a departmental orientation:

- *Departmental responsibilities*—the origins, overall function, and both long-term and short-term goals
- *Department structure*—the identification of specific functions and the incumbents in specific positions
- *Disciplinary procedure*—an outline of the general disciplinary procedure, sample infractions, and ramifications of same
- *Grievance procedure*—steps to follow, people to contact, time frames, and examples of legitimate grievances
- *Hours of work*—starting and quitting times and alternative work arrangements
- *Interrelationship between one's own department and other departments*—a description of the flow of work between departments and the key individuals to contact in other departments
- *Job duties and responsibilities*—a description of exact tasks to be performed, expected frequency of performance, areas of responsibility, and interrelationship with other jobs, both within the department and with other departments
- *Meal and break periods*—how meal and break periods are scheduled and the frequency and duration of breaks
- *Meal money*—eligibility for meal money, the maximum amount allowed, and procedures for obtaining reimbursement
- *Overtime*—requirements, eligibility, frequency, and scheduling
- *Personal telephone calls*—under what circumstances personal telephone calls are permitted
- *Personal visitors*—where personal visitors may be met and identification requirements

• *Reporting relationships*—direct and indirect reporting relationships and who is in charge during absences of those normally in charge

• *Smoking regulations*—both restrictions and areas where smoking is permitted

• *Time records*—sign-in sheets, and records of sick days, vacation days, and personal days

• *Vacation scheduling*—how vacations are scheduled, who approves vacation requests, and how far in advance requests should be made

It is advisable to have a topical checklist for these categories, similar to the one used on the employee's first day of work, in order to make certain that no topic is omitted. Giving a copy to the new employee so that he can take notes as you talk is also advised.

Materials Used

If the new employee will be working in a supervisory or managerial capacity, be certain to provide her with a copy of the organization's HR policies and procedures manual. Take time to familiarize the individual with the overall content, explaining how and when the manual is to be used. Also mention who to contact if clarification is needed. Advise the new person of any upcoming group training in the proper use of this important company tool.

If appropriate, also provide a departmental table of organization. Go over it with the employee, describing the primary functions of each position and individual.

In addition, provide the employee with work manuals, instructions, or other printed materials relative to his specific job.

Timing

This departmental orientation should take place sometime during the first few days of work. If the job is in a small company and the organizational orientation takes place during the afternoon of the first day and the morning of the second day, the departmental orientation can be scheduled for the afternoon of the second day. Large companies with full-week organizational orientations often sandwich in departmental orientations on the afternoon of the employee's third day of work.

Introducing employees to the organization first gives them a chance to adjust to the overall environment before learning about detailed departmental information.

Evaluating the Success of an Orientation Program

You may think your company's orientation program is great, but if employees do not find it worthwhile or fail to come away with an understanding of the salient features, then such efforts will have been wasted.

Your program should be evaluated in terms of its content and presentation, and the overall results. Obtain feedback by surveying participants at the end of each session. Then review and compare the survey results over a period of time. Sample questions and statements might include:

1. Which segment of the orientation did you find most informative? Least informative?

2. Which segment of the orientation did you find most interesting? Least interesting?

3. List three things you learned about this organization as a result of the orientation.

4. On a scale of 1 to 5, with 1 representing excellent and 5 signifying poor, rate the following:

- Duration
- Format
- Location
- Number of participants
- Quality of handouts
- Quality of visuals
- Range of topics
- Relevance of topics
- Room set-up
- Selection of speakers
- Timing

5. As a result of the orientation, do you fully understand your benefits?

6. As a result of the orientation, do you fully understand the contents of the employee handbook?

7. For each of the following categories, indicate whether you feel there was (1) too little time spent, (2) just enough time spent, or (3) too much time spent:

- An overview of the organization's history and current status
- The company's overall functions
- The organizational structure
- The organization's philosophy, goals, and objectives
- Each employee's role in helping to achieve company goals
- Benefits and employee services offered
- Standards of performance, rules, regulations, policies, and procedures
- Safety and security practices

8. On a scale of 1 to 5, with 1 representing the most effective and 5 signifying the least effective, rate each presenter in terms of ability to convey the subject matter, sustain your interest, and respond to questions. [List presenters, by title and topic each addressed.]

9. On a scale of 1 to 5, with 1 representing the most helpful and 5 signifying the least helpful, rate the usefulness of the tour.

10. On a scale of 1 to 5, with 1 representing the highest and 5 signifying the lowest, describe your level of interest in the orientation overall.

11. What suggestions do you have for improving the organizational orientation program? Please be specific.

12. Please provide a summarizing statement reflecting your overall evaluation of the orientation program.

Ask presenters for their feedback, as well. In addition to responding to the questions asked of participants, query presenters about:

- The overall structure of the program
- The balance of information
- The completeness of information
- The clarity of information
- The relevance of information
- The tone of the program

Approximately three months after orientation is completed, distribute questionnaires to the managers responsible for the work of new employees. This will provide some additional insight as to the effectiveness of the program overall and the applicability of specific information imparted.

Evaluating program feedback can help you determine how close you are coming to meeting intended objectives.

Cyberspace Orientation

Ideally, orientation should occur when an employee first joins a company, but sometimes this is just not feasible. For example, companies hiring a few people each month cannot conduct an organizational orientation each time someone new comes on board. And large, rapidly expanding businesses that hire hundreds of people each month may have orientation each week, but with so many people attending, it becomes difficult to answer specific questions.

What can companies like these do to make sure new employees do not miss out on the orientation experience? They might join a growing number of businesses conducting cyberspace orientation: a means for new employees to access relevant information from an internal HR Web page.

Cyberspace orientation allows new employees to log on to a guide that takes them through any one of several areas typically covered in conventional orientation programs. For example, employees who need help completing complicated benefits forms can click on the "benefits" icon. They will find out how to fill out the forms, where to send them, and what to do next. Employees unclear on a point in the employee handbook can click on "employee handbook," search the menu for the topic in question, double-click, and probably find what they are looking for. If not, they can locate the name of a person to call for help. Lists of company services, divisions, departments, contact people, vendors, and agents, and organizational charts, complete with photographs of division and department officers, might also be available.

Of course, missing is the face-to-face contact that is so basic to orientation programs: the opportunity for two-way communication, exchanging information, questions and answers, and ideas. Cyberspace orientation may be helpful when standard orientation is not practical. It is best viewed as a stopgap or support measure until employees can attend the traditional orientation program. Cyberspace orientation is also useful after orientation is over to answer employees' remaining questions.

Summary

A comprehensive orientation program for new employees consists of three main components: the first day of work; a formal organizational orientation program, and a less formal departmental orientation. Businesses that evaluate their orientation programs in terms of content, presentation, and overall results will ensure more effective employer-employee relations.

To supplement traditional orientation programs, some organizations are turning to cyberspace orientation: an intranet system of providing new employees with valuable company- and job-related information.

Chapter 14
Sample Orientation Programs

The purpose of an orientation program is to help new employees feel welcome and knowledgeable about the organization. Beyond that, each company will place a different emphasis on the mix of participants, location and setting, content, departmental representation, format, timing, and duration, depending on its size, complexity, and objectives. Following are five samples to illustrate different approaches to organizational orientation.

Sample One: A Medium-Sized Bank

Participants

There are a maximum of twenty exempt and nonexempt new employees at each session.

Location and Setting

Orientation is conducted in a training room at the bank's headquarters. Employees are seated at rectangular tables arranged herringbone style, with five chairs at each table.

Content

There are four segments to each orientation program: a general session, tour, benefits segment, and a session on policies and procedures.

General Session

This segment provides new employees with a comprehensive view of employment at the bank through discussions and presentations covering the banking industry in general and this bank in particular; a synopsis of what the bank offers its employees; and a summary of what the bank expects of its employees. More specifically, the first area—an overview of banking—covers the following:

• A description of the banking industry: what it entails, how it compares with other financial businesses, and what makes one bank more successful than another.

• A summary of the history of the bank, citing its origins, tracing its growth, noting its major accomplishments, and describing its present standing in the banking community.

• A description of the bank's philosophy and objectives.

• Frequently used banking terminology.

• An overview of the bank's structure and hierarchy.

• General information regarding the interrelationship between various departments and functions.

• A statement concerning the bank's equal employment opportunity and affirmative action policies.

The second segment is a summary of the benefits that employees may expect. Because the bank offers so much in the way of benefits, and since there are many other topics that are discussed during this first session, only the following benefits are described at this point in the program:

Employees' club	Special bank services
Holidays	Training and development
Leaves of absence	opportunities
Payday	Tuition reimbursement
Personal days	Vacation
Sick days	

Since employees are eligible for insurance coverage immediately upon hire, there is an in-depth discussion of the following:

Life insurance	Savings incentive plan
Medical and disability	Travel accident insurance
insurance	Other related plans or
Pension plan	coverage

The third main area mentioned at this overview session concerns what the bank expects of its employees. Once again, the intent here is to familiarize; a more intense session pertaining to rules and policies follows in the third week. In this regard, the following bank policies and procedures are mentioned:

- Grading system
- Importance of customer service
- Job posting
- Performance review process
- Promotions
- Rules regarding such matters as attendance and punctuality
- Salary increase guidelines
- Standards of performance
- Transfers
- Safety and security practices

Tour

Following the general session, employees are taken on a tour of the bank's major departments and one typical branch. Seeing a department in action serves to supplement the information provided in the general session. Arrangements are made in advance for representatives of each department to guide the employees through the department, explaining how it operates. Specific departmental literature is also distributed at this time.

In addition to a tour of key bank departments, employees are shown the employee cafeteria and executive dining room, employee lounge, exercise facilities, medical unit, and child care facilities. The hours, functions, and any eligibility requirements for each unit are described.

Detailed Benefits Session

This session provides detailed information regarding all of the bank's employee benefits. Since all areas of insurance were covered in detail during the general session, this segment elaborates on other, noninsurance benefits, including:

- *Employees' club*—its purpose, what it offers, how events are publicized, and who to contact for additional information
- *Holidays*—eligibility, specific dates, any unique stipulations pertaining to absences the day before or after a holiday, and adding holidays onto vacations or leaves of absence

- *Leaves of absence*—types of leaves, maximum duration, eligibility, and effect on employment status, seniority, salary, and benefits
- *Payday*—frequency, method, check cashing, advances, and paydays occurring during vacations or leaves of absence
- *Personal days*—eligibility, number of days allowed, purpose, and required procedure
- *Sick days*—eligibility, number of days permitted, uses, and required procedure
- *Special bank services*—eligibility and required approval for free checking, travelers' checks, safe deposit boxes, installment loans, and advanced checking
- *Training and development opportunities*—programs available, enrollment procedure, eligibility, frequency, and correlation with career planning
- *Tuition reimbursement*—eligibility, types of courses, grade requirements, registration fees, books, maximum number of courses or credits, and procedure
- *Vacation*—eligibility, formula for calculation, and unique stipulations pertaining to holiday additions or leaves of absence

Detailed Policies and Procedures Session

This session provides detailed information regarding the bank's policies and procedures. Because an overview was presented in the first general session, this more detailed segment elaborates, and more specifically explains, the bank's policies relevant to all employees. It includes the following topics:

- *Grading system*—purpose and correlation with salary
- *Importance of customer service*—why it is important, whom it affects, and possible ramifications of poor customer service
- *Job posting*—purpose, eligibility, types of jobs posted, how long jobs are posted, requirements, and procedure
- *Performance review process*—purpose, frequency, measurement factors, correlation with standards of performance, and salary increases
- *Promotions*—eligibility requirements, procedures, correlation with grading system, and salary increase guidelines
- *Rules regarding such matters as attendance and punctuality*—importance, possible ramifications of poor attendance and/or punctuality, requirements, and procedure

• *Salary increase guidelines*—procedure, eligibility, frequency, correlation with performance review process, and standards of performance

• *Standards of performance*—purpose, measurement factors, correlation with performance review process, and salary increases

• *Transfers and other changes in job classifications*—eligibility, voluntary and involuntary changes, procedures, correlation with grading system, and salary increase guidelines

• *Safety and security practices*—procedures and guidelines

Departmental Representation

An HR representative, a senior vice president, and three department heads interact with the attendees during the general session. The tour is led by an HR representative joined by several department representatives. The benefits segment is conducted by a benefits specialist, and policies and procedures are explained by an HR representative and a member of senior management.

Format

One-half hour of socializing is followed by a combination of lecture, discussion, question-and-answer periods, slides, videotape presentations, overheads, charts, and handouts.

Timing

The orientation begins on the afternoon of the first Monday of every month.

Duration

The schedule for the orientation is as follows:

Day 1:	P.M.—General session
Day 2:	A.M.—General session
	P.M.—Tour
Day 3:	A.M.—Tour
	P.M.—Departmental orientation
Week 2:	A.M.—Benefits
Week 3:	A.M.—Policies and procedures

Sample Two: A Small Publishing Company

Participants

Two to five exempt and nonexempt new employees attend each orientation session.

Location and Setting

New employees sit at a round table in the conference room.

Content

There is a general session followed by a tour.

General Session

The general session begins at 9:30 A.M. with the director of HR welcoming the new employees to the company. She chronicles the history of the business, distributes copies of its primary publications, and introduces the vice president. The vice president talks about senior management's philosophy and the organizational hierarchy, explaining how vital each employee is to the success of the company. He also explains the company's commitment to EEO and how proud they are to have a diversity-driven work environment. The director of HR shows a twenty-minute film, highlighting what she and the vice president have said thus far.

Following a short break, the HR director hands out booklets explaining employee benefits and services, including all insurance-related information, regarding medical, disability, pension plans, vacation days, and other time off. She also assists the new employees in completing required benefits forms. She does the same with the employee handbook, explaining its contents and collecting the signed form at the back that signifies understanding of its contents.

At 1:00 the employees are provided with a buffet lunch. While they are eating, the HR director and the vice president conduct an informal discussion about the company in general and answer questions about both the organization and specific jobs.

Tour

At 2:00 the new employees are escorted by the HR director on a tour of the building. Included in the tour is a visit to the company's six main departments, a stop at the cafeteria, a look at the exercise room, and a peek in at the child care facility.

The two-hour tour ends back in the conference room. Employees are given packets identifying each department and its staff, information relevant to the exercise room, such as type of equipment and hours of use, information about the cafeteria (e.g., hours of operation and sample prices), and criteria for and cost of using the child care facility. The HR director answers any final questions before ending the orientation at 4:30 P.M.

Departmental Representation

The HR director and the vice president conduct the general session. The HR director leads the tour.

Format

A brief social period is followed by a combination of lecture, completing forms, discussion, questions and answers, a film, and handouts.

Timing

Orientation takes place on the first Monday of every other month.

Duration

Each orientation session lasts one day.

Sample Three: A Large Telecommunications Company

Participants

Separate orientation sessions are simultaneously conducted for exempt and nonexempt new employees. Group size averages twenty-five to thirty nonexempt and fifteen to twenty exempt employees.

Location and Setting

Nonexempt sessions are held in rooms in the training department. Tables are arranged in rows, classroom style. Exempt sessions begin in a conference room at company headquarters at a long, oval-shaped board table. Subsequent exempt sessions are conducted at satellite locations.

Content

Sessions for nonexempt new employees begin with three consecutive days devoted to general information, what the company expects of its employees, and what the company offers its employees.

General information topics include:

- A historical view of the company
- Organizational products and services
- Company goals and philosophies
- Diversity, equal employment opportunity, and affirmative action
- Categories of employment
- Hours of work
- Inclement weather expectations
- Jury duty
- Payday
- Safety
- Termination

Topics covered under company expectations include:

- Attendance and punctuality
- Attire
- Confidentiality
- Customer relations
- Drugs and alcohol
- Office maintenance and damage to company property
- Outside employment
- Personal change notifications
- Teamwork
- Telephone use

What the company offers its employees encompasses:

- Bereavement leave
- Company-sponsored workshops
- Holidays
- Insurance
- Performance reviews

- Personal days
- Promotional opportunities
- Recreational activities
- Reimbursement of expenses
- Salary increases
- Severance pay
- Sick days
- Tuition reimbursement
- Vacation

Many of these topics are contained in the employee handbook. New employees are asked to complete and return by the fourth day of orientation the "acknowledgment" indicating understanding of the handbook contents.

The fourth day of the orientation deals exclusively with benefits. Employees were given a summary of benefits on the first day, and so are able to review the contents in advance and develop some familiarity with the complexities of the medical, dental, and life insurance plans. In addition to discussing plan offerings, employees attend an in-depth discussion of other company benefits such as:

- Direct deposit plan
- Disability
- Employee assistance program
- Pension plan
- Savings and incentive plan
- Tax-deferred annuity program

The fifth and final day of orientation involves a tour of company headquarters. Employees spend about fifteen minutes touring each department. A manager describes the primary function of each department and how it interrelates with other units. To make the tour more meaningful, new employees are given, in advance, a listing of departments with the corresponding names of department heads and managers, their extensions, and a brief description of each function. At the end of the tour, employees return to the training room, where the HR representative answers any final questions.

The first five days of orientation for exempt new employees are similar to the nonexempt program, except that professional-level employees discuss, and are asked to sign, a noncompete agreement. They are also given an overview of the HR policies and procedures manual and are scheduled to attend a separate training workshop in the manual's use before orientation ends.

Departmental Representation

Nonexempt sessions are led by several representatives from human resources. Participating also are department heads on a rotating basis, the company's EEO officer, and a vice president. Exempt sessions at company headquarters are opened by an executive vice president and led by the HR vice president. Several department heads make presentations, as does the company's EEO officer. Subsequent sessions at satellite locations are conducted by an HR officer. All tours are conducted by members of the human resources department, with brief presentations by department managers.

Format

Both groups receive a combination of lecture, discussion, question-and-answer periods, films, videotape presentations, overheads, charts, handouts, and small group projects. The last are especially useful as employees work at deciphering the various benefit plans.

Timing

Orientation begins on the first and third Monday of every month.

Duration

Nonexempt organizational orientation sessions take five days, with three consecutive days (Monday, Tuesday, and Wednesday) in the first week, and two days the following week (Monday and Friday). Exempt sessions last nine days. The first four days are similar in content to the nonexempt session; however, the exempt tour is far more extensive. The first day of the tour is at company headquarters, but the other four days, conducted over the next four weeks, are spent at satellite offices, two of which are in other states.

Sample Four: A Midsized Tech Company

Participants

Each time an applicant is hired, an "orientation" is scheduled.

Location and Setting

The one-on-one orientation session takes place in the human resources conference room.

Content

It may be difficult to think of a meeting with one person as an orientation, but that is precisely what this midsized company does. Actually, orientation begins weeks before a person's first day on the job. Once a job offer has been extended and accepted, the company sends the person a packet including benefits information and forms, a copy of the employee handbook, and a brochure describing the company's history, current status, and goals.

On the morning of her first day, the employee meets with the HR director for breakfast in the restaurant of a nearby luxury hotel. Joining them is the executive vice president, who reviews the company's status, talks a little about the competition, and outlines the organization's immediate and long-term goals.

After breakfast, the new employee and the HR director return to the office of the latter, where they spend the balance of the morning discussing benefits and reviewing the employee's completed forms. The director also answers questions about the employee handbook and asks the new employee to sign the handbook acknowledgment.

By now it is 12:30. The new employee's manager has made arrangements for lunch in the company's adjoining café. While eating, they discuss job specifics. The manager also points out or introduces other employees with whom the new employee is likely to have contact.

From 2:00 until 4:30 the HR director takes the new employee on a tour, showing her where all the departments are located and introducing her to other employees. At the end of the tour, they return to human resources, where the director hands her a directory of names and numbers and an organizational chart (if she is an exempt employee). The employee is encouraged to ask any final questions before the day ends at 5:00.

Departmental Representation

The HR director conducts the orientation session; the executive vice president spends about an hour talking with the new employee about the company's status and goals.

Format

Since basically only two people are involved, the format is informal. The HR director supplements verbal information with handout materials.

Timing

The new employee goes to human resources for orientation on her first day of work.

Duration

Orientation takes one full day.

Sample Five: A Small Manufacturing Company

Participants

Orientation is required of all new employees within the first three months of hire. It is also open to incumbents who want a refresher. Participation is limited to ten employees per session. No distinction is made between exempt and nonexempt employees.

Location and Setting

A round table in the president's conference room is used.

Content

Orientation begins at 8:30 A.M. with a welcome and introductory remarks by the president. She describes her own tenure with the company, including the jobs she held on her way up to the presidency. Many of these are jobs now held by orientation attendees. She concludes her presentation with some slides highlighting the company's beginnings, current standing, and goals. Throughout, her message emphasizes the importance of teamwork.

Employees are then given a packet of benefits information, including insurance forms. The HR vice president takes the group through each form, making certain everyone completes it correctly. In addition, he explains all company insurance-related benefits: medical, dental, life, and business travel accident insurance for exempt employees. He describes noninsurance benefits, such as the employee stock ownership plan (ESOP) and the tax-advantaged savings plan (401K).

Following the benefits segment is a coffee break. Then employees are taken on a tour of the facility by a member of operations. It is strictly a walk-through tour, with little more than the name of the department and department head offered. At the end, employees are given a directory of departments, names, and numbers.

Employees are on their own for lunch. At 2:00 they return to the president's conference room for a general session covering the employee handbook. The HR vice president covers the contents, page by page, answering questions along the way. Topics include:

• *Corporate principles and philosophies*: mission, vision, values, EEO and affirmative action, diversity, harassment, customer relations, solicitation/distribution, ethics, gifts from suppliers, proprietary information, security

• *General information*: locations, classification of staff members, personal safety, HR records, hours of work, attendance, supper allowance

• *Pay procedures*: payday, direct deposit, overtime, holiday pay, vacation pay, required deductions

• *Benefits* (other than those already covered): employee assistance program, health and fitness program, achievement awards program, employee recognition program, scholarship program, discount at the company store

• *Communication resources*: newsletter, the "president's letter," telephone directory, bulletin boards, grievances

• *Time allowance*: vacations, holidays, bonus days, sick days, family and medical leave of absence, personal leave of absence, bereavement absence, jury duty, military leave of absence

• *Career development*: performance planning and appraisal system, merit increases, education, promotions and transfers, job posting

• *Professionalism*: telephone use, reimbursement of business expenses, leaving the work area, courtesy, and appearance

If the participants are receptive, there is impromptu role playing of certain topics (e.g., "grievances" and "customer relations").

At 4:30 P.M., the first day of the orientation ends.

The next morning, the HR vice president begins by asking attendees to highlight what took place the day before. After a half-hour recap, he introduces three department heads, each making a forty-five minute presentation about the respective unit and how it affects the rest of the organization. At noon, employees are treated to lunch. They are joined by the president, who answers any final questions.

Departmental Representation

Most of the program is conducted by the HR vice president. The president makes welcoming remarks and returns on the second day to answer remaining questions. An employee from operations conducts the tour. Department heads make brief presentations on a rotating basis.

Format

The format is quite informal. In fact, employees are encouraged to "dress down."

Timing

Employees are asked to contact human resources any time during the first three months of employment. HR will then schedule a session when there are enough participants.

Duration

The orientation lasts for a day and a half.

Summary

Companies differ in their approach to orientation. The number and mix of participants, location and setting, content, departmental representation, format, timing, and duration vary according to an organization's size and objectives. Although some company programs are clearly superior to those of others, all new employees need a formal introduction to their employers.

Appendix A
Sampling of Job Ads

Although job ads vary in terms of content, approach, layout, and specific design, all ads should contain certain key elements. This includes information about the company (even blind ads should describe the organization), job requirements, and responsibilities. This holds true even for job titles that seem to speak for themselves. In addition, include a brief statement about benefits and compensation, as well as contact information. Also, make reference to equal employment opportunity. Of course, the overall appearance should be eye-catching and easy to read.

Following are three ads illustrating degrees of effectiveness.

Job Ad Number 1: Accountant/Bookkeeper

Part Time

Travelex America, an international leader in travel related financial services has an opportunity for an Accounting/Bookkeeper, 4-8 pm M-F, great location, A/P & A/R, GL exp. needed. MS Excel a must. Hi-energy, take charge person to handle large wire transfers in foreign currency transactions. College students/returnees welcome to apply. Please include salary req. No Phone Calls Please. Send/fax resumes to:

Travelex America, Inc.
1305 Franklin Avenue,
Suite 100
Garden City, NY 11530
Attn: Human Resources
Fax: (516) 294-5747

Equal Opportunity Employer/ Drug Free Workplace

Part Time

Source: Reprinted with permission of Travelex America, Inc.

Overall Appearance: Vertical placement of the job title invites investigation. Contents easy to read. Bold bars at the top and bottom of the ad serve to both contain the text and remind readers that the position is part time.

Job Specifications: Use of accounting "language" draws experienced applicants. Work schedule concisely stated.

Information About the Organization: Clearly stated in one sentence at the beginning of the ad.

Benefits and Compensation: No mention of benefits or compensation.

Contact Information: Clearly states how and to whom.

EEO Information: Addition of "Drug Free Workplace" is a nice touch.

Job Ad Number 2: Human Resource Generalists

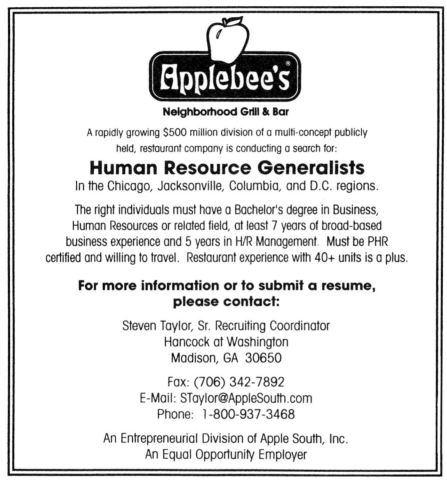

Neighborhood Grill & Bar

A rapidly growing $500 million division of a multi-concept publicly held, restaurant company is conducting a search for:

Human Resource Generalists

In the Chicago, Jacksonville, Columbia, and D.C. regions.

The right individuals must have a Bachelor's degree in Business, Human Resources or related field, at least 7 years of broad-based business experience and 5 years in H/R Management. Must be PHR certified and willing to travel. Restaurant experience with 40+ units is a plus.

For more information or to submit a resume, please contact:

Steven Taylor, Sr. Recruiting Coordinator
Hancock at Washington
Madison, GA 30650

Fax: (706) 342-7892
E-Mail: STaylor@AppleSouth.com
Phone: 1-800-937-3468

An Entrepreneurial Division of Apple South, Inc.
An Equal Opportunity Employer

Source: Reprinted with permission of Apple South, Inc.

Overall Appearance: Logo identifies company and attracts reader's attention. Varying size and boldness of print and use of white space effectively isolates information and makes the ad easy to read.

Job Specifications: Requirements are clearly identified. Number of years' experience identifies level of the job. Duties are not identified.

Information About the Organization: Succinctly stated at the beginning of the ad. Further identification as an entrepreneurial division of Apple South at the end provides clarification.

Benefits and Compensation: No mention of benefits or compensation.

Contact Information: Clearly states whom to contact and choices of fax, e-mail, or phone (800 number is a nice touch).

EEO Information: Minimally stated.

Job Ad Number 3: Plant Training Manager

Source: Reprinted with permission of Copeland Corporation.

Overall Appearance: Visually captivating. Reference to both international and U.S. locations immediately following job title is intriguing. Clever statement following job title. Spacing between paragraphs makes lengthy text easier to read.

Job Specifications: Detailed description of duties clearly indicates scope and level of responsibility. Requirements are explicit, yet flexible.

Information About the Organization: Not provided.

Benefits and Compensation: Reference to an "ideal climate for growth encourages creative thinking and rewards excellence" is likely to make qualified candidates believe it would be worth their while to apply.

Contact Information: Makes it clear that applicants should submit resumés by mail or fax only.

EEO Information: Addition of "m/f/d/v" and statement regarding the company's commitment to workforce diversity is effective.

Appendix B
Job Posting Form

Job Posting Notice

Job title:
Division/Department:
Location: Job no.:
Summary of primary duties
  and responsibilities:

Exemption status: Grade/salary range:
Work schedule:
Working conditions:
Qualifications/requirements:

Closing date:

Job Posting Eligibility Requirements

To qualify for job posting, you must:
1. Be employed by Valdart, Ltd. for at least twelve consecutive months.
2. Be in your current position for a minimum of six consecutive months.
3. Meet the qualifications/requirements listed above.
4. Have received an overall rating of satisfactory or better on your most recent performance evaluation.
5. Notify your immediate supervisor/manager of your intent to submit a job posting application.

Job Posting Application Procedure

1. Complete a job posting application form, available in the Human Resources Department.
2. Return the completed form to the Human Resources Department and give a copy to your immediate supervisor/manager by the closing date noted above.
3. You will be contacted within three working days after the closing date for an interview.

Appendix C
Job Posting Application Form

Job Posting Application

(Please print or type)   Date:
Name: Telephone ext.:
Current job title: Current div./dept.:
Summary of current duties and responsibilities:

Current grade: Current salary:
Current supervisor/manager:
Position applied for: Job no.

Job Posting Eligibility Requirements

To qualify for job posting, you must:
1. Be employed by Valdart, Ltd. for at least twelve consecutive months.
2. Be in your current position for a minimum of six consecutive months.
3. Meet the qualifications/requirements listed on the job posting notice for this position.
4. Have received an overall rating of satisfactory or better on your most recent performance evaluation.
5. Notify your immediate supervisor/manager of your intent to submit a job posting application.

Job Posting Application Procedure

1. Submit the original copy of this form to the Human Resources Department; submit the yellow copy to your immediate supervisor/manager; keep the white copy for yourself.
2. You will be contacted within three working days after the closing date for an interview.

Appendix D

Work Environment Checklist

Physical Working Conditions
- Extensive standing
- Ventilation
- Exposure to chemicals or fumes
- Space
- Noise level
- Types of machinery or equipment

Geographic Location of the Job
- Permanent
- Temporary
- Rotational

Travel
- Purpose
- Degree of advance notice
- Locations
- Frequency
- Duration
- Means of transportation
- Reimbursement

Work Schedule
- Full time
- Part time
- Contingency
- Job sharing
- Flextime
- Compressed workweek
- Telecommuting
- Days of the week
- Shift
- Meal breaks and other scheduled breaks

Appendix E
Job Description Form

Job Description

Job title: Location: Work schedule:

Department: Division: Reporting relationship:

Salary range: Grade: Exemption status:

Summary of Duties and Responsibilities

Primary Duties and Responsibilities:

(E) = essential functions (N) = nonessential functions

Percentage
of time
devoted to
each task

____%   1.
____%   2.
____%   3.
____%   4.
____%   5.
____%   6.
____%   7.
____%   8.
____%   9.
____%   10.

Performs other related duties and assignments as required.

***Education, prior work experience,
and specialized skills and knowledge***

Physical environment/working conditions

Equipment/machinery used

Other (e.g., customer contact or access to confidential information)

Job analyst:
Date:

Appendix F

Application for Employment Form

Avedon Industries
An Equal Opportunity Employer M/F/V/D

APPLICATION FOR EMPLOYMENT

Avedon Industries considers applicants for all positions without regard to race, color, religion, sex, national origin, age, veteran status, non-job-related disabilities, or any other legally protected status.

(Please Print)

Name _____ Date_____

Address _____

Phone No. _____ Social Security No. _____

Position Applied For _____

Available to Work:
( ) Full Time   ( ) Days   ( ) Contingency Basis
( ) Part Time   ( ) Evenings   ( ) Telecommuting

Referral Source _____

Have you ever filed an application at Avedon Industries before? ( ) Yes ( ) No

Dates _____

Have you ever been employed by Avedon Industries before? ( ) Yes ( ) No

Dates _____

Do you have any relatives, other than a spouse, currently employed by Avedon Industries? ( ) Yes ( ) No If yes, please list their names _____

_____

Are you above the minimum working age of _____?
( ) Yes ( ) No
If you are under the age of _____ can you furnish a work permit?
( ) Yes ( ) No

Are you legally permitted to work in this country? ( ) Yes ( ) No
If yes, will you be prepared to produce proof at the time of hire, in accordance with the Immigration Reform and Control Act of 1986?
( ) Yes ( ) No

Have you ever been convicted of a crime? A positive response will not necessarily affect your eligibility to be hired ( ) Yes ( ) No
If yes, please explain _____

_____

Can you perform the tasks required to carry out the job for which you have applied with or without accommodation? ( ) Yes ( ) No

As related to the position applied for, what language do you speak, read, and/or write? What is your degree of fluency?

_____

_____

What professional organizations or business activities are you involved with, relative to your ability to perform the position applied for?

_____

_____

Employment Experience

Please list present or most recent employer first. Include military service, if any.

Employer ——————————— Phone No. ———————————

Address ———————————————————————————

Position(s) ———————————————————————————

Manager ——————— Starting Salary ——————— Final Salary ———————

Dates Employed ———————————————————————

Reason for Leaving ————————————————————

Primary Responsibilities ————————————————

———————————————————————————————

– –

Employer ——————————— Phone No. ———————————

Address ———————————————————————————

Position(s) ———————————————————————————

Manager ——————— Starting Salary ——————— Final Salary ———————

Dates Employed ———————————————————————

Reason for Leaving ————————————————————

Primary Responsibilities ————————————————

———————————————————————————————

– –

Employer ——————————— Phone No. ———————————

Address ———————————————————————————

Position(s) _____

Manager _____ Starting Salary _____ Final Salary _____

Dates Employed _____

Reason for Leaving _____

Primary Responsibilities _____

_____

_____

Education and Training

List all schools attended, including trade, business, or technical institutions, beginning with the most recent.

Name/Location	No. Years Completed	Diploma/Degree

Please describe any additional academic achievements or extracurricular activities relative to the position applied for: _____

_____

Please identify any additional knowledge, skills, qualifications, publications, or awards that will be helpful to us in considering your application for employment:

_____

_____

_____

Please provide the name, title, address, and telephone number of three business references, other than current or former employers, who are not related to you.

1. _____

2. _____

3. _____

Special Notice to Disabled Veterans, Vietnam Era Veterans, and Individuals With Disabilities

Government contractors are subject to Section 402 of the Vietnam Era Veterans Readjustment Act of 1974, which requires that they take affirmative action to employ and advance in employment qualified disabled veterans and veterans of the Vietnam Era; and Section 503 of the Rehabilitation Act of 1973, as amended, which requires that they take affirmative action to employ and advance in employment qualified individuals with disabilities.

If you consider yourself to be covered by one or both of these Acts, and wish to be identified for the purposes of proper placement and appropriate accommodation, please sign below. Submission of this information is voluntary and failure to provide it will not jeopardize employment opportunities at Avedon Industries. This information will be kept confidential.

( ) Disabled   ( ) Disabled Veteran   ( ) Vietnam Era Veteran

Agreement

I certify that the statements made in this application are correct and complete to the best of my knowledge.

I understand that false or misleading information may result in termination of employment.

I authorize Avedon Industries to conduct a reference check so that a hiring decision may be made. In the event that Avedon Industries is unable to verify any reference stated on this application, it is my responsibility to furnish the necessary documentation.

( ) You may   ( ) You may not contact my present employer

( ) You may   ( ) You may not contact the schools I have attended for the release of my educational records

If accepted for employment with Avedon Industries, I agree to abide by all of its policies and procedures. If employed, I understand that I may terminate my employment at any time without notice or cause, and that Avedon Industries may terminate or modify the employment relationship at any time without prior notice or cause. In consideration of my employment, I agree to conform to the rules and regulations of Avedon Industries and I understand that no representative of Avedon Industries, other than the President or a designated Human Resources Officer, has any authority to enter into any agreement, oral or written, for employment for any specified period of time or to make any agreement or assurances contrary to this policy. If employed, I understand that my employment is for no definite period of time, and if terminated, Avedon Industries is liable only for wages earned as of the date of termination. I also agree to have my photograph taken for identification purposes if hired.

Signed _____

Date _____

– –

Interviewer   Date

Interviewer   Date

Interviewer   Date

Employed ( ) Yes   ( ) No

If employed: Title _____

Department _____

Starting Date _____

Starting Salary _____

Appendix G
Interview Evaluation Form

Applicant Evaluation

Applicant: Date Interviewed:

Position: Department/division:

Summary of relevant experience: _____

Summary of relevant education/academic degrees and/or achievements: _____

Relationship between position requirements and applicant's background, skills, and qualifications:

Position Requirements	*Applicant's Qualifications*
1. _____	_____
2. _____	_____
3. _____	_____
4. _____	_____
5. _____	_____
6. _____	_____
7. _____	_____
8. _____	_____
9. _____	_____
10. _____	_____

Additional relevant factors (e.g., test scores):

Overall evaluation: (   ) Meets job requirements
                         (   ) Fails to meet job requirements

Supporting comments: _____

_____

Interviewer: _____

Appendix H
Exempt Reference Form

This is a detailed employment reference form for exempt applicants. It may be submitted as a written request or conducted as a telephone reference. Although it is improbable that all questions will result in answers, the form targets a sufficient number of categories relevant to a professional-level position so that even if only half are answered, the prospective employer is likely to gain valuable insight into the candidate's qualifications.

Exempt Employment Reference

Applicant:_____ Position applied for:_____

Person contacted:_____ Title:_____

Company:_____ Phone no._____

Address:_____

- -

The above-named person has applied to us for employment. He/ She has listed you as a former employer, and has authorized us to conduct a reference check. We need your assistance in verifying and providing certain information regarding his/her work performance.

1. _____ worked in the _____
   department as a(n) _____
   from _____ to _____.
   ( ) Correct   ( ) Incorrect
   (If incorrect, please explain.)

---

2. His/Her primary responsibilities were:_____

_____

_____

3. He/She stated that his/her reason for terminating employment
   with your company was:_____.
   ( ) Correct   ( ) Incorrect
   (If incorrect, please explain.)

4. How would you evaluate his/her overall work performance?

5. What were his/her greatest strengths?

6. What areas required improvement and/or additional training?

7. What made him/her an effective supervisor/manager?

8. Describe a job-related situation involving pressure.

9. Describe how he/she handled a difficult job-related task.

10. Describe his/her management style.

11. Describe his/her decision-making style.

12. Describe his/her approach to time management.

13. Describe a situation involving delegation.

14. Describe a deadline he/she had to meet.

15. How did he/she handle repetitious tasks?

16. Describe how he/she responded to a new assignment.

17. Describe any work-related travel required, in terms of location, duration, and frequency.

18. This job calls for the ability to _____.
What experience did he/she have in doing this? [This question can be expanded to encompass several different factors. Use your job description as a guide.]

19. How effectively did he/she interact with peers? Senior management? Employees? Customers/Clients? Please be specific.

20. Would you rehire him/her? ( ) Yes   ( ) No. If no, why not?

21. Is there anything else we should know about his/her work performance?

Reference conducted by:_____ Date:_____

Appendix I
Nonexempt Reference Form

This detailed employment reference form for nonexempt applicants may be mailed or conducted by telephone. The form poses numerous competency-based and open-ended questions. If the person conducting the reference check is fortunate enough to encounter a former employer willing to take the time to answer these questions, the results will undoubtedly prove significant in making a hiring decision.

Nonexempt Employment Reference

Applicant:_____   Position Applied For:_____

Person Contacted:_____   Title:_____

Company:_____   Phone No._____

Address:_____

- -

The above named person has applied to us for employment. He/She has listed you as a former employer, and has authorized us to conduct a reference check. We need your assistance in verifying and providing certain information regarding his/her work performance.

1. _____ worked in the _____
   department as a(n) _____
   from _____ to _____.
   ( ) Correct   ( ) Incorrect
   (If incorrect, please explain.)

2. His/Her primary responsibilities were:

3. He/She stated that his/her reason for terminating employment
   with your company was:_____.
   ( ) Correct   ( ) Incorrect
   (If incorrect, please explain.)

4. How would you evaluate his/her overall work performance?

5. What were his/her greatest strengths?

6. Describe some tasks that he/she performed particularly well.

7. What areas required improvement and/or additional training?

8. How closely did you need to supervise his/her work?

9. Describe his/her ability to perform multiple tasks successfully. Please be specific.

10. How did he/she handle repetitious tasks?

11. Describe how he/she reacted to being given a new assignment.

12. Tell me about some of the questions he/she has asked when confronted with a new assignment.

13. Was there ever a time when he/she performed an assignment unsatisfactorily? Tell me about it.

14. How did he/she react to criticism? Give me a specific example.

15. How effectively did he/she interact with coworkers? With management?

16. How would you compare his/her work upon termination with his/her performance at the time of hire?

17. This job calls for the ability to _____.
    What experience did he/she have in doing this? [This question
    can be expanded to encompass several different factors. Use your
    job description as a guide.]

18. Would you rehire him/her? ( ) yes   ( ) no. If no, why not?

19. Is there anything else we should know about his/her work per-
    formance?

Reference conducted by:_____ Date:_____

Appendix J

Selection Checklist

SELECTION CHECKLIST

Instructions for Use

Apply the following rating scale to each of the factors evaluated:

  1 = exceeds the requirement or trait sought
  2 = meets the requirement or trait sought
  3 = fails to meet the requirement or trait sought
  4 = offers an alternative quality that may satisfactorily substitute
    for the requirement or trait sought
  5 = offers an alternative quality that does not satisfactorily sub-
    stitute for the requirement or trait sought

Be prepared to support each rating with job-related information and examples. Attaching a copy of the Interview Evaluation Form is acceptable.

Requirement or Trait	Rating		
	Candidate No.1	Candidate No.2	Candidate No.3
Work history			
Education			
Job-related intangibles			
Reactions to key questions			
Salary requirements			
Reasons for leaving previous employers			
Appropriate job match			

Appendix K
Checklist for New Employees

---

1. Functions of other workers situated nearby

2. Policies regarding pictures, plants, and other personal items

3. Desk supplies, including: pencils, pens and markers; pads and other paper goods; stapler; ruler; letter opener; paper clips; rubber bands; tape; scissors

4. Reference materials, including: dictionary; thesaurus

5. Equipment, including: calculator; computer; dictaphone machine

6. Supplies: location; procedure; exceptions

7. Telephone directory of departments and employees; primary contacts outside the organization

8. Phone system: prefixes, special codes, intercom systems, outside lines, transferring calls, holding calls, voicemail, conference calls

9. Rest rooms and water fountains

10. Coffee wagon: time; location; offerings; cost

---

11. Photocopy and fax machines: location; procedure for operation; changing paper; malfunction procedure

12. Paper files and backup disks: location; arrangement; procedure for signing out files

13. Cafeteria/executive dining room: location; food offered; cost; hours; reservations required (dining room); policy regarding guests (dining room)

14. Employee lounge: hours; activities; rules regarding use

15. Company car: who to contact for additional information

16. Expense accounts and reimbursable expenses: what expenses may be charged back to the company; limits on expenses; reimbursable expenses; expense reports

17. Exercise facilities and health program: location; equipment/workshops offered; eligibility; hours; requirements for use

18. Child and elder care facilities: location; eligibility; activities; caretakers; cost; who to contact for additional information

19. Nonemergency medical care: location; procedure

Index